"A solid introduction to the ecosystem of the far-right in Canada, which not only contextualizes the historical and contemporary landscape of right-wing extremism but also delves into the intricate web of conspiracy theories operating today. By employing a mixed-method approach, the authors offer a nuanced understanding of the ever-evolving far-right digital infrastructure that supports these extremist ideologies and allows them to thrive".

Amarnath Amarasingam, *Queen's University, Canada*

"This historically grounded account of the contours of right-wing extremism in Canada highlights the authors' observation that the myriad conspiracy theories that characterize the contemporary movement have a long lineage. The book also offers detailed analysis of the ways in which the array of distinct and intersecting conspiracy theories finds a broad audience through their online dissemination. This is an important contribution to the still limited Canadian scholarship, offering a strong empirical analysis of the actors and ideologies that constitute the movement in the 2020s".

Barbara Perry, *Faculty of Social Science and Humanities, Ontario Tech University, Canada*

The Canadian Far-Right and Conspiracy Theories

This book provides an empirical analysis, mapping, and assessment of Canadian right-wing extremist (RWE) groups and their conspiracy theories.

While the majority of studies on RWE groups focus on American and European actors, this book critically examines conspiracies disseminated by Canadian actors on different online sites and social media platforms. The authors deploy a mapping metaphor to chart the conspiratorial ideas that RWE groups create and share online. The book also examines the infrastructural terrain that supports mainstream and alternative platforms and the dark monetization structures that act as important conduits for this negative messaging. Theoretically, the study is situated within the concepts of dark social movements where dark participation on dark platforms often occurs. A conceptualization of conspiracy theories is developed by exploring four specific aspects: (1) topics, (2) targets, (3) concerns, and (4) actors. This concept is operationalized by applying it to BitChute and Telegram. The book also offers a historical understanding of different RWE groups and their ideological positions. In addition, it provides an empirical investigation of Google's autocomplete feature, Amazon books, the Dark Web, and several other alternative social media sites.

It will be of interest to researchers of Canadian politics, conspiracy theories, and the far-right.

Ahmed Al-Rawi is an Associate Professor of News, Social Media, and Public Communication in the School of Communication at Simon Fraser University, Canada. He is also the founder of the Disinformation Project, and his research interests are related to news, global communication, misinformation, and social media with emphasis on Canada and the Middle East. Al-Rawi is also a founding member of the Media & Digital Literacy Academy in Beirut.

Carmen Celestini is a Lecturer in the Religious Studies Department at the University of Waterloo, Canada. She has previously been a Postdoctoral Fellow at Queen's University, School of Religion and with the Disinformation Project at Simon Fraser University, and with the Centre on Hate, Bias, and Extremism. As a multi-disciplinary scholar, her research encompasses the overlapping belief systems of apocalyptic thought and conspiracy theories and the impact of these beliefs on politics in North America, extremism, Christian nationalism, hate, disinformation, and violence.

Nicole K. Stewart is an Assistant Professor in the School of Journalism and Mass Communication at Texas State University in Austin, USA, and formerly a researcher with the Disinformation Project at Simon Fraser University. Her research interests explore the social formations that emerge with the assemblage of publics and platforms.

Joseph M. Nicolaï is a PhD candidate in Communication and a Research Assistant with the Disinformation Project at Simon Fraser University, Canada. He is interested in questions of public participation and expertise, the social life of methods, and misinformation-related issues. His PhD thesis examines Canadian news reporting on vaccine hesitancy.

Nathan Worku is a Master of Public Health student at Simon Fraser University, Canada, where he worked with SFU's Disinformation Project as a research assistant. His research interests include health equity, health communication, and knowledge translation.

Routledge Studies in Fascism and the Far Right
Series editors: Nigel Copsey, Teesside University, UK
and Graham Macklin, Center for Research on Extremism (C-REX),
University of Oslo, Norway

This book series focuses upon national, transnational and global manifestations of fascist, far right and right-wing politics primarily within a historical context but also drawing on insights and approaches from other disciplinary perspectives. Its scope also includes anti-fascism, radical-right populism, extreme-right violence and terrorism, cultural manifestations of the far right, and points of convergence and exchange with the mainstream and traditional right.

Imagining Alternative Worlds
Far-right Fiction and the Power of Cultural Imaginaries
Christoffer Kølvraa and Bernhard Forchtner

The Transnational Making of Italian Neofascism
Matteo Albanese

Frege and Fascism
Stephen D'Arcy

Giving Credit to Dictatorship
Authoritarian Regimes and Financial Capitalism in Europe
during the Twentieth Century
Edited by Valerio Torreggiani and José Luís Cardoso

Importing Fascism
The Italian Community's Fascist Experience in Interwar Scotland
Remigio Petrocelli

The Canadian Far-Right and Conspiracy Theories
Ahmed Al-Rawi, Carmen Celestini, Nicole K. Stewart, Joseph M. Nicolaï, and Nathan Worku

For more information about this series, please visit: www.routledge.com/Routledge-Studies-in-Fascism-and-the-Far-Right/book-series/FFR

The Canadian Far-Right and Conspiracy Theories

Ahmed Al-Rawi, Carmen Celestini,
Nicole K. Stewart, Joseph M. Nicolaï,
and Nathan Worku

LONDON AND NEW YORK

First published 2025
by Routledge
4 Park Square, Milton Park, Abingdon, Oxon OX14 4RN

and by Routledge
605 Third Avenue, New York, NY 10158

Routledge is an imprint of the Taylor & Francis Group, an informa business

© 2025 Ahmed Al-Rawi, Carmen Celestini, Nicole K. Stewart, Joseph M. Nicolaï, Nathan Worku

The right of Ahmed Al-Rawi, Carmen Celestini, Nicole K. Stewart, Joseph M. Nicolaï, Nathan Worku to be identified as authors of this work has been asserted in accordance with sections 77 and 78 of the Copyright, Designs and Patents Act 1988.

All rights reserved. No part of this book may be reprinted or reproduced or utilised in any form or by any electronic, mechanical, or other means, now known or hereafter invented, including photocopying and recording, or in any information storage or retrieval system, without permission in writing from the publishers.

Trademark notice: Product or corporate names may be trademarks or registered trademarks, and are used only for identification and explanation without intent to infringe.

British Library Cataloguing-in-Publication Data
A catalogue record for this book is available from the British Library

ISBN: 978-1-032-81569-5 (hbk)
ISBN: 978-1-032-81948-8 (pbk)
ISBN: 978-1-003-50217-3 (ebk)

DOI: 10.4324/9781003502173

Typeset in Times New Roman
by codeMantra

Contents

Preface xi

Introduction 1

1 **RWE context** 3
   1.1 Introduction 3
   1.2 A historical overview RWE in Canada 4
   1.3 The development of conspiracy theories' scholarship 20
   1.4 Conceptualization of conspiracy theories 24
   1.5 Dark social movements, dark participation, and conspiracies 28
   1.6 Operationalizing conspiracy theories 33

2 **RWE actors** 46
   2.1 Situating RWE in Canada 46
   2.2 Far-right and hate influencers 51
   2.3 Right-wing extremism or terrorism? 54
   2.4 RWE groups in Canada 57
       2.4.1 White supremacists 59
           2.4.1.1 Neo-Nazis 59
           2.4.1.2 Accelerationists 61
           2.4.1.3 Identitarians 62
   2.5 Nationalists and patriots 65
   2.6 Militias 67
   2.7 Manosphere 69

3 **RWE sites** 87
   3.1 Introduction 87
   3.2 Platforms and means 89

3.3 Telegram 93
       3.3.1 Connecting conspiracies with other conspiracies 99
       3.3.2 Technology conspiracies: 5G, cryptocurrency,
             and platform surveillance 100
       3.3.3 #TheGreatAwakening 101
       3.3.4 Deep State, NWO, and political polarization 102
       3.3.5 #Savethechildren 103
       3.3.6 Race and religion 103
   3.4 BitChute 105
   3.5 Conclusion 118

4 Conclusion   124

Appendix: RWE sites   *141*
A1 Alternative SNS sites 141
    A1.1 4chan 141
    A1.2 8kun 143
    A1.3 Gab 145
    A1.4 Parler 147
    A1.5 Reddit 148
A2 Mainstream SNS sites 153
    A2.1 Facebook (currently Meta) and Instagram 153
        A2.1.1 Hashtag policies on Meta 153
    A2.2 Twitter (currently X) 155
    A2.3 YouTube 164
A3 Other sites 166
    A3.1 Amazon Book publishing 166
    A3.2 Dark Web and cryptocurrency 169
    A3.3 Google search 175
Index   *185*

Preface

This book is the product of a team of researchers from Simon Fraser University who worked for over seven months to present these findings and many more finetuning its presentation. I was extremely lucky to work with these dedicated researchers, and I would like to sincerely thank them for their commitment and hard work. It was a pleasure working with each of them, including Carmen Celestini (postdoctoral fellow), Nicole K. Stewart (doctoral candidate), Joseph M. Nicolaï (doctoral candidate), and Nathan Worku (MSc candidate).

This book has been made possible due to the generous funding I received from the Government of Canada, the Department of Heritage – the Digital Citizen Contribution program under grant no. R529384. The title of the project is "Understanding hate groups' narratives and conspiracy theories in traditional and alternative social media".

I would also like to thank Dr. Barbara Perry from Ontario Tech University and Dr. Richard Frank from Simon Fraser University for accepting to be research collaborators on this project proposal. They both provided advice and feedback on administrative and data collection matters.

I would like to especially thank one Canadian individual researcher who preferred to remain anonymous. Your generosity and feedback were instrumental in implementing and finalizing this project.

Finally, special thanks go to the excellent work of the graphic designer, Song Tong, and the administrative staff of Simon Fraser University for their patience and assistance.

We hope this modest contribution to the literature of mapping right-wing extremism (RWE) and their conspiracies in Canada assists journalists, policymakers, and the general public in better understanding hate, disinformation, and conspiracy theories within the Canadian context. We also hope that it opens further opportunities for researching these groups on new emerging online sites and/or in other geographical contexts.

Ahmed Al-Rawi, PhD

Introduction

This book provides an analysis of Canadian right-wing extremist (RWE) groups and their conspiracy theories with a particular emphasis on these groups during the COVID-19 global pandemic. While the majority of studies on RWE groups focus on American and European actors, this book empirically examines conspiracies disseminated by Canadian actors on social media sites. We deploy a mixed-method approach to map the conspiratorial ideas that RWE groups create and share online and to examine the infrastructural terrain that supports mainstream and alternative platforms and the dark monetization structures that act as important conduits for this messaging.

This is achieved in three major sections including context, actors and sites, which is followed by a conclusion that includes reflections and recommendations. In our conceptual discussion and analysis of RWE in Canadian history in Chapter 1, we did not limit our analysis to current RWE actors and conspiracies, which is discussed later. Our objective is not to provide an exhaustive history of RWE in Canada. Rather, this brief historical context provides a launch point to understand the contemporary landscape. We supplemented this with an examination of RWE actors in Chapter 2.

In Chapter 1, we look at conceptual issues in studying RWE and root the direction of our approach and reflections, briefly looking at the history of RWE in Canada. Reflecting on aspects of pre- and post-confederation, we show that tenets we often associated with RWE have been longstanding issues in Canada. We also see how RWE entities attempting to camouflage and manage their public image – in particular, for legal and political reasons – have been longstanding tactics. When we could, we also highlighted agency and resistance to RWE as being an integral part of the Canadian story.

In Chapter 2, we provide a geographical mapping of RWE presence and a chart of the major RWE actors in Canada. In terms of categorical differences, we offer classification of groups that are made up of other sub-groups including White supremacists, nationalists and patriots, militias, and manosphere ones. These broad four groups offer general distinct categories. Because of the conceptual overlap that often occurs, we offered a visualization and a justification of these crossovers.

Using deductive and inductive inquiry, we offer an original conceptual categorization of conspiracy theories in Chapter 1 developed through reviewing and systematically analyzing RWE content on BitChute and Telegram (Chapter 3). We operationalized the concept of conspiracy theories to show how it can be applied, for we show that conspiracies can be categorized based on four major elements: (1) sources, (2) actors, (3) targets, and (4) topics. We then use these conspiracies and categorization to help understand RWE in Canada more broadly.

In the Conclusion chapter, we offer reflections on our analysis and recommendations. Similar to how the context section highlights the role of resistance as being the other side of RWE in Canadian history, the conclusion offers a set of recommendations for future research and interventions.

In the Appendix, we provide an analysis of other social media platforms including mainstream sites such as Twitter, Facebook, YouTube, and Instagram, as well as alleged "free speech" or alternative platforms like Gab, Getter, Reddit, and 4Chan. We also examined features related to Google searches and Amazon books, among other sites and apps. We wanted to ensure we had a mixture of mainstream and alternative platforms, as well as a diversity of mediums: video, text-based, visual mediums, and forums. To achieve our goals, we deployed various digital tools to download the data and analyze it. Several methods and analysis techniques were used to cater to our various objects of analysis. Among these, in conjunction with traditional research approaches to manually analyze multimodal social media contents, we also used a number of Open Source Intelligence Tools to trace the cryptocurrency transactions of RWE group members, visualize the content, and conduct thorough searches on the Dark Web, as well as on alternative and traditional social media sites.

1 RWE context

1.1 Introduction

The presidential win by Donald Trump in November 2016 left the Canadian media seemingly surprised that right-wing extremism (RWE) is also a Canadian issue (Scrivens & Perry, 2017). Despite the fact that RWE in Canada is more widespread than initially thought (Scrivens & Perry, 2017), research on this topic is still limited, especially in relation to how these groups disseminate conspiracies online. This limited body of scholarship on RWE in Canada exists in English and French, both official languages (Barrett, 1989; Campana & Tanner, 2014; Dawson, 2019; Hubert & Claudé, 1991; Kinsella, 2001; Li, 1995; Nadeau & Helly, 2016; Nadeau, 2021; Nesbitt et al., 2021; Perry & Scrivens, 2015, 2019). Perry and Scrivens (2016, p. 820) rightly emphasize how the work conducted thus far is insufficient and remains relatively incomplete. Some explain this limitation as, at least partially, the result of Canadians' belief that RWE is simply not a part of the Canadian story (Parent & Ellis, 2014). While many studies focus on the presence of RWE online, there is little comprehensive analysis on specific groups, leaving an incomplete picture of their ideologies, networks, and violent nature (Perry & Scrivens, 2015).

This chapter offers a theoretical framework to situate the study of far-right communication in Canada. In the wider context of the difficulties of conceptualizing RWE, we find through historical analysis that Canadian RWE is not a new concept, and major tenets of this movement exist pre- and post-confederation. After we situate the context of RWE in Canada, we then narrow onto an approach that delves into RWE history, conspiracy theories, and conceptualizations of conspiracies, dark social movements in platform ecologies, and conclude with our methodological approach and novel codebook for studying platformed conspiracies. We find this a compelling methodology to approach and interpret RWE in Canada for a variety of reasons. For one, it highlights how not only the RWE phenomenon in Canada is far from novel but also shows that discussions of the ideological coordinate of RWE communication are better understood when looking at why, when, and where they occur within the emergent dark media ecosystems that provide a platform for ideas, including the spread of conspiracies, but also opens the door for remuneration for

RWE actors, specifically enabling them to remain in the business of conspiracy. Taken together, this helps us map RWE's ideologies and actors in Canada.

In terms of the contexts of study, we looked at conceptual difficulties in working on the questions of RWE and how they play out through a brief sketch of the history of RWE in Canada. In Canada, RWE is not an anomaly in an otherwise harmonious multicultural nation (Lund, 2014; Perry & Scrivens, 2018). However, locating its place in history and mapping its current place in Canada is not an easy task given contemporary debates around the best way to conceptualize RWE.

Below, we highlight the conceptual difficulties of working with the literature on RWE, which informs our historical analysis of groups in Canada as well as our current approach to the matter. Conducting a historical analysis of RWE groups in Canada requires us to be reflective of the descriptive categories used to describe historical events. In the context of our historical analysis, we had discussions about how to differentiate various situations, like a race riot stemming from labor struggles to how to situate extremism in different historical contexts.

1.2 A historical overview RWE in Canada

Attributes commonly associated with RWE, such as Islamophobia, xenophobia, racism, and anti-Semitism, among others, have long been a part of Canadian RWE groups (Parent & Ellis, 2014). Drawing from the conceptual framework outlined above, this section shows how the current persistence of RWE movements throughout Canada is indicative of longstanding forms of exclusion and racism that have already existed within the fabric of society (Lund, 2014).

What can be defined as RWE violence in Canada can be traced back to the 18th century (Perry & Scrivens, 2016). Race riots related to labor issues in the territory we now call Canada can be traced back to 1784 in Shelburne, Nova Scotia, where white loyalists from the United States, who sided with Britain during the U.S. War of independence, destroyed over 20 homes of free blacks. The riots have been interpreted as a response to struggling white workers facing Shelburne employers' preference to hire black men at a lower wage than white men (Ross, 1992; Hofmann et al., 2021). Satzewich (1989) argues that this form of racial violence was utilized as a tool to divide worker unity and justify exploitative labor relations. That is, instead of fostering a transcultural community in which laborers had common interests in combating exploitation–regardless of race, creed, or gender–white laborers were incited and organized around perceiving black labor as competitors over limited resources.

Through the 19th century, anti-Catholic sentiment was prevalent among White Anglophone protestants. An embodiment of this is found within the Irish Protestant fraternal organization known as the Orange Order (Ross, 1992; Perry & Scrivens, 2019). Established in Toronto in 1830, the Orange Order had ties to the administration in the city of Toronto and had aspirations for Protestants to further ascend into political power in Canada. There was a time when every police officer, firefighter, and mayor of Toronto was a member of the Order (Houston & Smyth, 1980). However, following a potato famine in the 1840s, the vast majority of the almost 40,000 Irish refugees who came to Toronto were Catholic (Hull, 2016). Discrimination against Catholics, and Irish Catholics in particular, became a way of life for some Orangemen. Toronto became known as Belfast North, as the "troubles" from Ireland manifested in Canada. The battle between the British Protestants of Northern Ireland, already established in Canada, met with the Irish Catholics south of Belfast, in Canada. The battles from the homeland entrenched themselves within Canada (McGowan, 1999). In this context, a culture of racism intermixed with political and economic benefits for those willing to identify with this culture. From 1867 to 1892, 22 riots took place in Toronto between the Irish Catholics and the Protestants. In some ways recalling Ignatiev's (1995) analysis on Irish in the U.S. context, Ross (1992) interprets these riots not simply as matters of racial strife but as issues stemming from political conflicts between the groups.

A presentation of 19th-century anti-Catholicism in Canada in terms of ideas alone, as if it was simply a matter of theological preference, would be disingenuous. During this period, it is worth recalling that the British Empire was not only engaged in ongoing conflicts with Catholic communities in Ireland but was also fighting Irish Catholics in the United States, which added to longstanding struggles with both Catholic France and Catholic Quebec. In the mid-19th century, an Irish-Catholic group describing themselves as the Fenians emerged in order to liberate Ireland from British Rule. While within the British Empire, including Canada, they had to operate as a secret organization, the Fenians within the United States actively organized a militia to take Canada by force, and they were allowed to operate openly and without fear of reprisal (Senior, 2021).

Similar to the many Chinese Benevolent Associations that emerged during this era, of which some are still active in Canada today, the Irish Catholics created the Hibernian Benevolent in the ashes of a St. Patrick's Day Toronto Riot in 1858. Because of the yearly riots, the Saint Patrick's Day parades were banned in Toronto in 1878 and they did not hold it again until over a hundred years later in 1988 (Berry, 2020). At the macro level, with British Empire suspicions over enemies at the gates and the fifth column or enemies within, we can better understand Orangemen positioning within various levels of the Canadian and British Empire administration. At the micro level, we can reflect on how "being an Orangemen", by adopting their attributes and joining their organizations, may have opened professional paths that might have otherwise been closed. In short, being an Orangemen opened the door for political and professional privileges in British Canada in a way that being a Fenian could not.

The nationalist organization, Canada First, was founded in the context of the Canadian Confederation of 1867 (Vigod, 2015; Wallace, 1920, p. 152). Beginning as a secretive organization they brought together a range of ideas on Canadian nationalism, including that Canada was "superior to its neighbor to the south because of the rigors of the northern climate and the pureness of its race" (Farrell, 1969, p. 17). As much as they may have been "drawn together by their distrust of the pervading spirit of selfishness and provincialism manifested by party warfare" (Farrell, 1969, p. 17), when answering in the positive that there was a "Canadian nation and when they attempted to answer questions as "What is a Canadian?"

or" they "equated this with Ontario provincialism" of an English-speaking variety (Farrell, 1969, p. 17). As Gagan (1970, p. 36–38) writes, they embodied an aggressive exclusivism of English-Canadian nationalism and behaved more like "Ontario First" or "Toronto First" in failing to recognize the diversity of their neighbors and instead replicated the "older racial and religious prejudices of pre-Confederation Canada West". Further evidence of this exclusionism in their national definition of Canada was the lack of any member from Quebec or the Maritimes (Farrell, 1969, p. 17). Their national exclusionism can be contrasted with more inclusive voices at the time, embodied in, for example, the Canadian politician Christopher Dunkin, among others (see Parliament of Canada, 1865, pp. 511–524) though Indigenous Canadians were always shunned.

Canada First transitioned from a secret organization to having a more public presence with the outbreak of the Red River Resistance (1869–1870) in what we now call the province of Manitoba. With the inauguration of Canada's first Prime Minister John A. Macdonald, the government attempted to finalize negotiations with the Hudson's Bay Company for the acquisition of the Northwest Territory (Hougham, 1953, p. 175). The project of Western consolidation was promoted by British Empire authorities who saw it as an effective deterrent to possible U.S. expansionism (Smith, 1995, p. 61). While Canada First attempted to rile up the national sentiment to the political project of the Canadian West, both the Government and the Hudson's Bay Company ignored the "sensitivities of the local half-breed settlers", the people living in the region, which led to the Red River Resistance (Hougham, 1953, p. 175). As one Canada First member put it "the indolent and the careless, like the native tribes of the country, will fall back before the march of a superior intelligence" (as cited in Farrell, 1969, p. 17). As evident in the Red River Resistance, this did not happen.

The crisis started in 1869 when the Canadian government sent a surveying party, led by an Orangemen, to prepare for the "annexation, large-scale land sales and white settlement" that ignored "traditional land claims and boundaries" (Smith, 1995, p. 61). The new Canadian government appointed the English-speaking Orangemen governor William McDougall to rule the territory. McDougall was opposed by the French-speaking mostly-Métis inhabitants of the settlement. For McDougall, adventurers and Irish Fenians from the United States had "stirred up and kept alive" discontent in the region with the intent to annex Métis territories as the United States had done in Oregon and Mexico (Smith, 1995, p. 62). Even before the land was officially transferred to Canada, McDougall's surveyors plotted the land as if pre-existing settlements and farmland were not there (Smith, 1995, p. 61). Moreover, their method of measurement was made according to the square Public Land Survey System, which went against the established French local traditions of land partition in the region and this incited fear among residents that their traditional land titles and rights were in danger of being overturned (Smith, 1995, p. 61). To prevent the newly designated Canadian governor and accompanying surveyors from entering the territory, the Métis under the leadership of Louis Riel established an armed blockade in order to limit access to the primary Red River Colony settlement Fort Garry in what is now Winnipeg, Manitoba (Smith, 1995, p. 61).

Soon afterward the Métis established their own government and constitution and tested the limits of Canada's emerging legal civil culture by negotiating directly with the leaders of Canada in Ottawa (Angus, 2005). With news of the "rebellion" reaching Ontario, Canada First created a separate front organization, the Northwest Emigration Aid Society, to help organize their public activities (Hougham, 1953, p. 176; Farrell, 1969, p. 19; Wallace, 1920, p. 153). In fact, Canada First quickly popularized defining the resistance in terms of a "rebellion" against the natural law and order of Canada (Hougham, 1953, p. 175). In the context of wider Anglo-Protestant pressure on the Cabinet, even Prime Minister MacDonald was recorded saying that if they could bring Riel to Ottawa he would be "one gone coon" (as cited in Smith, 1995, p. 67). In short, from the point of view of the Métis, the new government represented an extreme change to the status quo, while from the point of view of Canada First and its traveling companions, the Métis represented an extreme challenge to the idea of Canada itself.

While the details of the resistance are beyond the scope of this book, in 1869, then Prime Minister Macdonald proposed a three-pronged strategy to consolidate the confederation process of Canada and block possible U.S. expansion over areas where the new government of Canada had very little effective control (Smith, 1995, pp. 63–64). The first was to negotiate with the Métis to ensure that they had no fears of Canadian settlers taking their land and diminishing the role of their culture. The extent to which this was a success is debated. Some have highlighted how concessions were made, as evidenced in the following *Manitoba Act* of 1870 which offered Red River entry into the Canadian union as a province not as a territory and offered otherwise generous terms for including Métis concerns (Smith, 1995, p. 68). Others argue that Canadian civil culture accepted the Métis as long as they were willing to become "rights bearing Englishmen" and banished to the extent in which they declared to have an original self-constitution (Angus, 2005, p. 885). The second was to send a military expedition to make certain that the U.S. government and the Métis people were made aware of British support of the westward expansion. Third and final, Macdonald urged the quick construction of an all-Canadian, coast-to-coast railroad from the Atlantic to Pacific railroad in order to dislodge evolving north-south trade patterns and tie the West economically to the Canadian dominion. For the Canadian historian Innis (1941, pp. 394–397), the practical and political reality of the need and prohibitive economic cost of constructing a coast-to-coast railroad was one of the primary reasons for Canadian confederation in the first place.

With its incredible expense, the question of who was going to build the railroad became an ongoing question. These Chinese Canadian laborers were exploited through their integral construction of the railroad (Ross, 1992). As much as they were an expedient necessity from the eyes of those wanting to see the railway completed regardless of working conditions, they were viewed with suspicion by some white laborers. From the 1870s to the early 1930s, mainstream Canadian labor leaders consistently placed what they described as the problem of immigration near the top of their reform agenda (Goutor, 2008, p. 39). White supremacy and fearmongering became effective in politically organizing the white-working class against Chinese laborers (Ross, 1992). In the words of the Labor Reformer newspaper, competition from Asian immigrant workers would lead to the degradation or "Mongolization" of white workers who would need to be brought down to "Chinese standards" (as cited in Goutor, 2008, p. 39). In answering what this kind of labor competition means to "whites", the Labor Reformer writes it means that they "will live on rice, wear the least expensive clothing, give up their families and homes and pig together in dens [and] become the ignorant barbarians their competitors are" (as cited in Goutor, 2008, p. 39). In this analysis, the exclusion of Chinese from Canadian society in general, and in particular Chinese in the labor market, was presented as necessary for the protection of not only the material interests of the working classes but also the moral fabric of the Dominion of Canada (Goutor, 2008, p. 41). The pattern of weaving right-wing violence with labor issues continued when Japanese and Chinese communities fell victim to a wave of anti-oriental attacks in British Columbia during the late 19th and early 20th century (Ross, 1992).

Following the importation of Chinese workers to help build the Canadian Pacific Railway, hostility grew due to their alleged "unfair" competition in the labor market (Boswell, 1986, p. 363). For example, in 1883, near Lytton, B.C., a brawl between white and Chinese workers left nine Chinese men unconscious, with two later dying (Ross, 1992). As a result of the public's distrust of Chinese immigrants, including the fear that they would steal jobs from Canadians, the federal government reconsidered their legal status. In 1885, a Royal Commission, appointed by Prime Minister John A. MacDonald, studied whether restricting Chinese immigration would be in the best interest of Canada (Li, 2008). Following the results of the commission, the federal government passed the Chinese Immigration Act, imposing a tax on every Chinese person traveling to Canada while limiting the number of Chinese immigrants allowed (Lee, 2002). This differed with Japanese immigration because of an agreement between the two countries that Japan would limit its immigrants to Canada. Some residents in Vancouver made it explicitly clear that the Chinese were not welcome. One article from the Vancouver's Morning News published in 1886 urged the Chinese to spare Vancouver of "the evil which has cursed all Pacific coast towns" (as cited in Roy, 1976, p. 47).

In 1887, the Knights of Labor Society in Vancouver became heavily involved in a grassroots campaign to remove Chinese people from the city. The Knights of Labor was founded in 1869 in the U.S. city of Philadelphia by a group of garment cutters and throughout the 1870s expanded throughout the United States and Canada (Kealey & Gagnon, 2017). Unlike traditional craft unions, which tended to organize around improving the situation of their immediate members, the Knights of Labor pursued, in general, an extensive reform agenda that aimed to transform society regardless of race or gender (Kealey & Gagnon, 2017). Contrary to these general trends, the Vancouver chapter organized boycotts and defaced Chinese-associated businesses. The actions culminated in an attack on a Chinese labor camp that involved roughly 300 Knights of Labor members and sympathizers (Goutor, 2008, p. 64). Out of the large mob of attackers who numbered in the hundreds, only three members were arrested and all were later acquitted with the help of a Knights-sponsored lawyer (Goutor, 2008, p. 64). Goutor (2008, p. 64) argues that in general the Canadian labor movement defended "riots against alleged uncivilized immigrants by claiming the right of white workers to protect their livelihoods". This led to a situation where, on the one hand, they blamed the problem of capitalist oppression for the violence, while, on the other hand, the actual Canadian labor papers accepted "that immigrants, rather than the bosses" were the primary problem (Goutor, 2008, p. 64).

Different lenses of analysis can lead to vastly different interpretations of the above. For example, at the macro level of historical currents relating to national politics and global capitalism, Thobani (2000) argues that the anti-Chinese "head tax" and broader immigration policy reflected Canada's everyday racism and nativism. In the context where the very founding of Canada was through the colonization and genocide of Indigenous people, the racialized immigration policies can be interpreted as simply enabling the settlement of Europeans into their new self-proclaimed national territory (Thobani, 2000). At the more micro level of analysis, and thinking in particular through the lens of group-making projects, we can ask why would Canadian laborers, far from being elites in society, target groups suffering from even worse levels of inequality than themselves. Attempting to answer this type of historical question is difficult. As Baker (1997) writes, the "dead don't answer questionnaires". Despite this difficulty, it is worth at least recognizing that some Canadian laborers actively participated in a group-making project in which they were imagined as being more equal among their white employers and political leaders than their fellow Chinese laborers. As much as this may also be explained in terms of larger global trends and categories of analysis, as Thobani (2000, 2008) does, it is also important to recognize the changing local contexts and agency of people in accepting, resisting, and constructing alternatives to RWE.

The early 20th-century atmosphere of racial nationalism and labor insecurity in Canada helped inspire the Asiatic Exclusion League (AEL), a far-right group with the goal of preventing Asian immigration (Wynne, 1966). In 1907, thousands of people, led by members of the AEL, marched in front of Vancouver city hall to protest Asian Immigration (Price, 2007). The protest later resulted in riots targeting Japanese and Chinese neighborhoods in the city for over two days (Wynne, 1966; Roy, 1976). It should also be highlighted how far from being helpless victims, Japanese and Chinese communities were defiant during and after the riots. Japanese communities confronted the rioters on the street and served them with what then Prime Minister Laurier described as a "well deserved licking", while Chinese workers organized a protest against the riot by withdrawing their labor in its aftermath (Goutor, 2008, p. 30). The subsequent riot resulted in the federal government, then still under the auspices of British rule, creating a royal commission to investigate the economic losses sustained by the population in Vancouver (Gilmour, 2014).

These attacks reflected a radical means to defend the nation and what Anderson (1983) coined as the "imagined community". Anderson highlighted how the concept acts to both enlarge a category of belonging, creating a sense of allegiance across vastly different economic classes within a community, but also how it acts as a way to differentiate "one's own" community against others. In this framing, regardless of any concrete inequality between classes within a society, they are nevertheless given the attribute of a common groupism. In this way, for example, a white laborer and a white tycoon can see themselves as being equal between each other under the banner of whiteness but may feel in competition with racialized others. These forms of group-making projects may position competition or even conflict against other imagined groups rather than face wider inequalities within society itself (Nicolai, 2017).

After the First World War (1914–1918), there was a nationalist surge in Canada. After this "baptism of fire", there was a renewed attempt for Canada to move away from British control (Innis, 1941, p. 58). In this context, English-speaking Canadian public reacted unfavorably to a growing number of incoming non-British immigrants (Lund, 2014). The Komagata Maru incident in 1914 was one of the most racial discrimination cases in Canadian history, with the 376 passengers, predominantly Sikhs from India, being denied entry into Canada. The ship was sent back to India where the Indian Imperial Police attempted to arrest individuals on the ship, and a riot erupted, resulting in the deaths of 22 people. The denial to enter into Canada of those under British rule at the time was based upon arbitrary legislation to exclude Asians into Canada, the Immigration Act of 1910 (Roy & Sahoo, 2016). In 1918, as part of the War Measures Act, Prime Minister Sir Robert Borden outlawed many political and labor groups that were labeled as "extreme" (Berry, 2019). Many of these groups were run by non-British whites (Berry, 2019). As part of this move, many labor leaders were arrested for protesting and being members of outlawed unions: in one swoop canceling both labor voices as well as non-British whites in Canada (Berry, 2019).

Within this context, the Ku Klux Klan (KKK), initially titled the Reconstruction KKK, was able to tap into the underlying xenophobic sentiment by organizing a grassroot populist movement within white middle classes, using community leaders, workers, and the church to spread its message of white supremacy, Protestantism, and conservative social values (Schaefer, 1971; Lund, 2014; Parent & Ellis, 2014). The KKK was founded in 1865 at the end of the Civil War in the U.S. city of Pulaski, Tennessee by six Confederate soldiers, who claimed that the group was simply a prankster group to light the spirits of the war-torn region (Baker, 2011). The group was concerned with the impact of post-war Reconstruction on Southern culture and began to target Northern whites, and people of color, before eventually morphing into a paramilitary movement (Baker, 2011, pp. 6–7). In 1871, the U.S. Congress passed the KKK Act to protect voters and the 14th Amendment, and with the passing of this Act, the KKK dissipated in the United States (Baker, 2011, p. 8).

In the North American context, the KKK is perhaps the oldest and most infamous hate group (SPLC, 2021). The symbolism for the organization typically is a red flag with a white cross featuring a diamond with a red blood drop at the center. After the murder of Mary Phangan in the U.S. state of Georgia in 1913, and the threat of mob violence after the life sentence, and not death penalty sentencing of her accused murder, Leo Frank, a Northern Jew, The Knights of Mary Phangan were founded. The Knights lynched Frank, in 1915 after breaking into the prison where he was serving his sentence and lynched him in front of a crowd in Phangan's hometown. This event was the catalyst of the revival of the KKK, by former Christian minister William Simmons (Baker, 2011, p. 104). By 1924, membership in the KKK rose to four million members, bound together by Protestant faith; the group focused their ire and violence on people of color, Jews, and Catholics (Baker, 2011, p.8), citing nationalism, and faith the KKK with its sheer numbers influenced the immigration laws of United States, in the 1920s.

The organization expanded its operations into Canada, establishing branches in Ontario, Saskatchewan, Quebec, Alberta, and British Columbia (Hofmann et al., 2021). The Klan appeared under various names, such as the Canadian KKK and the KKK of the British Empire (Parent & Ellis, 2014). These branches all followed the same racial ideology to the original chapters in America but had a narrower focus on their allegiance to Canada and the Union Jack (Perry & Scrivens, 2016). Roman Catholics were disqualified from joining because it was believed that their first allegiance would be toward the Pope in Rome rather than their own country (Racine, 1973). All members were required to be white and Protestant while pledging to uphold white supremacy and nationalist principles (Racine, 1973; Perry & Scrivens, 2016).

In 1925, the Canadian KKK set up its national headquarters in Toronto, Ontario. In the wake of the American Civil War (1861–1865), ex-members of the Confederate army who fought to preserve the system of slavery founded the Klan as an insurgent movement to promote white supremacy and resist the post-war reconstruction era (Schaefer, 1971). After the Klan declined in strength in 1871, it re-emerged in 1915 following inspiration from the film The Birth of a Nation (Schaefer, 1971; Lennard, 2015). They promoted themselves as a fraternal structure, holding meetings and rallies across Ontario (Bartley, 1995). Initially, the Klan found their strongest support in southwestern Ontario, where they often targeted black people with racist attacks (Bartley, 1995). Members and supporters embraced the animosity toward those who didn't fit within the mould of British Protestant Canadian nationalism (Cline, 2019). Within a year, the Klan became one of the fastest-growing social organizations in the country (Lund, 2014). The KKK made its mark in the Saskatchewan political sphere by playing a pivotal role in the downfall of the ruling liberal establishment during the 1929 provincial election (Lund, 2014). Kwak (2020) links the current Canadian conservative discourse to right-wing populism and the emboldening of white nationalism in Canada, using race-neutral terms such as "heritage" and "common values" to draw more general support (Kwak, 2020, p. 1) in a wider context where who gets to define the common in heritage is a site of ongoing struggle.

By infiltrating the conservative party and energizing the public debate on immigration and sectarian schools, the KKK found a broad base of support. Membership in the Saskatchewan chapter was over 25,000 in the late 1920s and even included a Member of Parliament, Walter Davy Cowan (Lund, 2014; Parent & Ellis, 2014). In Alberta, the KKK had significant influence under the leadership of the Imperial Wizard, John James Maloney, a seminarian who helped revive the Klan in Saskatchewan (Appleblatt, 1976; Waldman, 2017). After Maloney successfully campaigned for Daniel Knott to be mayor of Edmonton, they celebrated by burning a cross on election night. Knott would continue to approve of the cross burnings across the city (Pitsula, 2013). Alberta's Klan membership surged in 1932 as Maloney's influence grew (Appleblatt, 1976; Pitsula, 2013). He mainly focused his attacks on the Catholic Church and French-speaking minorities across the prairies during this time. In the spring of 1932, Maloney published his newspaper in Edmonton called T*he Liberator*, which would continue to spread "Patriotic-Protestantism" messaging (Pitsula, 2013). In this way, the Klan shared political overlap with the Orange Order, gaining popularity in areas with an established Orange Order stronghold. They also engaged in violent anti-Catholic campaigns throughout Canada, threatening those who did not conform to their beliefs (Cline, 2019). Catholic churches became the targets of arson, notably at a Cathedral in Quebec City in 1922. In 1924, at a Catholic school in Winnipeg, Manitoba, ten students were killed following a fire set by the Klan. In 1926, the Klan was also responsible for detonating a Catholic church in the city of Barrie, Ontario (Ross, 1992; Parent & Ellis, 2014). Membership in the Klan declined in the early 1930s as their momentum and influence in the political sphere began to diminish (Newton, 2014).

The KKK and subsidiary groups played a significant role in mainstreaming hate, with the political campaigns and election (1989–1992) of former KKK Grand Wizard David Duke being a prime example. These are important "goals" for many of the larger RWE groups and the political parties which are currently at play in the extremist landscape. In 2007, the Regina Leader-Post reported that Regina resident Christian Waters, a high-ranking officer of the Canadian branch of the Brotherhood of Klans, started the organization which grew to 250 members in Saskatchewan and 3,500 members across Canada (Rhodes, 2018). A *CBC* article illustrates how the threaded history of the KKK led to remnant members moving into cyberspace in the early 2000s and paved the way for a number of successor groups with similar ideologies (Manasan, 2020).

This white supremacist variety of the above can be traced to British Israelism. British Israelism suggested that the people of the British Isles are the direct descendants of the Ten Lost Tribes in Ancient Israel, and therefore God's chosen people (McFarland & Gottfried, 2002; Perry & Scrivens, 2016). Before moving to further describe this movement, it is worth to pause and reflect on the historical context of the emergence of the concept in terms of a group-making activity. The idea that the peoples of the British Isles can be understood as an inclusive category can be interpreted as disparaging other important attributes such as the existence of independent movements. It is worth recalling that longstanding historical struggles between Ireland, Scotland, and England – among other groups within the region – have had different approaches with group-making projects as is evident still today. Returning to the development of the concept of British Israelism, this idea has been interpreted as having given rise to the Christian Identity movement that believes that white people were direct descendants of Ancient Israel. Those who ascribe to the Christian Identity movement also believe that Jews are the source of all evil and the children of the Devil (McFarland & Gottfried, 2002; Parent & Ellis, 2014). Additionally, they believe that non-white people have no souls and, thus, should either serve whites or be exterminated (Quarles, 2004). From its historical roots until today, the far-right utilizes racial essentialism as a justification for the idea of the natural hierarchies among groups. As a result, systematic discrimination among racial, ethnic, and religious groups is seen as an inevitable result of this natural hierarchy (Quarles, 2004; Parent & Ellis, 2014) rather than as a process of contestations over different group-making visions.

British Israelism dismisses those of the Jewish faith, but interpretations of the roles that those of the Jewish faith play in world events or apocalyptic narratives can be interpreted through political and hate ideologies. One such religious interpretation is related to Christian Zionism, a belief system that is based within apocalyptic narratives from the Book of Revelation with John Bale's *The Image of Both Churches* (1545), where he wrote that the conversion of Jews to Protestantism was essential for God's plan. Bale's work and that of John Foxe soon took an important role in the Protestant apocalyptic hermeneutics. In 1609 Thomas Brightman's *Apocalypsis Apocalypseos,* he built upon this narrative and argued that Puritans needed to convert the Jews, as they would eventually join the Puritan army to perish Islam in the battle of Gog and Magog (Ezekiel 38–39). As interpretations of the Book of Revelation continued by Protestant theologians, the enmity against Islam grew (Smith, 2012). In the 1970s, Hal Lindsey's bestselling nonfiction book, *The Late Great Planet Earth*, added the notion that for the Ultimate Battle to begin, Israel needed to build the Third Temple on its previous site. The obvious issue here is that the Dome of the Rock is in this location (Durbin, n.d.). In the modern era, Christian Zionism is expressed by conservative Christians, mostly white evangelicals (Northey, 2015, p. 94), who believe that an Israeli nation is the fulfillment of biblical prophecy and as the nation expands, and it is understood as evidence that God's covenant with the people of Israel continues. This biblical interpretation about the land of Palestine and its people aided in the making of the Palestinian Nakba with the help of some Canadian politicians and Zionist figures (Engler, 2010), and it led Christian Zionists to believe it is their duty, as Christians, to continuously support Israel at the expense of Palestinians' right to live in Palestine. Linked to a contemporary interpretation of the Book of Revelation, Christian Zionists believe that the establishment of the nation of Israel is one of many steps to the battle of Armageddon and the return of Christ. More often following the 9/11 events, many Christian Zionists argued that Israel was the representative of Western values in the Middle East, and the act of terrorism in the United States was not only interpreted as a domestic threat but was also included in their understanding of the Israeli-Middle East conflict whether in Canada or the US (Engler, 2010; Walberg, 2017; Smith, 2012). With the lobbying power of Zionists and conservative Christians both in the United States and in Canada, far-right and Zionist beliefs are closely aligned when Israel and the Middle East are involved and have greatly impacted international relations and anti-Palestinian policies. These religious interpretations can also be utilized by anti-Islam and anti-immigration RWE groups who can spread their ideologies when events such as the October 7, 2023 attack by Hamas on Israel and the subsequent Israeli destruction of Gaza and its settlers' attacks against Palestinians in the West Bank. In relation to current Canadian RWE figures, Ezra Levant is considered one of the promoters of not only far-right ideologies in Canada and abroad but also Zionism (Walberg, 2017, p. 239), often invoking his "Jewish Holocaust heritage" (Dart, 2022, p. 116).

In the 1930s, the global rise of Nazism and fascism had spillover effects in Canada (Ross, 1992; Perry & Scrivens, 2016). In the Canadian context, the economic collapse during the Great Depression drew some people towards fascism who blamed their woes on racial or ethnic minorities (Reid, 1933). While there was resistance to anti-Semitism and fascism (see Canadian League Against War and Fascism, ca. 1935), Jews, in particular, were a significant target because some people viewed them as greedy and dishonest economic competitors (Nadeau, 2011). Aspects of these wider issues can be found in the province of Quebec that had a significantly large and established Jewish community (Weinfeld et al., 2012). Adrien Arcand, a prominent Canadian journalist, became a major fascist leader and champion of anti-Semitic propaganda. After losing his job as a reporter Arcand launched his own newspapers, including his populist newspaper Let Goglu (Nadeau, 2011). The newspaper was known for mocking famous people in society, including political figures such as William Lyon Mackenzie King. In 1929, in Quebec without a public school system and where schools were run either by the Catholic church or by Protestant churches, he used his newspaper to attack the Taschereau government for setting up a separate Jewish school system in the province's city of Montreal. He published an editorial on why the plans for Jewish schools are a danger to society, following it up with several anti-Semitic editorials in the months that followed (Nadeau, 2011; Théorêt, 2017). Arcand viewed Jewish people as a threat to national sovereignty, saying they would plot to dominate the world (Nadeau, 2011). In 1930, Arcand received Conservative Party funding to campaign for them and his newspapers created smear campaigns against Liberal candidate William Lyon Mackenzie King in exchange for funding. Arcand's reputation surged following an impressive conservative win of Bennet, for which he took credit (Nadeau, 2011; Théorêt, 2017).

Inspired by Hitler, Arcand's followers and others created several Nazi and fascist parties throughout Canada (Ross, 1992; Nadeau, 2011; Théorêt, 2017). One such group was the Swastika Club that was concerned with Jewish families travelling to the predominantly "Anglo-Saxon" beaches in Toronto, Ontario (Arato, 2021). The group became known for openly displaying Nazi symbols to make visiting Jews feel unwelcomed (Arato, 2021). In response, 1933 young Jewish Canadians organized a mass protest at the beaches which confronted counter-protesters from the Swastika Club. A couple of weeks later a riot of approximately 10,000 people broke out between the Swastika Club and young Jews after Swastika Club members displayed the swastika flag during a baseball game in Toronto (Levitt et al., 2018). Levitt et al. (2018) mention how the riots revealed the growing anti-Semitic attitudes toward Jews during the Great Depression and only six months after Hitler took power in Germany.

In 1934, Arcand established the Christian National Social Party, a fascist and anti-Semitic organization that advocated for the banishment of Jews to the Hudson Bay area (Nadeau, 2011; Théorêt, 2017). In a March 25, 1935 article, Arcand's newspaper *Le Patriote*, wrote that Jews in Canada could neither be citizens nor vote or be elected into politics, so they had two choices. First, they could accept the conditions of being British subjects in Canada and move to the Hudson Bay area, or they could leave for Palestine (Theoret, 2019. p. 256). Arcand expressed his anti-semitism as an attack on Christianity and its potential demise at the hands of the Jewish faith taking over Canada's religious landscape. He justified the use of the swastika as a rallying call against the Jews and in his interpretation, a symbol in support of Christian strength (Theoret, 2019. p. 256). In 1937, students associated with the Christian National Party went on a series of raids, smashing Jewish-owned shops in Montréal, with several more attacks on Jewish-owned property throughout Quebec (Ross, 1992). In 1938, Nazis and other racist clubs around Canada made efforts to unite into one National Unity Party (NUP) under the leadership of Arcand (Nadeau, 2011; Théorêt, 2017). After getting arrested on May 30, 1940, the National Unity Party was subsequently banned for attempting to overthrow the state. At his internment camp, he spoke out about how he would help rule Canada when Hitler conquered it (Repka & Repka, 1982). Following his release in 1945, Arcand remained quiet until 1949 when he announced he would be a candidate in his local federal riding for the NUP. His platform remained the same in that he called for a Christian government. Arcand lost the election and in 1953 he ran again and failed to secure the electorate's support. In the Cold War era of the 1950s, Arcand published a 22-page booklet, *La Republique Universelle*, where he claimed that two world wars had established a foundation for the "world revolution of the Jews". These theories were mostly drawn from the *Protocols of the Elders of Zion* that creates an international conspiracy led by the Jews (Theoret, 2019. p. 265).

The end of the Second World War (1939–1945) brought with it contrasting and conflicting interpretations of how it should be remembered. One site of struggle was over the Holocaust. While as researchers we know that the Holocaust did in fact occur, there was and is a global Holocaust denial movement. In the Canadian context, a major voice in the 1970s Holocaust denial movement came from Ernst Zündel (Atkins, 2009; Southern Poverty Law Center, 2021). Between 1945 and 1957, there was a surge of immigration out of Germany, including over 35,000 Holocaust survivors and their descendants travelling to Canada (Tingler, 2016). After witnessing the collapse of the Nazi Third Reich in 1945, Zündel immigrated to Canada in 1958 to avoid the military draft (Tingler, 2016). Germans were unpopular in Canadian society during this time with polls showing Canadians opposing German immigration. In this context, some Germans felt there was a lack of distinction between the Nazis and non-Nazis in media portrayals of Germans (Freund, 2006). In 1961, Zündel met Adrien Arcand, whom he credited for helping him better understand his German heritage. Zündel's meetings with Arcand changed the way he viewed media portrayals of Germans and re-cast his ethnic nationalism in a more combative and rebellious mould (Tingler, 2016; Théorêt, 2017). In 1968, he campaigned to be a candidate for the Liberal Party of Canada. He used this platform to protest the alleged anti-German propaganda in society (Atkins, 2009; Tingler, 2016). After withdrawing from the campaign, he later moved to Toronto where he grew to be a central figure for Holocaust denialism in Canada (Tingler,

2016). In 1978, he formed the "The Concerned Parents of German Descent", distributing propaganda to ethnic Germans while also protesting against Holocaust memorialization in the media (Atkins, 2009; Tingler, 2016). Zündel received broad media coverage in the 1980s after setting up his own publishing company, Samisdat Publishers, becoming one of the largest global distributors of hate material. His publishing company distributed material which included Holocaust denialist literature and pro-Nazi memorabilia (Goldschläger, 2012; Tingler, 2016).

Far from being marginal or unknown in Canada, a 2013 Canadian Security and Intelligence Service noted that Zündel was "considered one of the most notorious distributors of hate material in the world" (Thompson, 2017, p. 78) and referenced him as being the patriarch of the white supremacist movement in Canada. Zündel would go through a series of trials, one for the propagation of malicious and knowingly false content, which included publishing Richard Harwood's book *Did Six Million Really Die?* (Harwood, 1982; Goldschläger, 2012; Tingler, 2016). Zündel welcomed the public charges as free publicity, claiming the trial would serve as an opportunity to expose the alleged Holocaust controversy (Tingler, 2016). The trial served as an important test on the policing of hate speech and the limits of freedom of speech in Canada (Butovsky, 1985; Goldschläger, 2012; Tingler, 2016). After being convicted, the decision was later overturned on a technicality. This led to another trial in 1988, where he was convicted again. However, after spending two years in prison, he would be acquitted by the Supreme Court of Canada in 1992 (Goldschläger, 2012; Tingler, 2016). After his final appeal was rejected in 1994, Zündel failed to acquire Canadian citizenship and was deported back to Germany in 2005 (CBC, 2005; Southern Poverty Law Center, 2021).

In the 1960s, significant changes were made to Canada's immigration laws. These ended restrictions on Asian and European immigrants. Surges in immigration, coupled with high unemployment and rampant inflation, created frustration and anxiety in Canada (Perry & Scrivens, 2016; Hofmann et al., 2021). While the election of Prime Minister Pierre Elliot Trudeau marked the beginning of a shift in Canada's national identity to a multicultural one, racial tensions still reached dangerous heights (Ross, 1992; Wayland, 1997; Hofmann et al., 2021). In 1965, KKK violence continued with the vandalism of a Black Baptist church in Ontario, including the burning of a cross and graffiti (Parent & Ellis, 2014). Other neo-Nazi groups, such as the Western Guard Party, carried out anti-Semitic and racist attacks in the 1970s (Ross, 1992). Neo-Nazi groups belong to the "white power movement", using "symbols and ideology of Nazi Germany to imagine a white ethnostate" (Belew & Gutiérrez, 2021, p. xv).

As part of this wider context, in 1973 The Church of the Creator was established by Ben Klassen, promoting racism and anti-Semitism (Parent & Ellis, 2014). Deriving his beliefs from the Christian Identity movement, Klassen claimed it was wrong to think that Jews were the "chosen people" as it undermines the white race (McFarland & Gottfried, 2002; Parent & Ellis, 2014). Across North America, the movement can be found in small churches, Bible study groups, and political groups that are identity based. Christian Identarions share three key beliefs, that white "Aryans" are descended from the tribes of Israel and are doing the work of

God, and that Jews are not connected to the tribes of Israel but are viewed instead as the children of the Devil. In their understanding, the Devil mated with Eve in the Garden of Eden creating Jews. The third belief is that humanity is living in the era of the apocalypse, where the ultimate battle between good and evil will take place, in the form of Aryans battling the Jewish conspiracy and its allies so that the world may be redeemed and rewarded with an era of peace (Barkun, 1997). The group developed the concept of the Racial Holy War (RAHOWA), a term that has inspired other far-right groups across the world. Led by singer George Burdi, the idea of RAHOWA was spread into Canada by the Canadian Rock band RAHOWA, which sought to advance white power (Michael, 2006; Parent & Ellis, 2014). Though the Church Of The Creator claimed to be non-violent, it has been a catalyst for promoting and organizing neo-Nazi functions throughout Canada (Jackson, 2018).

In the 1980s, Aryan Nations spread to Canada from America. The national leader at the time, Terry Long, attempted to build a training camp in Caroline, Alberta. This camp would be similar to the Aryan Nations camp in Hayden Lake, Idaho, USA, which brought together individuals from various extremist groups, survivalists, and members of the Aryan Nation's prison ministry. The group was based on strong Christian Identity theology and spread its faith through prisons across America, and through doing so became foundational in the development of the Aryan Brotherhood (Ellis, 2015, p. 58.) The Brotherhood is a neo-Nazi prison gang that began in California in the 1960s (ADL, n.d.). Symbols for the Brotherhood include a shamrock often combined with a swastika, the initials AB, or their numerical equivalent 1 and 2 (ADL, n.d.). The Aryan Brotherhood is not a listed terrorist organization in Canada.

Crew 38 was the recruitment arm of the Hammerskins, which is described below. New recruits to the group spend time "shadowing" a member in what they called "hang outs". If the group approves of the new member, they are given a membership in Crew 38. If the recruit proves their loyalty to the group, they will be offered full membership in the Hammerskins. This process of proving loyalty can be a very long process; therefore, the Crew 38 can be classified a group of its own, closely associated with the Hammerskins. Hammerskin Nation is a well-organized, widely dispersed, dangerous skinhead group that was formed in Dallas, Texas in the late 1980s (ADLa, n.d.). The name and symbol for the group are derived from Pink Floyd's 1979 album "The Wall". The album was later turned into a film that tells the story of how the rock singer becomes a drug addict and turns to fascism (ADLa, n.d.). The film includes a scene where Pink Floyd performs a song about lining up "queers", "Jews", and "coons", "up against the wall" to shoot them (ADLa, n.d.). The film is fiction and Pink Floyd does not support fascism, the Hammerskin Nation borrowed inspiration to create its logo/flags/ banners that feature "two red, white and black crossed hammers" (ADLa, n.d.). The Hammerskins in the 1990s were present in Montreal (Perry & Scriven, 2016), and chapters of Northern Hammerskins and the Vinland Hammerskins engaged in a series of assaults and weapons offenses across Canada in the 1990s (Perry & Scriven, 2016).

Racial hierarchies that position white people as superior are embedded into many far-right ideologies and documented extensively. The Aryan Resistance Movement

(ARM) is an umbrella term for a group of neo-Nazi movements. The most famous is the White Aryan Resistance (WAR) that was founded by Tom Metzger in 1983. Metzger argued that nations should be racially based and promoted to his membership that their loyalty should be to their race, and not their country (Michael, 2016, p. 35). Metzger himself was labeled a neo-Nazi, but he adhered to "third positionist" ideology, that is highly critical of capitalism (Michael, 2016, p. 36). The Canadian version of WAR initially provided security for anti-immigration meetings, and soon morphed into part of ARM and carried out sophisticated media operations. Active and savvy on the Internet, WAR and ARM used the medium to recruit and spread their ideology (Wilson, 2017).

Another RWE group adhering to racist and anti-Semitic beliefs established in the 1980s was Blood & Honour (B&H), and is now a listed terrorist entity in Canada with strong roots in the country (Public Safety Canada, 2024). Its members support fascist, anti-Semitic, white supremacist ideologies (Public Safety Canada, 2024). The members are often identified as racist skinheads, white power skinheads, or neo-Nazi skinheads. Many members of B&H are also gang members and affiliated with white nationalist organizations. B&H was founded in 1987 by Ian Stuart Donaldson and Nicky Crane, who originally came together in the late 1970s through an English punk rock band titled Skrewdriver (Pollard, 2016, p. 401). The organization is also frequently referred to in German ("Blut und Ehre"), the letters "B" and "H", or the alphabetical equivalents ("2" and "8" or "28"). The selection of "Blut and Ehre" comes from Hitler's youth motto, and the two organizations share a red, white, and black color scheme. The B&H logo often includes the words with a triskele symbol in the place of an ampersand, but there are a number of variations on this logo, including the substitution of the kopf symbol in the place of the triskele. As noted above, Canadian Kyle McKee was the leader of B&H, as well as its armed branch, Combat-18 (the number 18 representing the alphanumeric code for Adolf Hitler; 1=A and 8=H), and was a primary figure in leading the expansion of these groups into Edmonton in 2012 (Humphreys, 2012).

Similarly, The Heritage Front is a Canadian neo-Nazi, white supremacist group that was founded in 1989 (Brean, 2008). The group disbanded in 2005 (Brean, 2008). The group focuses on bringing awareness of the "reality of race" to the world and preaches for racial separatism, and anti-immigration (Burstow, 2003, p. 417). The group was founded by Wolfgang Droege, who based the mandate of the organization on the creation of a white ethnostate (Burstow, 2003, p. 417). Originally founded in 1989, the group quickly became one of the strongest voices in RWE in Canada (Burstow, 2003, 419). Members oppose race mixing, multiculturalism, liberal immigration policies, communism, and homosexuality (Burstow, 2003, p. 418). Heritage Front had close ties with other groups in Canada such as the Church of the Creator, Aryan Nations, and the Hammerskins. The Heritage Front was based in Toronto with regional groups across the country (Burstow, 2003, p. 419). Groups such as The Heritage Front and WAR respond to a "grievance with aggression" through violence in the hope of submission to the perceived threat. In the case of these groups, it could be a perceived notion of harm to white male privilege or power position in society due to lax immigration laws (Perry &

Scriven, 2016, p. 7). This too can be seen in Christian extremists who envision their battle against a perceived enemy to protect God, country, and family (Perry & Scriven, 2016, p. 8). This articulation of saving both the nation and their God can be articulated in a sense of persecution or destruction of their religion, but can also be a mobilization tool for political means.

Still active, White Lives Matter (WLM) is a movement that promotes the idea of a "white genocide" fueled by "mass third world immigration, integration by force and 24/7 race mixing propaganda" (Mettler, 2016). The WLM movement has been interpreted by the SPLC (2021) as being a "racist response to the civil rights movement Black Lives Matter". The now-defunct website (whitelivesmatter.com) claimed that WLM is not a white supremacist, but rather believes that "ethnic Europeans are worth preserving" (Mettler, 2016). WLM has a presence on most mainstream platforms, and it has a strong physical and digital footprint in Canada primarily on Telegram. The regions with Telegram channels range from Alberta and Toronto. A slogan that is frequently used on various WLM Telegram channels is: "We declare war against the anti-white system". As our previous work illustrates, fear, othering, and brotherhood are central means this group uses to mobilize their followers (Stewart et al., 2023). The WLM has become important because of its mainstreaming of RWE issues and the connections that it provides to non-RWE individuals and groups.

Finally, it is important to reflect on the above RWE groups in relation to the notion of Christian nationalism, which is considered a contemporary political issue in Canada with umbrella groups such as the Liberty Coalition Canada (LCC) propagating a parallel Christian nation within Canada. The LCC is a group of several clergies who have banded together to promote and proselytize a conservative Christian worldview of politics, law, and culture guided by the notion that Christ rules all nations and to advocate for transformation in Canadian society to reflect the biblical principles and laws. To accomplish this, they have created training programs for Christians to run for political office, organize protests against LGBTQ2SA education in schools, and anti-COVID19 mandates. They have created podcasts and social media campaigns to achieve these goals and to have an audience reach far greater than the borders of Canada, in an attempt to inspire Christians globally. The LCC uses conspiracy and disinformation intertwined with conservative biblical values, laws, and interpretations to create a Canadian Christian nationalist state, combatting the perceived persecution and prosecution of Christians in Canada.

Recently, Christian nationalism is a term that has become mainstream, with some conservative Christians adopting the phrase as a positive political belief system and a duty of their faith. While most definitions link this movement to America, it is not purely American in its application by believers. Christian nationalism has been used as a mobilization tool to "save the nation" and for moral panics that have led to the marginalization of LGBTQ2SA communities, banning of books, women's healthcare, and attacks on the public school system and immigration process. A 2024 poll in the United States found that as the Christian Nationalism movement's presence became bolder in the political process that Americans were beginning to reject the politics of this movement. Thirty percent of Americans were opposed,

37% skeptical of Christian Nationalism, with Republicans more than three times more likely to support the movement than Democrats (Contreras, 2024). Christian nationalism serves as both a vision of the history of a nation and its future, which delineates who are true citizens and who believe their culture is under attack by enemies, both foreign and domestic. This vision of the history of America and Canada is that of the two nations founded by white, traditionally Christian men, who founded their countries on Christian principles. Those designated as the enemies of this national Christian culture are understood to be evil racial, religious, and cultural outsiders who threaten the traditional white, conservative Christians (predominantly males) through persecution and usurpation of their power positions. The destruction and degradation of the culture of the nation comes through "progressive" immorality (Gorski & Perry, 2022). Here we can see connections with RWE groups through notions of power, racism, misogyny, and "patriotism" that denote domestic enemies, based not on citizenship but on hate rhetoric.

In brief and based on the above historical context, we see how the spread of RWE is not simply a question of floating ideas in the public that convert individuals by force of reason alone. In cases beyond rhetoric, there are also political and economic underpinnings that give these ideas traction. Canada First in the 1860s and its more politically acceptable political fronts came about to challenge Métis and Francophone political and ownership rights to land. Instead of seeing the import to recognize the rights of Métis and others at the time of confederation, the more radical wings painted them as threats to the integrity of the nation. In relation to late 19th- and early 20th-century immigration from Asia, racist white pride movements, traits often associated with RWE, came about in part from white laborers fearing losing their labor position in relation to "cheaper" labor. This was a position promoted not only by some Canadian commercial interest but also by grassroot labor organizations. Being a Protestant Orangemen, long-time recognized for their distaste for Catholics, opened doors to employment within the police forces in cities such as Toronto. Ernst Zündel was quite literally in the business of peddling conspiracies in print for profit. Below, we briefly discuss early conspiracy research and the pathologizing approach of Richard Hofstadter, and how this "paranoid style" was later taken up. Next, we briefly look at the cultural and philosophical turn to researching conspiracy theories through the lens of scholars like Mark Fenster, Peter Knight, Jodi Dean, Michael Barkun, Charles Pigden, and M R. X. Dentith.

1.3 The development of conspiracy theories' scholarship

Early conspiracy theory research in the 1930s and 1940s was outlined by scholars like Katharina Thalman, whose work expands on the earlier work of Jack Bratish and Mark Fenster (Butter & Knight, 2019). Frankfurt School scholar Theordor Adorno identified the personality types he considered more susceptible to the "irrational practice of conspiracy theorizing" (Butter & Knight, 2019, p. 34). Sociologists like Leo Loewenthal and Norbert Guterman equated conspiracy beliefs to the complexities of modernity (Butter & Knight, 2019). While these early political psychologists and sociologists were largely speaking about conspiracy, they failed to locate a label for what they were studying, until in 1940, when Karl Popper described what he referred to as *the conspiracy theory of society* (Butter & Knight, 2019). According to Popper, an oversimplification of historical causation "committed the intellectual error of ascribing agency to improvisational forces" (Butter & Knight, 2019, p. 34).

The rise of McCarthyism during the 1950s set the tone for another generation of researchers and journalists – Edward Shils, Seymour Martin Lipset, and Richard Rovere – who regarded conspiracy theories as "irrational", "unscientific", and "harmful" for democracy (Butter & Knight, 2019). This led to a shift in research by pluralist political scientists who began to draw a link between these irrational, unscientific conspiracy beliefs and anti-democratic extremism (Butter & Knight, 2019). This way of understanding conspiracy led to the work of Richard Hofstadter's conceptualization of a more "paranoid style", giving way to an era of researchers who discarded the neutral sociological of perspective in favor of pathologizing conspiracy theories.

In the 1960s, Richard Hofstadter's (2012) paranoid style whereby the paranoia felt by believers is not a personal attack directed toward them as individuals, but an attack against the community. Hofstadter inextricably linked paranoia and conspiracy theory, creating an approach, a "style", that pathologized and marginalized conspiracy theories (Butter & Knight, 2019). Hofstadter (2012) positions conspiracists from this time as people who believed the nation was taken from them and they were fighting to get it back. Hofstadter (2012) underscored the importance of style, aesthetic, and narrative dimensions, but the approach impeded research because it pathologized and marginalized the conspiracies (Uscinski, 2018).

In *The Political Style of Conspiracy: Chase, Sumner, and Lincoln*, Michael Pfau modified Hofstadter's work by distinguishing paranoid style as an "exception to the rule" and Gordon Wood made the case that theorizing conspiracies is a rational activity, not within the fringes of society, but "rooted in the social mainstream" (Uscinski, 2018, p. 36; see also, Butter & Knight, 2019). The pathologizing paradigm has been challenged since the 1990s with greater appreciation for the fact that conspiracies are widespread in nature and have "potentially serious consequences" (Uscinski, 2018, p. 36). Early research, like the assumptions held by Hofstadter, "tended to take for granted that conspiracy theories are held by distinctive kinds of people with identifiable and flawed characteristics, and most work in the field holds that belief in conspiracy theories is irrational" (Uscinski, 2018, p. 37). Unfortunately, Hofstadter's conceptualization of conspiracy theories "impeded historical research for decades", leaving historians to either frame conspiracies as pathological or dismiss the "anxieties that fuelled them" (Butter & Knight, 2020, p. 30).

In the late 1990s, the fields of cultural history and cultural studies took up the study of conspiracy, largely in response to its pervasive nature in modern entertainment such as television, film, and Internet newsgroups (Butter & Knight, 2019). This first wave of cultural studies work included scholars like Jodi Dean, Mark Fenster, and Peter Knight (Butter & Knight, 2019). Jodi Dean observed how conspiracies about subjects like aliens permeated into culture and led to a broader distrust of institutions (Butter & Knight, 2019). Mark Fenster (1999) interprets conspiracy theories as effective when politics are interpreted through a lens by those individuals and groups for whom politics are inaccessible. Fenster understood inaccessibility to mean rendering politics as something impenetrable, hidden beneath a veil of secrecy. Fenster (1999) also notes that although "conspiracies" can be wrong and appear simplistic in their presentation of "answers," they may harbor a problem or issues that need to be discussed or addressed. Beneath the conspiracy could be issues such as structural inequities, an unjust political order, a dysfunctional civil society, or an exploitative economic system (Fenster, 1999). The conspiracy could provide a response to these issues for the adherents when society as a whole or the social safety net does not. Those who feel disenfranchised will seek out others who understand or feel the same and create a community or social group of like-minded individuals. A common thread among these cultural study theorists was an assertion that the task was "not to condemn popular manifestations of conspiracy theory, but to understand their appeal and assess their cultural significance" (Butter & Knight, 2020, p. 31).

The most conservative study in this field came from Michael Barkun's book *A Culture of Conspiracy: Apocalyptical Visions of Contemporary* America (Butter & Knight, 2019). While Barkun does not overtly challenge the pathologization of conspiracy theories, he does discuss how conspiracies have moved from the fringes to the mainstream (Butter & Knight, 2019). Barkun (2013, p. XI) argues that there are different types of conspiracy theories with the most prevalent being "improvisational conspiracism". This exists when there are significant subcultures or a group within a larger culture that holds beliefs or interests outside of the mainstream. Mainly rising or appearing during times of crisis, improvisational conspiracism is composed of heterodox religion, esoteric and occult beliefs, fringe science, and radical politics, and it has a potent influence on politics within the nation (Barkun, 2013, p. XI). What brings these various ideas like fringe science and heterodox religion together, is what Barkun (2013, p. 2) refers to as "stigmatized knowledge", which is a belief that secret hidden evil forces are controlling human destinies. A scapegoat always plays the role of evil within a conspiracy theory. Barkun (2013) refers to this as a systemic conspiracy, when a conspiracy is believed to have broad-based goals, such as to take over the control of a country, a specific region, or the entire world. While these goals may seem quite grandiose, a single organization seems to be at the center of these plans and is envisioned as completing them through the infiltration and subversion of existing institutions (Barkun, 2013, p. 53).

In categorizing types of conspiracies, Barkun (2013) identifies three important distinctions including *event conspiracies*, *systemic conspiracies*, and *superconspiracies*. Event conspiracies are restricted to a "limited, discrete event or set of events" such as the Kennedy assassination conspiracy or the spread of AIDS through black communities (Barkun, 2013, p. 6). Event conspiracies contend that an evil group is responsible for a single, or even multiple events, with a singular objective (Barkun, 2013, p. 50). Systemic conspiracies have wide-arching goals to secure control of a country, region, or the entire world – a common scenario with conspiracies targeting the machinations of Jews, Masons, and the Catholic Church (Barkun, 2013). When various forms of conspiracies come together, they are called superconspiracies (Barkun, 2013). Multiple conspiracies are "linked together hierarchically" and eventually nested within each other. At the top of the hierarchy is an all-powerful evil force, and it manipulates and controls conspiratorial actors lower on the hierarchy (Barkun, 2013, p. 6). Conspiracy theories share discursive narrative styles, logics, tropes, and myths (Byford, 2011; Marwick & Partin, 2022). Importantly, these "big tent" conspiracies like QAnon weave conspiracy theories together and change as current events evolve (Marwick & Partin, 2022).

When individuals begin to take a conspiracy seriously, there is inherently less trust in the institutions of the nation. The conspiratorial plot is evident in the churches, universities, government, banks, and the media. Due to these institutions not being trusted, the believer turns to the ideas and groups that are condemned by these very institutions (Barkun, 2013). de Wildt and Aupers (2024) argue that contemporary conspiracy culture is different in that it is less about the "other" and is now directed at the institutions of modern society. The authors mention that modern conspiracists produce and reconstruct cultural meaning, through the mixing of rationalism, and a strong sense of the metaphysical. This mainstreaming of conspiracy and distrust in institutions and positions of authority helps to foment the normalization, institutionalization, and commercialization of fringe ideologies and conspiracies, forming not only an alternative rationality but also alternative blueprints for society.

Early works by Karl Popper and Richard Hofstadter have made it all too easy to situate conspiracy theories as "irrational", "pathological", "delusional", or "extremist". Recent work often assumes a philosophical approach (see Dentith, 2023) or a cultural sociological perspective that assumes an agnostic stance toward an empirical analysis of conspiracy theories. Frederik Jameson's concept of "cognitive maps" represents "social systems that have become too complex to represent" or even consider as a totality. Conspiracy theories demand answers to the most pressing questions of our times; they represent the resonant ideal of the current Zeitgeist, calling upon us to consider what is really going on in "global politics, economy, and the media landscape" so we can make meaningful sense out of these stories and the opaque structures of power that "fuel the collective imagination about a (global) conspiracy". This subsequently demands understanding conspiracies as media practices recontextualized through new media, shaping content and form, as well as "their place in public discourse".

From the lens of analytical philosophy, Charles Pigden challenged Karl Popper's notion that "conspiracy theories are necessarily mistaken" (Butter & Knight, 2019, p. 39). Pigden, David Coady, and Lee Basham all argued "conspiracy theories are not *prima facie* irrational", and that historical examples illustrate how some conspiracies can be "construed as successful" (Butter & Knight, 2019, p. 39). Analytical philosophy questions rationality and contends that "conspiracy theory" is far from neutral or objective "but a pejorative dismissal of an allegedly 'crippled epistemology'" (Butter & Knight, 2019, p. 40). This philosophical line of analysis implored researchers to consider whether or what parts of a conspiracy might have "potential validity" – an argument that has been more recently taken up by the philosopher Matthew Dentith (Butter & Knight, 2019, p. 39).

1.4 Conceptualization of conspiracy theories

Conspiracy theories are commonly understood as a form of communication, to inform, and a tool for mobilization, to foster community (Yablokov, 2014). These conspiracy narratives often express perceived injustice, an articulation of fears both real and imagined, which are then propagated to mobilize wider social movements. These theories have provided a vehicle for the expression and symbolic representation of the fears of the extreme right.

While the term *conspiracy* is often not defined, according to Michael Barkun (2013, p. 3), a "*conspiracy belief* is the belief that an organization made up of individuals or groups was or is acting covertly to achieve some malevolent end". Weeks and Garrett (2014, p. 402) liken *conspiracy theories* to political rumors – "unverified stories or information statements people share with one another". In the past, conspiracy beliefs have been linked to personality types and social stresses, but more recent research shows conspiratorial beliefs can "emerge from both situational triggers and subtle context variables" (Theocharis et al., 2023, p. 3416). The term "conspiracism" acknowledges that conspiracy theories contain narrative elements (parts of a theory rather than a fully constructed theory) and not every individual or group who participates in the culture of a conspiracy necessarily believes the entire narrative (Mahl et al., 2023). Importantly, some actors and groups engage with conspiracy theories for alternative motives such as attention, money, or entertainment (Mahl et al., 2023). Lars de Wildt and Stef Aupers (2023) question portrayals of conspiracy theories, noting that conspiracists and their quote-unquote "radical beliefs" are often *pars pro toto* generalizations accumulated from the most extreme aspects or participants, as if these representations are accurate of the larger conspiracy culture. These extremist views and participants also include the grievances of males in their patriotism woven into the impetus for resistance and mobilization, saving not only the traditional gender roles, their virility, but the nation itself (Ashcraft, 2022). Importantly, both conspiracy theories and misinformation "tend to be endorsed by right-wingers" (Boulianne & Lee, 2022, p. 33).

Conspiracy theories are often interpreted as an attack on modern liberal democracy; they do raise ideas of injustice, either real or perceived. Within this articulation of injustice comes also an emotional response of fear which can be manifested through isolation or acts of resistance. These fears can be about power structures, values, morals, and the reduction of traditions and religions. Robertson (2022) argues that religion and conspiracy theories both demarcate the other, the domination of one group over an "uncivilized" other, and both claim to hold the ultimate truth (Robertson, 2022, p. 652). The missionary or proselytization of this ultimate truth among conspiracists can resemble that of religious missionaries, yet this same ultimate truth can lead to radicalization, extremism, and acts of resistance that can be manifested through violence, hate speech, and moral panics that harm marginalized communities.

In defining the far-right and the use of fear and conspiracy for mobilization, important commonalities need to be acknowledged. First, there are common tropes of the need to make the nation more ethnically homogenous and demand a return to more traditional Christian values and gender roles. Descriptions of those in power and national institutions are seen as being under the control of elites who place internationalism before the nation. Elites or powerful individuals are described by the extreme right as putting their own self-interests ahead of those they represent. This notion of fear and dread is an important component of the power of conspiracy theories, in that they can provide an "answer" or rationale as to why these fears manifest. Linked to politics, religion, and racism, conspiracy theories have served as justification for political mobilization, activism, and in some cases, physical violence. For example, conspiracy theories played on the fears brought forward by the pandemic. The public's concerns about uncertainty about the virus, the economic impacts, and their mortality were preyed upon by conspiracies that used narratives of racism, xenophobia, and antisemitism. Here, the ideologies of RWE resonated with the conspiracies falsely blaming the virus on intentional plots by foreign entities that integrated with RWE notions of "alien threats". The links between conspiracies placing the blame for the pandemic and the resulting remedies, such as mandates and vaccines, converged with mainstream and populist concerns and perceived injustices about different issues.

Current racist rhetoric online is focused on this conspiracy and migration, with RWE describing unauthorized immigrants as a securitization threat or even an existential threat to national security. This threat is mobilized through metaphors, policy tools, analogies, stereotypes, and emotions, by politicians, media, and influencers via their words and actions. With the Great Replacement theory, the securitization threat is articulated through a consistent description of unauthorized immigrants as "military aged men from Islamic nations or enemy nations" and a lack of women or children crossing borders, creating a narrative of invasion, rather than a human crisis at national borders. The process of securitization and the response to the threat rhetoric can create a conspiratorial convergence, where both the public and political response can initiate a rhetorical, practical, and philosophical tool to legitimate the mobilization, creation, and expansion of security regimes and populist political response. Here, populist actors can act as the voice of those who feel threatened and disenfranchised from the politics as usual policies. The image created of the unauthorized immigrants is that of cells of militarized men who will rise up to attack the nation, while simultaneously leaving their children and women unprotected and dismissed in their homelands. This image is consistent with the gendered discussion within nationalism.

Further, this gendered understanding of both unauthorized immigration as a national security threat and the conspiracy theory intertwined leads to a populist response that positions masculinity as aggrieved. This emotional understanding of virility under attack is one of the strongest propagators of populism in the 21st century. With moral panics, conspiracy theories, notions of religious persecution and prosecution, and liberal progressive politics attacking the power position of males and undermining their ability to protect God, country, and family the grievance of white, CIS Christian males have numerous conduits of expression. This masculine grievance is intertwined with race, socio-economic status, sexuality, religion, ethnicity, and citizenship. In North America, this grievance is articulated predominately by white, heterosexual, Christian males (Ashcraft, 2022). Ashcraft (2022) argues that this emotion of masculine grievance in the 21st century has become the reason why populism has become a political response globally. The conspiratorial convergence and political response to the perceived attack on maleness has created a maelstrom on and offline and is apparent in our research.

Politically, populism and conspiracy are usually connected. Historian Michael Kazin (1998, p. 1) defines populism as "a language whose speakers conceive of ordinary people as a noble assemblage not bounded narrowly by class, view their elite opponents as self-serving and undemocratic, and seek to mobilize the former against the latter". Public policy scholar Nathan Jessen (2018, p. 680) argues that populists are critics of power, and conspiracy theories provide a mode for that criticism. In essence, the populists feel that the government and those in authority do not represent the people or the silent majority. Through conspiracy theories, populists are given an identity for the hidden controlling factors preventing their representation. The link between conspiracy and populism can be found in the features both address. Populism provides a mechanism to mobilize people against the established power structures and the values of a society. Predominantly appealing to a sense of resentment against a perceived injustice in society, it calls for radical change and the elimination of hierarchical structures in society. In essence, populism provides a conduit to express unfairness and injustice, but it also serves as a recourse and remedy (Betz & Johnson, 2004, p. 313). Populism emphasizes the sovereignty of the people, promotes attacking the elite and ostracizing the "other", and invokes nationalism. In this respect, nationalism is not merely defined by official borders but can articulate an understanding of people united by geolocation, traditions, values, and community. This can take a negative turn when nationalism is articulated by RWE which envisions the people of the nation through a narrow and exclusive identity, such as white, male, heterosexual, and protestant Christian (Bjork-James, 2020). However, the term Christian values here mostly works as a cohesive mechanism for Christians regardless of denomination or dogma. Conspiracy theories can be dark social movements that operate as tools to spread nationalism and populism through fear of a crisis of identity and creating a perceived enemy through politics and ethnonationalism.

There is an articulation of the enemy as both elites and politically liberal in our data as well as the focus on two significant global conspiracy theories: the Great Reset and the Great Replacement. The Great Replacement theory is the belief that through immigration white people will be replaced in the geopolitical unit of a nation (Feola, 2021, p. 529). This particular conspiracy theory has evolved into a moral panic across social media platforms, with violent events and immigrant encampments in Europe being shared across social media platforms as a warning to North America. This moral panic mirrors the tale that began the conspiracy theory itself. The term "Great Replacement" was coined by French author Renaud Camus in his 2011 dystopian novel *Le Grande Replacement*. In 1992, Camus visited an old village in France and noted that the demographics had changed significantly since his last visit; this change led him to believe that French citizens were being replaced by immigrants. Initially, Camus founded his own political party in

France in 2002, with the party platform advocating "re-immigration" and the end to all immigration to France. The re-immigration process would see any individual who had immigrated to the country including any family members to their country of origin, resulting in the removal of all non-white people. In 2017, he expanded his re-immigration ideology by creating the National Council of Resistance. The Council was a pan-European movement established to stop the Great Replacement across the continent and to defeat, what he referred to as the "replacist totalitarianism" that a great cabal was attempting to instill to create a submissive populace that would submit to a New World Order. His book, *Le Grand Replacement*, was a rallying call and warning to all Western civilization about the coming destruction of their world through continued immigration (Celestini, 2023).

The book itself creates a dystopian vision of the future that comes to fruition through industrialization, secularism, or reduction of Christianity in society, the loss of national cultures. Based upon an earlier novel by Jean Raspail, *The Camp of Saints,* Camus' book became the impetus to the "you will not replace us" chant at the Unite the Right Rally in Charlottesville, Virginia. In fact, Camus was so inspired by the "resistance" of the RWE at the Rally that he wrote a second book on the Great Replacement titled. *You Will Not Replace Us* shortly after the rally (Celestini, 2023). The impact of this conspiracy theory is not only through violent acts, such as the death of Heather Heyer at the Unite the Right Rally, but also through resistance narratives of increasing birthrates of white women. Low birth rates among white women in Western civilizations are understood to be the catalyst for white replacement. When the Supreme Court of the United States' landmark decision on *Roe v Wade* was released, Great Replacement conspiracists cheered this as a victory for the resistance (Celestini, 2023). This celebration is linked to the populist component of this conspiracy theory and the resulting moral panic. The Great Replacement was also intertwined with COVID-19 conspiracy theories, including the idea that the vaccines were a mechanism of white population control. This particular conspiracy theory is a form of conspiratorial convergence where various conspiracy theories or those holding conspiratorial beliefs combine their beliefs to find common ground. In essence, it is the interconnection and blending of separate conspiracy theories, where those who believe differing conspiracies recognize shared elements or connections; this could be themes, actors, or motivation, leading to a belief that theories are not isolated but interconnected within a larger conspiracy (Celestini & Amarasingam, 2023).

The use of this conspiracy theory is one of the many scare tactics used to spur nationalism and populism. Yet, some who are believers in the Great Replacement Theory do conceive of a cabal who are forcing immigration to create a New World Order. In fact, Renaud Camus, once wrote that the "global elite" were planning to attack white people in society and replace them with immigrants to gain control of the world (Camus, 2011). The notion that whites are being replaced in Western countries positions this conspiracy in the political realm, not only within the confines of immigration policies, but also to the idea that the nation, including its values, traditions, and political power, is being taken from one group, and given to others (Feola, 2021, p. 530). Politically this conspiracy theory is understood as a mechanism for one political party to remain in power over another, via a voting bloc of immigrants. This trope links to Hofstadter (2012) and political paranoia of disenfranchisement, as well as Fenster's (1999) definition of conspiracy as voiceless and disenfranchised from the political realm.

In recent years, the spread of misinformation has taken center stage in the public arena, occasionally referred to as "information pathologies" – a trifecta of false information, propaganda, and conspiracy theories (Culloty & Suiter, 2021). These information pathologies have become heavily implicated in the subversion of national politics and the amplification of social dichotomies (Culloty & Suiter, 2021). In this wider context, far-right movements and the "diffusion" of disinformation have grown significantly since the 2016 presidential election in the United States (Yang & Fang, 2021). More recently, right-wing pundits and "celebrities" routinely accuse popular social media sites of censoring conservative opinions (Buckley & Schafer, 2021).

1.5 Dark social movements, dark participation, and conspiracies

To better situate how conspiracy theories move through digital platforms, we examine these "bad actors" with a focus on so-called dark social movements (Culloty & Suiter, 2021, p. 2). "Bad actors" is a term for people or groups that "intentionally create and propagate disinformation", including through social movements (Culloty & Suiter, 2021, p. 11). Similar to internetworked social movement (ISM) theory, dark social movements include identity, ideology, and network formation (Langman, 2005, p. 45), all of which are motivated by political and ideological interests, often around subjects like anti-immigration or Islamophobia (Culloty & Suiter, 2021). Platforms allow counter-narratives to materialize and provide a platform for extremists to air grievances through relationships that form around a common enemy (Perry & Scriven, 2016, p. 68). While it is difficult to measure or define "ideologically motivated violent extremism", these dark social movements share a "framework of beliefs, ideas, concepts, and literature that cuts across far-right groups which makes it possible to identify actors within this ideology" (Amarasingam et al., 2021, p. 7). During the pandemic, dark social movements in Canada anchored onto "anti-lockdown and anti-public health measure movements", likely as a way to "lure anti-vaccine activists and conspiracy theorists to their cause" (Amarasingam et al., 2021, p. 7). Movements that predated the pandemic pivoted or created groups to "co-opt and/or subvert others" (Amarasingam et al., 2021, p. 10). The anti-mask, anti-lockdown, and anti-vaccination movements have coalesced into networks, and while some members may leave organizations when COVID-19 dissipates, the sense of distrust in institutions and the feeling of disenfranchisement will not simply disappear, which could lead to continued conspiratorial beliefs. Others who are now fully networked will remain connected to "extremists as they move to the next issue", which will likely be some semblance of a return to common RWE preoccupations like "anti-immigration, Islamophobic and antisemitic views, policies and violence" (Amarasingam et al., 2021, p. 10). Amanda Garry et al. (2021) argue that conspiracy and extremist ideologies are different, but they can intersect: "while conspiracy theories may not have mass radicalizing effects, they are extremely effective at leading to increased polarization within societies" (Garry et al., 2021, p. 156). Conspiracy theories expose enemies and those who are unaware of the truth by an in-group that prioritizes their knowledge of truth, their morality, and most importantly, their role as the social heroes who will save the world.

Dark social movements often form identities and build collective action around conspiracies. While dark social movements continue to create political and social gains, the ISMs tend to focus on building collective identities and articulating resistance through symbolic or cultural grounds, rather than traditional political channels. Social movements emerge from existing conditions in society and amplify "causes" or injustices laid upon the "other" to create strategic agendas that produce an "alternative social imaginary" (Langman, 2005, p. 44). The collective identity of RWE on social media platforms is constructed through interaction, negotiation, and the opposition to "others". Through the sharing of information, these groups create a notion of "we" and delineate who the "them" are, creating well-defined borders of in- and out-groups. The creation of the collective identity is relational to the creation of the collective enemy or the other. These collective identities create social boundaries that are used by the RWE movements to illustrate the moral, cognitive, affective, and behavioral differences between "us" and "them" (Perry & Scriven, 2016, p. 79). Through the denigration of the other, a common cause, threat, or fate is the catalyst to motivate people to act together to protect their collective (Perry & Scriven, 2016. p. 72). The internet and social media platforms provide a community where individuals can express their deconstructions, or interpretations of the official versions of the truth, as well as interact with other accounts of reality.

Social movement theory and social media scholarship exist in dichotomies around those who are optimistic (Castells, 2012; Shirky, 2008) versus those who see social media as superficial and unproductive in the development of social movements (Gladwell, 2010). In more recent years, social movement theories have grown to include internet-based social movements and cyberactivism. Despite this divisiveness, it is important to recognize that internet-based social movements are positive and negative in nature. The advent of the internet created an entanglement between RWE groups and technology, which has expanded ISM numerically and globally "to publicize messages of hate" (Perry & Scriven, 2016, p. 77). According to Perry and Scriven (2016, p. 68), the globalized nature of the internet mimics the globalized understanding of the threat to the "rightful authority and even survival of the white race and the white culture". Within this virtual public sphere, dark social movements connect instantaneously to build strategies, spread ideologies, and frame causes of injustices (Langman, 2005, p. 44). Alternative platforms allow counter-narratives to materialize and provide a stage for extremists to air grievances through relationships that form around a common enemy (Perry & Scriven, 2016, p. 68). On Telegram, RWE groups operate as dark social movements that strategically appeal to "mainstream sensibilities" to recruit and grow movements (Tetrault, 2021, p. 1). Communication technologies propel mobilization structures that are fluid, open, and participatory (Langman, 2005). Individuals are recruited into social movements through four factors: (1) the framing of information; (2) a personal identity that is receptive to this informational framing; (3) a location that is conducive to activism; and finally, (4) ties to social actor networks with similar concerns (Langman, 2005, p. 52). Framing and meaning construction are helpful for understanding the sociopsychological processes in the formation of digital coalitions. This framing develops a relatable belief system for participants and provides grievances and motivations that are well-defined, linked, and extend to create a collective identity and solidarity among group members. Within the theory of framing and meaning, the role of media is integral to building movements as relational frames that encompass the role of media in the discourse between the individual members, the movement as a whole, and the movement within the public sphere (Langman, 2005, p. 44).

Social media platforms also provide a conduit to connecting like-minded individuals who can then work in tandem in their dark participation on forums, blogs, and news media comment sections (Waisbord, 2020, p. 1032). Here, dark participation can take the form of media manipulation, misinformation, hate speech, and harassment (Westlund, 2021, p. 1). Social media platforms, including dark social media sites, have enabled users to express and communicate their hatred, through content liberation. According to Westlund, the threshold for users to express their hate has been lowered significantly on social media platforms, which has allowed coordinated groups to intentionally express hate speech (Westlund, 2021, p. 2). Newly emerging technology as well as the social architecture of social media and the internet as a whole has created a world where there is a very low threshold for the production of hate speech via dark participation. These expressions of hate can have a significant impact on both individuals and coordinated groups. There will always exist those who will take advantage of such platforms through systemic exploitation, regardless of the safety protocols enacted. Dark participation can have an impact on societies and democracies through hate speech, conspiracy theories, and incivility (Westlund, 2021, p. 4). Dark participation is not only text based but can also include images, audio, and video messaging (Frischlich et al., 2021, p. 2). Defining dark participation is affected by online norms, so what is acceptable on one platform such as 4chan would be deemed completely unacceptable on another social media site, such as Twitter. This is complicated further when one considers the various perspectives or roles that exist in determining or interpreting the messages in that there is a sender, a receiver, and a target (Frischlich et al., 2021, p. 2).

In 2014, *The Guardian* argued they had found a large number of manipulative, and planned posts in their comment sections, which were eventually linked to the Russian government or associated groups. By 2015, the use of "troll farms", "web brigades", and "troll armies" had been well documented, as were their intentions of having influence on the Western public and journalists (Quandt, 2018, p. 40). Not all of these participants are political foreign actors, they can also be organized state propagandists, religious groups, or extremists. Their misinformation campaigns can be used to attack certain groups or individuals (Quandt, 2018. p. 41). This practice is what Quandt defined as "dark participation" which can also take the form of fake information through the impersonation or imitation of news sources. This imitation plays upon the public trust in these legacy news media sources (Quandt, 2018, p. 41). Due to the content moderation on sites like *The Guardian*, planned posts can be moderated, and silenced, yet the content liberation found on alternative social media sites allows conspiracy theories and planned tandem dark participation to flourish.

The three dimensions that envelop so-called dark platforms include infrastructure ostracization, exile congregation, and content liberation (Zeng & Schäfer, 2021). A central feature of dark platforms is infrastructure ostracization (Zeng & Schäfer, 2021, p. 3), which unfolds through platform processes like shadowbanning and deplatformization.

The motivation behind dark participation is varied and depends on if it is an individual or a group. Individuals are driven by "genuine personal hate for others or the sheer pleasure of making others suffer" (Quandt, 2018, p. 42). Planned group attacks may appear random, but they are controlled in their delivery, as group members are following "specific tactics" to spread their narrative (Quandt, 2018. p. 42). Large-scale campaigns to manipulate are obviously strategic in nature but have a dark logic and process (Quandt, 2018, p. 42). For individuals, personality characteristics are also a driving force for dark participation. For example, individuals who display online disinhibition effect, or the power of anonymity, comment without the fear of ramifications for their words and are one of the main forces behind toxic behavior online. The sensation of being invisible and/or anonymous can cause people to push social boundaries without the fear of repercussions (Kowert, 2019, p. 2). Dark participation that causes harm to others is considered toxic behavior, and fundamentally the outcome of dark participation is toxicity (Kowert, 2019, p. 3). When anonymous individuals come together online, members can encourage each other to participate in group norms, even if those norms are toxic or harmful (Kowert, 2019. p. 2). Feelings of empowerment through anonymity are not the only personality traits that can affect toxic online behaviour; sadism, a sense of inferiority to others, depression, and/or social extraversion can also be catalysts to the toxicity of dark participation (Kowert, 2019, p. 2).

The actions of conspiracy theorists can be highly motivated and organized, leading them to have motivation to engage in the production of citizen journalism online (Quandt, 2018, p. 40). This can lead to the type of commentary found in dark social sites like Telegram, and BitChute content providers analyze world events through various lenses. Quandt (2018, p. 40) argues that the rise of this "dark participation" grows parallel to the rise of populism in Western democracies. Frischlich et al. (2021, p. 3) in their research used three aspects of ideological motivations in dark participation, namely political ideology, political frustration or anger, and their perceived feelings of political inefficacy or disenfranchisement. The study found that psychopathy and Machiavellianism increased uncivil participation, but narcissism had no effect (Frischlich et al., 2021, p. 7). Conspiracy theories have been linked to "anti-democratic attitudes, prejudice, and non-normative political behavior" (Sternisko et al., 2020, p. 1), and given the similarities to the toxicity of dark participation, conspiracy is the ideal conduit for spreading misinformation and hate speech. The Great Replacement theory is an example of the power of conspiracy to further white nationalism. Distrust and a sense of disenfranchisement from society's institutions are foundational for conspiracy theories to seem legitimate and believable.

Ihlebæk and Holter (2021) interviewed participants of dark web news media sites and found that their actions were instigated by political fear or concern. This fear constituted a significant aspect of the users' narratives and understanding of the world (Ihlebæk & Holter, 2021. p. 1209). They found that the dark participants believed that media was not covering the political issues "correctly" and those who felt as they did, many of who are far-right actors, were being silenced and ridiculed by these same legacy media outlets (Ihlebæk & Holter, 2021, p. 1209). When the legacy media are not providing "objective reporting" (reporting how far-right dark participants experience the world factually or emotionally), these participants seek alternative news sources that do (Ihlebæk & Holter, 2021, p. 1209). As alternative social media sites, they have provided an outlet for dark participants to find their communities and a voice for their worldviews via alternative news and information sources.

This alternative source often mimics legacy news sites or mainstream social media platforms like YouTube, through text and video that are very similar in presentation, but without similar journalistic rigor or integrity. The purveyors of these imitative news performances often articulate their position as an alternative voice, and the providers of "news" that legacy media does not present (Westlund, 2021, p. 2). These performances often articulate the news through a conspiratorial lens, which provides an explanation and the cause of what is occurring in world events. People are drawn to conspiracy theories and movements that serve to fulfill their situational relevant needs and concerns (Sternisko et al., 2020. p. 4). This positioning is integral to the dissemination and appeal of their messaging. Schulze found in their research that the strongest predictors for right-wing alternative media were political interests and attitudes regarding immigration. Further Noppari et al. (2019) found that those who engaged in alternative media in Finland were skeptical of systems and institutions, critical of political agendas, and were overall discontent. Noppari et al. (2019) also found that these users turned to alternative media for added information and entertainment. As a result, emotions of anger, suspicion, and hostility emerge. In essence, the dark participants feel that the serious threat and immorality that society is facing are not being articulated by the media as viable, and their anger fuels them to speak out in the comment sections, social media, and to find alternative news sources (Ihlebæk & Holter, 2021, p. 1215). Furthermore, the dark participants stated that alternative news sources, as actors outside of the establishment, were understood as more trustworthy (Ihlebæk & Holter, 2021, p. 1216). In other words, alternative social media sites as an alternative news and information source provide a confirmation and recognition of the dark participants' worldviews, fears, and anger (Ihlebæk & Holter, 2021, p. 1217) because conspiracy theories are outcomes of dark participation.

It is important to mention that strategic dark participation is prevalent in the comment sections of articles and is the work of troll factories, right-leaning counter-publics, and extremists (Frischlich et al., 2019, p. 2015). Dark participation on legacy news sites offers commentators an audience to agitate while harnessing the power of the media brand (Quandt, 2018, p. 41). The power this kind of agitation has is illuminated by the practice of dark participants on German news sites who use the term Lügenpresse, or press of liars. On German news sites, the anti-Islam, anti-refugee group Pegida posted comments on articles to promote anti-immigration. This dark participation was a planned and consistent attack on the media but provided a platform for the dissemination of a cohesive narrative directing Pegida's ideology to a larger audience while sowing distrust in the news media (Quandt, 2018, p. 42). Pegida's commentary is a form of cyber hate, which is a concerted effort by hate movements or campaigns targeted at groups based on race, ethnicity, gender, or religion (Quandt, 2018, p. 41).

1.6 Operationalizing conspiracy theories

It should be noted that our research focuses on the role of RWE and conspiracy theories in Canada – an under-developed area of study within the scholarship of conspiracy theories and RWE movements. In thinking about how to study this question, we deductively and inductively developed a conceptualization of RWE conspiracies by exploring four specific aspects:

1. Topics;
2. Concerns;
3. Targets;
4. Actors.

In terms of method, we employed a deductive approach by borrowing from previous research we consulted on conspiracy theories. In addition, we used inductive inquiry by examining the raw data that we collected from different social media sites, allowing more sub-topics, issues, and actors to emerge from the data. To achieve our goals, we used traditional content analysis that employs both quantitative and qualitative approaches as both are needed to better understand the content. We also used the API of Hatebase to assess the amount of hate on Reddit, and mostly employed multimodal analysis in terms of analyzing BitChute videos, emojis on Telegram and Reddit, and memes on Twitter and elsewhere. We also employed a number of digital methods for the examination of each social media platform or site, depending on their affordances. For the Dark Web research, for instance, we used The Onion Router (TOR) and subscribed to a commercial digital tool, Beacon Dark Web search engine offered by Echosec Systems, to identify and retrieve relevant data after which we qualitatively examined the sample. In addition, we used Pushshift API for Reddit data and Python scripts for Twitter and Parler data collection. We also used descriptive statistics to report frequencies and figures. In some cases, we employed Python to process large datasets and extract relevant meaning from them such as the most frequent Twitter hashtags. In addition, we used a manual reverse engineering approach to explore the algorithmic rules found on Google's autocomplete search engine as well as different social media sites like Instagram regarding the use of certain hashtags.

34 *The Canadian Far-Right and Conspiracy Theories*

The four areas addressed in our manual coding of data serve to designate the overall communication, what fear or injustice is being acknowledged, who the "enemy" or other is, and who is the cause of this perceived injustice. In general, conspiracy theories are created by actors, focusing on specific topics, serving to articulate a matter of concern, for example, a fear or an injustice whether real or perceived, and providing a target to confront, an "enemy" (Chart 1).

Using the above four-part conceptualization, we then retrieved the major topics, concerns, targets, and actors spread by Canadian RWE. This was achieved through a deductive and inductive inquiry of RWE content, specifically on Telegram and BitChute (see Chapter 3). By conceptualizing the components that makeup conspiracies, it is easier to examine the dark platform ecosystem and map the conspiracy theories within them. After analyzing the data, we developed Figure 1.1 to visualize our conceptualization of conspiracy theories.

While topics such as islamophobia or antisemitism may be understood as specific topics, other topics such as the Great Reset, Great Awakening, and New World Order (NWO) can be understood as being wider umbrella topics.

One such umbrella term is the Great Reset. The term gained traction from a 2016 video released by the World Economic Forum (WEF), which asked economists to describe the future. Shortly after posting the video, the WEF removed it from their social media accounts, and the video in 2016 made very little impact in the conspiracy realm. Later in May 2020, the WEF held a virtual conference with politicians, economists, and public figures to discuss structural reforms to global capitalism – a Great Reset in light of the pandemic and economic effects. WEF leader Klaus Schwab and economist Schwab and Malleret (2020) published a book

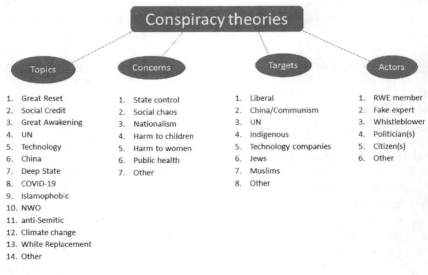

Figure 1.1 Conceptualization of conspiracy theories.
Source: Created by the authors.

under the same title. Within the predictions of the economists was that in 2030 people would "own nothing and be happy", and they would rent material goods which would be delivered to their door by drones, and that the world would need to both protect democracy and re-envision immigration due to climate change draughts and making areas inhabitable. Conspiracy theories that support climate denialism often assert that a powerful organization is "lying or spreading misinformation for personal gain, or that they are suppressing alternative theories by presenting a united front" (Walker, 2023, p. 29). Based on a video released in 2016, Klaus Schwab interviewed then Prince Charles on a WEF podcast where the two discussed the need for a "Great Reset" due to the implications of the COVID-19 pandemic on the world. The term the Great Reset was linked back to the 2016 video, and conspiracists linked the lockdowns to the idea of owning nothing, having everything delivered to our homes, and eventually to the enslavement of humanity, to a one-world dictatorial government of elites. The contrasting conspiracy to the Great Reset is the Great Awakening, which is the belief that humanity would awaken to the threat of the one-world order and rise up to destabilize the Great Reset, and defeat those who would rule over the enslaved population. The Great Awakening will come as those who know the "truth" spread their knowledge to others, creating a global wave of resistance to the New World Order.

Canadian Prime Minister Justin Trudeau also discussed the Great Reset in a short video on the WEF's program. Conspiracists quickly linked the Great Reset to a worldwide, communist cabal that wanted to destroy so-called free-enterprise capitalism (Schuller, 2021, p. 195). Both of these conspiracy theories are global in nature and have been linked to the COVID-19 pandemic and the preventative measures that were put into place, in particular in relation to lockdowns and mask mandates. The preventative measures involved in mitigating the effects of COVID-19 were interpreted as "evidence" of the eventual take-over of Canada by an evil cabal through their actions to restrain freedoms, both individual and religious. The Great Reset conspiracy theory during the pandemic provided a conduit to the mobilization of the sensation and language of perceived oppression during lockdown mandates, "provided an epistemic foundation that matched the scale of the global crisis" and used language that provided an aura of authority and potential control that was appealing to those on the political right and those holding antidemocratic ideologies (Christensen & Au, 2023, p. 2349).

Similar to the WEF, the United Nations has been interpreted as a conduit to a New World Order since its establishment in 1945. The UN was not seen as a world organization for the betterment of humanity, but as a tool to enslave humanity by the Global Elite. Throughout the Cold War the UN was interpreted as an enemy infiltrating national institutions and today with policies such as Agenda 21 and the Sustainable Development Goals, conspiracists believe it is an attempt to force immigration (similar to the Great Replacement Theory) as well as enforce the taking of weapons and land ownership from the citizenry (similar to the Great Replacement theory). Others believe that Agenda 21 and the more current Agenda 2030 are a means for population control by the United Nations. Agenda 21 and 2030 are plans by the United Nations to address current global environmental and development issues and to initiate steps to prevent further issues in the future.

The opposite of these conspiracies is the Great Awakening, a prominent aspect of the QAnon conspiracy. Similar to redpilling, the Awakening occurs when collectively people become aware of the "real" battle transpiring within the political realm of deep states. QAnon, regularly referred to on social media as "Q", started as a "fringe phenomenon" but has evolved into a mainstream movement that propagates false information related to COVID-19 and the Black Lives Matter protests (Roose, 2021). "QAnon is a wide-ranging, completely unfounded theory that says that President Trump is waging a secret war against elite Satan-worshiping pedophiles in government, business and the media" (Wendling, 2021). Initially, QAnon was linked specifically to the United States and 45th President Donald Trump, yet now it is linked to international governments, and world events such as the war between Russia and Ukraine. Once enough individuals are "awake" to the cabal controlling world politics and pedophiles who are human trafficking of children, then an apocalyptic uprising will occur destroying the evil cabal. The Great Awakening has grown from its roots on Reddit, r/greatawakening where those who were discovering the QAnon conspiracy could pose questions, to a book supposedly written by 12 QAnon insiders; the Great Awakening is the siren call of QAnon conspiracists to share the truth of this historical battle, and saving the world (Overwijk & de Zeeuw, 2023). What started as a largely online movement has now infiltrated the offline world with followers participating in events like the January 6 Capitol riot (Roose, 2021).

Based on our research, QAnon leaders/followers are present on a wide variety of online platforms, typically using the letter "Q" as platforms like Twitter have banned the hashtag #QAnon. Romana Didulo, Canada's QAnon "Queen" uses a range of alternative platforms (Telegram, BitChute, etc.) to mobilize followers (CBC News, 2021). Didulo claims to be the "sovereign of the republic of Canada" and has encouraged the following to send "cease-and-desist letters across North American on her behalf" to "stop COVID-19 restrictions" (CBC News, 2021). In late 2021, Didulo encouraged her online followers to "shoot to kill" anyone administering COVID-19 vaccinations to children (CBC News, 2021) and her followers attempted citizen arrests on police officers in Peterborough Ontario, for perceived treason due to supporting COVID-19 mandates (Celestini et al., 2023). QAnon followers have also participated in the anti-vaccine trucker protest in 2022, also known as the "freedom convoy" (Ling, 2022).

From the telephone to 5G, technological advancements have been a breeding ground for conspiracy theories. The main conspiracies addressed by our conceptualization incorporate the modern versions of conspiracies related to technology, such as the social credit system. Technology in our approach included micro-chips, the Internet of Things spying on people, the use of QR codes to control the population through banking, identification, and tracking of people. Fears of China link to these technological fears through their power as a nation, the control of their population, and the implementation of the social credit system.

Aside from these wider umbrella themes, many associated conspiracies are present. Substantial attention has been placed on the ideological asymmetries that circulate on social media (Freelon et al., 2020) related to topics like Islamophobia, anti-immigration, climate change, QAnon, and COVID-19 (Culloty & Suiter, 2021). As mentioned above, the COVID-19 pandemic, in particular, proliferated the number of "conflicting reports, hoaxes, and conspiracy theories" in the digital sphere, prompting the World Health Organization to declare an "infodemic" – when an abundance of conflicting claims makes it difficult for the public to know "what to believe" (Culloty & Suiter, 2021, p. 1). From these topics, our conceptualization flows through to the concerns or fears that are being articulated. Many of these concerns reflect the perceived political disenfranchisement many conspiracists feel, that their voices are being silenced and the government in power is not reflecting their world views. These concerns are also linked to the turmoil or chaos that global elites would use to declare emergency powers to enslave humanity in times of social chaos or public health emergencies through declaring martial law or new powers of state control. These concerns also reflect understandings of patriotism and nationalism often articulated through traditional gender roles and the male protection of women and children.

Conspiracy theories sometimes delineate who the hero is, or a true citizen of the nation, but they also define who the enemy is. This definition of the perceived enemy is the focus of our "targets" in our conceptualization. As our research was on RWE, liberals, communists (such as China), and the UN were understood as historical targets. Conspiracy theories are inherently anti-Semitic, with *The Protocols of the Elders of Zion* as well as Islamophobic, forming the foundation for many components of conspiracy theories. The category of "Actors" in our conceptualization defined the source of spreading the conspiracy theory, and these included fake experts, extremists, those declaring themselves as whistleblowers, or "internet researcher" citizens. While in the past conspiracy theorists were often dismissed in the public realm, today we are witnessing politicians using the pulpit of their Parties to spread, reinforce, and validate conspiracy theories so we reflected this reality within our Actors category.

While classic conspiracy theory attempts to "make sense of the political world", we find that "new conspiracism piles bare assertion on bare assertion" as evidenced by QAnon's mash-up of conspiracies (Rosenblum & Muirhead, 2019, pp. 20–27). A common QAnon conspiracy entailed Donald Trump trying to "drain the swamp" of the "deep state" – a theory suggesting the democratic party of the United States contains a secret "cabal" of "elites conspiring behind the curtain of social reality". Conspiracy theories are narratives employed to express injustice and articulate real or imagined fears. Conspiracies are also a vehicle for mobilization and a lens to interpret political and motivational tools for populist and militia movements. "A militia is an extralegal paramilitary group that trains, dresses, and prepares for combat, sometimes as part of a movement and sometimes as an unaffiliated group" (Belew & Gutiérrez, 2021, p. xv). Not all conspiracy theories result in radicalization, nor do they spur political action or mobilization, but many conspiracies across

North America are entwined in both (Garry et al., 2021). We focus on conspiracies because it "is one of the most pervasive and prominent worldviews of our time", and there is an urgent need to take "conspiracy culture seriously, instead of dismissing it as irrational or invalid" (De Maeyer, 2019, pp. 21–23). While there is substantial work on conspiracy, our work fills a gap in the literature by providing insight into the online conspiratorial topics circulating in Canada. To do this, we applied our conceptualization model to two social media platforms, BitChute and Telegram. This approach was used to operationalize the concept of conspiracy theory and ensure that we could analyze its spread and RWE's content in both video and text/image (meme)-based platforms. The varying mediums would allow our framework to be tested in longform and shortform videos where audiences were able to engage in the material.

References

ADL. (n.d.). Aryan brotherhood. *Anti-Defamation League*. https://www.adl.org/education/references/hate-symbols/aryan-brotherhood

ADLa. (n.d.). The hammerskin nation. *Anti-Defamation League*. https://www.adl.org/education/resources/profiles/hammerskin-nation

Amarasingam, A., Carvin, S., & Phillips, K. (2021). Anti-lockdown activity: Canada country profile. *Institute for Strategic Dialogue*. https://www.isdglobal.org/wp-content/uploads/2021/12/Anti-lockdown-canada-ISD.pdf

Anderson, B. (1983). *Imagined communities: Reflections on the origin and spread of nationalism*. London: Routledge.

Angus, I. (2005). Louis Riel and English-Canadian political thought. *University of Toronto Quarterly*, *74*(4), 884–894.

Appleblatt, A. (1976). JJ Maloney and the Ku Klux Klan. *The Chelsea Journal*, *2*(1), 47.

Arato, R. (2021). *Righting Canada's wrongs: Anti-semitism and the MS St. Louis: Canada's anti-semitic policies in the twentieth century*. Lorimer.

Ashcraft, K. L. (2022). *Wronged and Dangerous: Viral Masculinity and the Populist Pandemic*. Policy Press.

Atkins, S. E. (2009). *Holocaust denial as an international movement*. New York: ABC-CLIO.

Baker, A. (1997). "The dead don't answer questionnaires": Researching and writing historical geography. *Journal of Geography in Higher Education*, *21*(2), 231–243.

Baker, K. J. (2011). *Gospel according to the Klan: The KKK's appeal to protestant America, 1915–1930*. Lawrence: University Press of Kansas.

Barkun, M. (1997). *Religion and the racist right: the origins of the Christian Identity movement* (Rev. ed.). University of North Carolina Press.

Barkun, M. (2013). *A culture of conspiracy: Apocalyptic visions in contemporary America* (2nd ed.). University of California Press.

Barrett, S. (1989). *Is God a racist?: The right wing in Canada*. Toronto: University of Toronto Press.

Bartley, A. (1995). A public nuisance: The Ku Klux Klan in Ontario 1923–27. *Journal of Canadian Studies*, *30*(3), 156–174. https://doi.org/10.3138/jcs.30.3.156

Belew, K., & Gutiérrez, R. A. (Eds.). (2021). *A field guide to white supremacy*. University of California Press.

Berry, D. (2019). One big union. In *The Canadian Encyclopedia*. Retrieved from https://www.thecanadianencyclopedia.ca/en/article/one-big-union

Berry, D. (2020). St. Patrick's day in Canada. In *The Canadian Encyclopedia*. Retrieved from https://www.thecanadianencyclopedia.ca/en/article/st-patrick-s-day-in-canada

Betz, H. G., & Johnson, C. (2004). Against the current—Stemming the tide: The nostalgic ideology of the contemporary radical populist right. *Journal of Political Ideologies, 9*(3), 311–327.

Bjork-James, S. (2020). White sexual politics: The patriarchal family in white nationalism and the religious right. *Transforming Anthropology, 28*(1), 58–73.

Boswell, T. E. (1986). A split labor market analysis of discrimination against Chinese immigrants, 1850–1882. *American Sociological Review, 51*(3), 352. https://doi.org/10.2307/2095307

Boulianne, S., & Lee, S. (2022). Conspiracy beliefs, misinformation, social media platforms, and protest participation. *Media and Communication, 10*(4), 30–41.

Brean, J. (March 22, 2008). Scrutinizing the human rights machine. *National Post*. Retrieved from https://archive.ph/20080324231719/https://www.nationalpost.com/news/story.html

Buckley, N. & Schafer, J.S. (2021). "Censorship-free" platforms: Evaluating content moderation policies and practices of alternative social media. *SOC ARXIV*. https://doi.org/10.31235/osf.io/yf9qz

Burstow, B. (2003). "Surviving and thriving by becoming more 'groupuscular': the case of the Heritage Front". *Patterns of Prejudice*. 37.4: 415–428.

Butovsky, A. (1985). The Holocaust on trial in Canada. *Patterns of Prejudice, 19*(3): 34–36.

Butter, M., & Knight, P. (2019). *The history of conspiracy theory research: A review and commentary*. Oxford University Press https://doi-org.libproxy.txstate.edu/10.1093/oso/9780190844073.003.0002

Butter, M., & Knight, P. (2020). Conspiracy theory in historical, cultural and literary studies. In Butter, M., & P. Knight (Eds.), *Routledge handbook of conspiracy theories*. London: Routledge.

Byford, J. (2011). *Conspiracy theories: A critical introduction*. Springer.

Campana, A., & Tanner, S. (2014). The radicalization of right- wing Skinheads in Quebec. *TSAS: Canadian Network for Research on Terrorism, Security and Society*, No. 14-07. https://doi.org/10.13140/2.1.5093.5681

Canadian League Against War and Fascism (ca. 1935). Toronto, Ontario.

Camus, R. (2011). Le Grand Remplacement.

Castells, M. (2012). *Networks of outrage and hope: Social movements in the Internet age*. John Wiley & Sons.

CBC. (2005, March 1). Zundel turned over to German authorities. *CBC NEWS*. https://www.cbc.ca/news/canada/zundel-turned-over-to-german-authorities-1.529567

CBC News. (2017, July 6). Who are the proud boys? Retrieved from https://www.cbc.ca/player/play/984404035633

CBC News. (2021, November 10). 2 years after banning other Canadian hate groups, Facebook deletes Quebec far-right group. *CBC News*. https://www.cbc.ca/news/canada/montreal/far-right-quebec-group-facebook-1.6244609

Celestini, C. (2023, August). Where did the great replacement theory come from? *Sojourners Magazine*.

Celestini, C., & Amarasingam, A. (2023). Reviving the violet flame: The New Age conspiratorial journey of Canada's Queen Romana Didulo. *Studies in Religion/Sciences Religieuses, 0*(0). https://doi-org.proxy.lib.uwaterloo.ca/10.1177/00084298231209700

Celestini, C., & Amarasingam, A. (2023). Reviving the violet flame: The new age conspiratorial journey of Canada's Queen Romana Didulo. *Studies in Religion/Sciences Religieuses, 0*(0). https://doi-org.proxy.lib.uwaterloo.ca/10.1177/00084298231209700

Christensen, M., & Au, A. (2023). The great reset and the cultural boundaries of conspiracy theory. *International Journal of Communication (Online)*, *17*, 2348.

Cline, T. (2019). "A clarion call to real patriots the world over": The curious case of the Ku Klux Klan of Kanada in New Brunswick during the 1920s and 1930s. *Acadiensis: Journal of the History of the Atlantic Region / Revue D'histoire De La Region Atlantique*, *48*(1), 88–110. https://doi.org/10.1353/aca.2019.0004

Contreras, R. (2024). Poll: Most Americans cool to Christian nationalism as its influence grows. *Axios*. https://www.axios.com/2024/02/28/poll-christian-nationalism-americans-reject

Culloty, E., & Suiter, J. (2021). *Disinformation and manipulation in digital media: Information pathologies*. London: Routledge.

Dart, R. (2022). The Canadian Red Tory tradition: Janus. In T. Bar-On & B. Molas (Eds.), *The right and radical right in the Americas: ideological currents from interwar Canada to contemporary Chile* (pp. 107–128). Lanham, MD: Lexington Books.

Dawson, L. L. (2019). The study of new religious movements and the radicalization of home-grown terrorists: Opening a dialogue. *Terrorism and Political Violence*, *22*(1), 1–21.

De Maeyer, J. (2019). Taking conspiracy culture seriously: Journalism needs to face its epistemological trouble. *Journalism*, *20*(1), 21–23.

Dentith, M. R. X. (2023). The future of the philosophy of conspiracy theory: An introduction to the special issue on conspiracy theory theory. *Social Epistemology*. https://doi-org.libproxy.txstate.edu/10.1080/02691728.2023.2173538

de Wildt, L., & Aupers, S. (2024). Participatory conspiracy culture: Believing, doubting and playing with conspiracy theories on Reddit. Convergence, 30(1), 329–346.

Durbin, S. (n.d.). Christian Zionism in the United States, 1930–2020. In *Oxford research Encyclopedia of religion*. Oxford University Press. https://doi.org/10.1093/acrefore/9780199340378.013.1205

Ellis III, J. O. (2015). Right-Wing Extremism in Canada. *Countering Violent Extremism*, 55.

Engler, Y. (2010). *Canada and Israel: Building apartheid*. Vancouver: Fernwood Publishing.

Farrell, D. R. (1969). The Canada First movement and Canadian political thought. *Journal of Canadian Studies/Revue d'études Canadiennes*, *4*(4), 16–26.

Feola, M. (2021) "You will not replace us": The Melancholic nationalism of whiteness. *Political Theory*, *49*(4), 528–553.

Fenster, M. (1999). *Conspiracy theories: Secrecy and power in American culture*. University of Minnesota Press.

Freelon, D., Marwick, A., & Kreiss, D. (2020). False equivalencies: Online activism from left to right. *Science*, *369*(6508), 1197–1201.

Freund, A. (2006). Troubling memories in nation-building: World War II memories and Germans' inter-ethnic encounters in Canada after 1945. *Histoire Sociale/Social History*.

Frischlich, L., Boberg, S., & Quandt, T. (2019). Comment sections as targets of dark participation? Journalists' evaluation and moderation of deviant user comments. *Journalism Studies*, *20*(14), 2014–2033.

Frischlich, L., Schatto-Eckrodt, T., Boberg, S., & Wintterlin, F. (2021). Roots of Incivility: How Personality, Media Use, and Online Experiences Shape Uncivil Participation. *Media and Communication*, *9*(1).

Gagan, D. P. (1970). The relevance of "Canada First". *Journal of Canadian Studies/Revue d'études Canadiennes*, *5*(4), 36–44.

Gladwell, M. (2010). Small change. *The New Yorker*, 4.

Garry, A., Stern, L., & Silverman, D. (2021). QAnon conspiracy theory: Examining its evolution and mechanisms of radicalization. *Journal for Deradicalization: A Multidisciplinary Journal for Research on Extremism & Terrorism*, *26*(3), 154–168.

Gilmour, J. F. (2014). *The history of Canada series: Trouble on main street: Mackenzie King reason race and the 1907 Vancouver riots*. Penguin Canada.
Goldschläger, A. (2012). The Trials of Ernst Zündel. In R. S. Wistrich (Ed.), *Holocaust Denial* (pp. 109–136). De Gruyter.
Gorski, P. S., and Perry, S. L. (2022) *The flag and the cross: White Christian nationalism and the threat to American democracy*. Oxford University Press.
Goutor, D. (2008). *Guarding the gates: The Canadian labour movement and immigration*. Vancouver: University of British Columbia Press.
Harwood, R. (1982). *Did six million really die?* Canada: Institute for Historical Review.
Hofmann, D. C., Trofimuk, B., Perry, S., & Hyslop-Margison, C. (2021). An exploration of right-wing extremist incidents in Atlantic Canada. *Dynamics of Asymmetric Conflict*, 1–23. https://doi.org/10.1080/17467586.2021.1876900
Hofstadter, R. (2012). *The paranoid style in American politics*. New York: Vintage.
Hougham, G. M. (1953). Canada First: A Minor Party in Microcosm. *The Canadian Journal of Economics and Political Science / Revue Canadienne d'Economique et de Science Politique*, 19(2), 174–184.
Houston, C. J., & Smyth, W. J. (1980). *The sash Canada wore: A historical geography of the Orange order in Canada*. University of Toronto Press.
Hubert, D., & Claudé, Y. (1991). *Les skinheads et l'extrême-droite*. VLB.
Hull, K. (2016). Concerns at home, concerns abroad: Irish and English political ephemera in southern Ontario. *International Journal of Historical Archaeology*, 20(4), 768–780. https://www.jstor.org/stable/26174295
Humphreys, A. (2012, April 17). Violent racist gang expands into Edmonton. *National Post*. https://nationalpost.com/news/canada/violent-racist-gang-expands-into-edmonton
Ignatiev, N. (1995). *How the Irish became White*. London: Routledge.
Ihlebæk, K. A., & Holter, C. R. (2021). Hostile emotions: an exploratory study of far-right online commenters and their emotional connection to traditional and alternative news media. *Journalism*, 22(5), 1207–1222.
Innis, H. A. (1941). Recent developments in the Canadian economy. In C. Martin (Ed.), *Canada in peace and war* (pp. 58–85). Oxford University Press.
Jackson, P. (2018). Conspiracy theories and Neo-Nazism in the cultic milieu. In A. Dyrendal, D. Robertson, & E. Asprem (Eds.), *Handbook of conspiracy theory and contemporary religion* (pp. 461–489). Leiden: Brill.
Jessen, N. (2018). Populism and conspiracy A historical synthesis of American countersubversive narratives. *American Journal of Economics and Sociology*, 78(3), 675–715.
Kazin, M. (1998). *The populist persuasion: An American history*. Ithaca: Cornell University Press.
Kealey, G. S., & Gagnon, M. -A. (2017). Knights of labor in Canada. In *The Canadian Encyclopedia*. https://www.thecanadianencyclopedia.ca/en/article/knights-of-labor
Kinsella, W. (2001). *Web of hate: Inside Canada's far right network*. Toronto: Harper Collins.
Kowert, R. (Ed.). (2019). *Video games and well-being: Press start*. Springer Nature.
Kwak, L. J. (2020). Problematizing Canadian exceptionalism: A study of right-populism, White nationalism and Conservative political parties. *Oñati Socio-Legal Series*, 10(6), 1166–1192.
Langman, L. (2005). From virtual public spheres to global justice: A critical theory of internetworked social movements. *Sociological Theory*, 23(1), 42–74. https://doi.org/10.1111/j.0735-2751.2005.00242.x
Lee, E. (2002). Enforcing the borders: Chinese exclusion along the U.S. borders with Canada and Mexico, 1882–1924. *The Journal of American History*, 89(1), 54. https://doi.org/10.2307/2700784

Lennard, K. (2015). Old purpose, "new body": "The birth of a nation" and the revival of the Ku Klux Klan. *The Journal of the Gilded Age and Progressive Era, 14*(4), 616–620. https:// www.jstor.org/stable/43903547

Levitt, C., Shaffir, W., & Gee, M. (2018). *The riot at Christie Pits.* Toronto: New Jewish Press.

Li, P. S. (1995). Racial supremacism under social democracy. *Canadian Ethnic Studies, 27*(1), 1–17.

Li, P. (2008). Reconciling with history: The Chinese-Canadian head tax redress. *Journal of Chinese Overseas, 4*(1), 127–140. https://doi.org/10.1353/jco.0.0010

Ling, J. (2022, February 8). 5G and QAnon: How conspiracy theorists steered Canada's anti-vaccine trucker protest. *The Guardian.* https://www.theguardian.com/world/2022/feb/08/canada-ottawa-trucker-protest-extremist-qanon-neo-nazi

Lund, D. E. (2014). Keeping Canada British: The Ku Klux Klan in 1920s Saskatchewan. *Nova Religio, 18*(4), 122–123. https://doi.org/10.1525/nr.2015.18.4.122

Mahl, D., Zeng, J., & Schäfer, M. S. (2023). Conceptualizing platformed conspiracism: Analytical framework and empirical case study of BitChute and Gab. *New Media & Society, 0*(0). https://doi.org/10.1177/14614448231160457

Manasan, A. (November 28, 2020). The rise of the Ku Klux Klan in Canada and why its lasting impact still matters. *CBC - The Sunday Magazine.* https://www.cbc.ca/radio/sunday/the-sunday-magazine-for-november-22-2020-1.5807350/the-rise-of-the-ku-klux-klan-in-canada-and-why-its-lasting-impact-still-matters-1.5807353

Marwick, A. E., & Partin, W. C. (2022). Constructing alternative facts: Populist expertise and the QAnon conspiracy. *New Media & Society,* 14614448221090201.

McFarland, M., & Gottfried, G. (2002). The chosen ones: A mythic analysis of the theological and political self-justification of Christian identity. *Journal for the Study of Religion, 15*(1), 125–145. https://www.jstor.org/stable/24764349

McGowan, M. G. (1999). *The waning of the Green Catholics, the Irish, and identity in Toronto 1887–1922.* Montreal: McGill Queen's University Press.

Mettler, K. (2016, August 31). Why SPLC says White Lives Matter is a hate group but Black Lives Matter is not. *The Washington Post.* Retrieved from https://www.washingtonpost.com/news/morning-mix/wp/2016/08/31/splc-the-much-cited-designator-of-hate-groups-explains-why-white-lives-matter-is-one/

Michael, G. (2006). RAHOWA! A history of the world church of the creator. *Terrorism and Political Violence, 18*(4), 561–583.

Michael, G. (2016). This is war! Tom Metzger, White Aryan resistance, and the lone wolf legacy. *Focus on Terrorism,* 14, 29–62.

Nadeau, J. F. (2011). *The Canadian Fuhrer: The life of Adrien Arcand.* Toronto, ON: James Lorimer & Company.

Nadeau, F. (2021). Rupture ou continuité? La matrice idéologique de l'extrême droite québécoise. In D. Helly (Ed.), *Rupture ou continuité? La matrice idéologique de l'extrême droite québécoise* (pp. 89–142). Marquis (Classiques des sciences sociales).

Nadeau, F., & Helly, D. (2016). Une extrême droite en émergence? Les pages Facebook pour la charte des valeurs québécoises. *Recherches Sociographiques, 57*(2–3), 505–521. https://doi.org/10.7202/1038437ar

Nesbitt, M., et al. (2021). Introduction to Canadian terror. *Manitoba Law Journal, 44*(1).

Newton, M. (2014). *White robes and burning crosses: A history of the Ku Klux Klan from 1866.* McFarland.

Nicolai, J. (2017). Rewiring UNESCO's world heritage centre and rural peripheries: Imagined community and concrete inequality from France's Corsica to China's Heyang. *International Journal of Communication, 11,* 4541–4558.

Noppari, E., Hiltunen, I., & Ahva, L. (2019). User profiles for populist counter-media websites in Finland. *Journal of Alternative & Community Media*, 4(1), 23–37.

Northey, W. (2015). Christian Zionism. In Dart, R. (Ed.), *Canadian Christian Zionism: A tangled tale* (pp. 93–99). Dewdney, BC: Synaxis Press.

Overwijk, J., & de Zeeuw, D. (2023). The new clarity: Awakening in the post-truth era. *New Formations*, 109(109), 129–146. https://doi.org/10.3898/NEWF:109.09.2023

Parent, R., & Ellis, J. (2014). Right-wing extremism in Canada. Canadian Network for Research on *Terrorism, Security and Society*, 14(3), 1–44.

Parliament of Canada. (1865). Parliamentary debates on the subject of the confederation of the British North American provinces. 3rd session, 8th provincial parliament of Canada. Hunter, Rose & Co., Parliamentary Printers.

Perry, B., & Scrivens, R. (2015). *Right-wing extremism in Canada: An environmental scan*. Ottawa, ON: Public Safety Canada.

Perry, B., & Scrivens, R. (2016). Uneasy alliances: A look at the right-wing extremist movement in Canada. *Studies in Conflict & Terrorism*, 39(9), 819–841.

Perry, B., & Scrivens, R. (2018). A climate for hate? An exploration of the right-wing extremist landscape in Canada. *Critical Criminology*, 26(2), 169–187.

Perry, B., & Scrivens, R. (2019). *Right-wing extremism in Canada*. Springer Nature.

Pitsula, J. M. (2013). *Keeping Canada British: The Ku Klux Klan in 1920s Saskatchewan*. UBC Press.

Pollard, J. (2016). Skinhead culture: The ideologies, mythologies, religions and conspiracy theories of racist skinheads. *Patterns of Prejudice*, 50(4–5), 398–419.

Price, J. (2007). "Orienting" the empire: Mackenzie King and the aftermath of the 1907 race riots. BC studies. *The British Columbian Quarterly*, (156/7), 53–81.

Public Safety Canada. (2024). Currently listed entities. *Government of Canada*. Retrieved from https://www.publicsafety.gc.ca/cnt/ntnl-scrt/cntr-trrrsm/lstd-ntts/crrnt-lstd-ntts-en.aspx

Quandt, T. (2018). Dark participation. *Media and Communication*, 6(4), 36–48.

Quarles, C. L. (2004). *Christian identity: The Aryan American bloodline religion*. McFarland.

Racine, P. N. (1973). The Ku Klux Klan, Anti-Catholicism, and Atlanta's Board of education, 1916–1927. *The Georgia Historical Quarterly*, 57(1), 63–75.

Reid, E. (1933). The effect of the depression on Canadian politics, 1929–32. *American Political Science Review*, 27(3), 455–465.

Repka, W., & Repka, K. M. (1982). *Dangerous patriots: Canada's unknown prisoners of war*. New Star Books.

Rhodes, B. (2018, April 16). As Valentine's Day mall plot sentencing begins, new details from court records. *CBC News*. https://www.cbc.ca/news/canada/nova-scotia/halifax-shopping-centre-attack-lindsay-souvannarath-sentencing-1.4618021

Robertson, D. G. (2022). Crippled epistemologies: Conspiracy theories, religion, and knowledge. *Social Research*, 89(3), 651–677. https://doi.org/10.1353/sor.2022.0052

Roose, K. (2021, September 3). What is QAnon, the viral pro-trump conspiracy theory? *The New York Times*. Retrieved from https://www.nytimes.com/article/what-is-qanon.html

Rosenblum, N. L. & Muirhead, R. (2019). *A lot of people are saying: The new conspiracism and the assault on democracy*. Princeton University Press.

Roy, P. E. (1976). The preservation of peace in Vancouver: The aftermath of the anti-Chinese riot of 1887. BC studies. *The British Columbian Quarterly*, (31), 44–59.

Roy, A. G., & Sahoo, A. K. (2016). The journey of the Komagata Maru: National, transnational, diasporic. *South Asian Diaspora*, 8(2), 85–97.

Satzewich, V. (1989). Racisms: The reactions to Chinese migrants in Canada at the turn of the century. *International Sociology*, 4(3), 311–327.

Schaefer, R. T. (1971). The Ku Klux Klan: Continuity and change. *Phylon*, *32*(2), 143. https://doi.org/10.2307/273999

Schuller, S. (2021). World conspiracy literature and antisemitism. TRANSIT 13.1. Available online at https://transit.berkeley.edu/2021/schuller-conspiracyliterature/ (last accessed at 010323).

Schwab, K., & Malleret, T. (2020, July). *COVID-19: The great reset*. Geneva: Forum publishing.

Scrivens, R., & Perry, B. (2017). Resisting the right: Countering right-wing extremism in Canada. *Canadian Journal of Criminology and Criminal Justice*, *59*(4), 534–558. https://doi.org/10.3138/cjc-cj.2016.0029

Senior, H. (2021). Fenians. In *The Canadian Encyclopedia*. https://www.thecanadianencyclopedia.ca/en/article/fenians

Shirky, C. (2008). *Here comes everybody: The power of organizing without organizations*. Penguin.

Smith, J. P. (1995). The riel rebellion of 1869: New light on British liberals and the use of force on the Canadian frontier. *Journal of Canadian Studies/Revue d'études Canadiennes*, *30*(2), 58–73.

Smith, R. O. (2012). Anglo-American Christian Zionism: Implications for Palestinian Christians. *The Ecumenical Review*, *64*(1), 27–35. https://doi.org/10.1111/j.1758-6623.2012.00142.x

Southern Poverty Law Center. (2021). Ernst Zundel. https://www.splcenter.org/fighting-hate/extremist-files/individual/ernst-zundel

SPLC. (2021). Atomwaffen division. *Southern Poverty Law Center*. https://www.splcenter.org/fighting-hate/extremist-files/group/atomwaffen-division

Sternisko et al., Sternisko, A., Cichocka, A., & Van Bavel, J. J. (2020). The dark side of social movements: Social identity, non-conformity, and the lure of conspiracy theories. *Current Opinion in Psychology*, *35*, 1–6.

Stewart, N. K., Al-Rawi, A., Celestini, C., & Worku, N. (2023). Hate influencers' mediation of hate on telegram: "We declare war against the anti-white system". *Social Media+ Society*, *9*(2), 20563051231177915.

Tetrault, J. E. C. (2021). Thinking beyond extremism: A critique of counterterrorism research on right-wing nationalist and far-right social movements. *The British Journal of Criminology*, *62*(2), 431–449.

Theocharis, Y., Cardenal, A., Jin, S., Aalberg, T., Hopmann, D. N., Strömbäck, J., ... & Štětka, V. (2023). Does the platform matter? Social media and COVID-19 conspiracy theory beliefs in 17 countries. *New Media & Society*, *25*(12), 3412–3437.

Théorêt, H. (2017). *The Blue shirts: Adrien Arcand and Fascist anti-semitism in Canada*. Ottawa: University of Ottawa Press.

Theoret, H. (2019). The rise and fall of Adrien Arcand: Antisemitism in 20th century Quebec. *Antisemitism Studies*, *3*(2), 231–272. https://doi.org/10.2979/antistud.3.2.03

Thobani, S. (2000). Closing ranks: Racism and sexism in Canada's immigration policy. *Race & Class*, *42*(1), 35–55. https://doi.org/10.1177/030639600128968009

Thobani, S. (2008). Reading TWAIL in the Canadian context: Race, gender and national formation. *International Community Law Review*, *10*(4), 421–430.

Thompson, N. (2017, August 7). Ernst Zundel, deported from Canada on Holocaust denial charges, dies at 78. *The Globe and Mail*. https://www.theglobeandmail.com/news/national/ernst-zundel-deported-from-canada-on-holocaust-denial-charges-dies-at-78/article35892595/

Tingler, J. (2016). Holocaust denial and holocaust memory: The case of Ernst Zündel. *Genocide Studies International*, *10*(2), 210–229.

Uscinski, J. E. (2018). The study of conspiracy theories. *Argumenta*, *3*(2), 233–245.

Vigod, B. l. (2015). Canada first. In *The Canadian Encyclopedia*. Retrieved from https://www.thecanadianencyclopedia.ca/en/article/canada-first

Waisbord, S. (2020). Mob censorship: Online harassment of US journalists in times of digital hate and populism. *Digital Journalism*, *8*(8), 1030–1046.

Walker, J. (2023). Learning together out of climate change denial. *New Directions for Adult and Continuing Education*, *2023*(178), 27–40.

Walberg, E. (2017). *The Canada-Israel Nexus*. Atlanta, GA: Clarity Press.

Waldman, A. (2017). Daniel Carlyle grant and the Ku Klux Klan in Winnipeg, 1928. *Manitoba History*, (85), 24+. Retrieved from https://link.gale.com/apps/doc/A520581857/AONE?u=anon~f3e90ae6&sid=-googleScholar&xid=a45d9a28

Wallace, W. S. (1920). *The growth of Canadian national feeling*. Toronto: University of Toronto Press.

Wayland, S. V. (1997). Immigration, multiculturalism and national identity in Canada. *International Journal on Minority and Group Rights*, *5*(1), 33–58.

Weeks, B. E., & Garrett, R. K. (2014). Electoral consequences of political rumors: Motivated reasoning, candidate rumors, and vote choice during the 2008 US presidential election. *International Journal of Public Opinion Research*, *26*(4), 401–422.

Weinfeld, M., Schnoor, R., & Koffman, D. (2012). Overview of Canadian Jewry. *The American Jewish Year Book*, *109/112*, 55–90.

Wendling, B. M. (2021, January 6). QAnon What is it and where did it come from? *BBC News*. https://www.bbc.com/news/53498434

Westlund, O. (2021). Advancing research into dark participation. *Media and Communication*, *9*(1), 209–214.

Wilson, J. (2017, April 4). Life after white supremacy: The former neo-fascist now working to fight hate. *The Guardian*. Accessed from https://www.theguardian.com/world/2017/apr/04/life-after-hate-groups-neo-fascism-racism

Wynne, R. E. (1966). American labor leaders and the Vancouver anti-oriental riot. *The Pacific Northwest Quarterly*, *57*(4), 172–179.

Yablokov, I. (2014). Pussy Riot as agent provocateur: conspiracy theories and the media construction of nation in Putin's Russia. *Nationalities Papers*, *42*(4), 622–636.

Yang, T., & Fang, K. (2021). How dark corners collude: A study on an online Chinese alt-right community. *Information, Communication & Society*, *26*, 1–18.

Zeng, J., & Schäfer, M. S. (2021). Conceptualizing "dark platforms". Covid-19-related conspiracy theories on 8kun and Gab. *Digital Journalism*, *9*, 1–23.

2 RWE actors

2.1 Situating RWE in Canada

Defining social objects is a challenge. Categories related to groups are one type of social object. Groups are sometimes defined by common associations or distinct attributes that distinguish one group from another. Unlike elements on a periodic table, fixed in agreed upon formulas, what specific attributes are selected in defining social objects over others may change depending on specific historical and local contexts. For example, definitions of what it means to be Canadian may refer to simply the presence or absence of citizenship, being born in the country, being Indigenous or Métis, having a set of cultural values or competences, among countless other possible defining attributes. Different individuals and institutions within Canadian society may have equally different definitions for what is particularly "Canadian".

There are also moments when these contrasting and conflictual definitions may generate context-based tests. Continuing with the example above, Canada Border Services Agency staff generally test for documents of citizenship such as a passport; not necessarily cultural knowledge, but to assess the Canadian status of incoming travelers. Similar issues arise when dealing with categorizing RWE groups. Following Brubaker (2004), researchers should be wary of repackaging common sense groupisms and existing categories, before labeling the process as a clear cut social science (see also Cicourel, 1964). Within the field of research on RWE and its related terms and categories, there has been pronounced reflection over these conceptual issues. In particular, longstanding debates have emerged over how to test what is, or what is not, RWE. In this context, this chapter outlines some of the conceptual challenges related to working with the history and contemporary situation of RWE groups in Canada.

As Carter (2005, p. 14) writes, "almost every scholar of right-wing extremism has pointed to the difficulties associated with defining the concept". The absence of "an agreed-upon definition of RWE means that scholars continue to disagree over" the essential attributes that warrants labelling an individual or group as part of the extreme or far-right (Carter, 2005, p. 14). These problems are not limited to the concept of RWE alone. Similar discussions have occurred over terms related to RWE such as extremism and "neo-facism". For neo-fascism, Gregor (2006) argues

DOI: 10.4324/9781003502173-3

the term has been abused by academics to such an extent that it no longer has descriptive power. On the attribute of extremism, Roberts (1994, p. 466) argues that there are still no "satisfactory operational indicators of extremism". For Roberts (1994), the adjective extreme is a relational concept that requires at least two points of reference. Applied to studies of social objects, Roberts (1994) argues that the concept of extremism is tethered to historical mainstream social norms. For example, what is extreme in the year 1522 does not necessarily equate to extremism in the year we are currently in. In attempts to solve these "definitional" problems, some scholars suggest selecting one common feature shared by RWE groups to subsume the rest. For example, writing within the context of Western Europe, Husbands (1981) defines RWE in terms of racial exclusionism, whereas Eatwell (2000) described racial nationalism as the core gravitational pull that brings otherwise different RWE groups together.

In contrast, others have attempted to rely on a much larger register of attributes to describe RWE. Within this approach, Mudde's (1995) review of definitions for RWE outlined over 50 different attributes. Out of this relatively large group of attributes, Mudde (1995) focuses on five attributes related to nationalism, xenophobia, racism, anti-democratic sentiment, as well as a call for a strong state (Mudde, 1995, pp. 206–207). Mudde (1995) uses the term "far right" as an "umbrella term" to describe the radical *and* extreme right (Ahmed & Lynch, 2024). The term *radical* "refers to a person whose critique of society goes to its roots, whether on the far left or far right" (Belew & Gutiérrez, 2021, p. xvi). Teasing apart the often fraught definitions attributed to "right-wing extremism" becomes an exercise in understanding the importance of definitions as conveyors of meaning, specificity, and exclusion (Carter, 2018). Carter (2005, p. 15) also argues that simply because some attributes seem to occur more than others "does not mean that they can be considered as constituting the foundations of a generally accepted definition". Moreover, one can imagine how left-wing extremism shares attributes of nationalism, xenophobia, racism, anti-democratic sentiment, and a call for a strong state, raising questions about the ability to easily define RWE groups.

Beyond the problems outlined above, it may be problematic to select some defining attributes at the expense of others which may dilute the overall importance of a number of issues, for example, while RWE is typically associated with attributes such as Islamophobia, anti-Semitism, anti-feminism, racism, and nationalism (Ging, 2019b; Perry & Scrivens, 2016). Articulations of nationalism may include nurturing positions related to "us" versus "them" by creating racial, cultural, and social hierarchies. In the larger historical context of the emergence of and subsequent gendering of the nation, the idea of the nation became attributed as a "motherland" or "fatherland", leaving some anti-feminists to blame feminists for belittling men and threatening the patriotic structure of society (Strong-Boag, 1996; Ging, 2019b).

Some nationalists that are overwhelming conservative Christian groups use feminism and women's rights as a basis for their arguments. In such cases, otherwise progressive social movements are used to vilify those perceived not to belong to their group category, such as unwanted immigrants, further reproducing "social and cultural hierarchies constructed on racial stereotypes informed by and informing gender" (Colella, 2021, p. 271). Stereotypes of racial and sexual identities blend together to create an "other" that is sexist and patriarchal that introduce the ideas of the sexualization of racism and racialization of sexism (Colella, 2021, p. 273). The selective use and support of feminist issues can construct a narrative to reinforce traditional norms of femininity and masculinity and patriarchal and heteronormative values (Colella, 2021, p. 271).

In the use of feminism and anti-gender discourse, nationalists become "both boundary makers and threshold figures" that support maleness, but neither woman or gender become the voice or power within politics (Colella, 2021, p. 273). In this framing, the sexual purity of women is symbolic of racial, economic, and political power, while the image of women as mothers simultaneously epitomizes hope for the nation through the childbirth and continuation of tradition and culture. Men who are not a part of this categorization, such as those who identify as LGBTQ2SA, or those in lower socio-economic positions are stigmatized as non-productive (Colella, 2021, p. 273). From this basis the identification of the nation is based on gender difference, where women are articulated as central to the nation and domestic spaces, as the reproductive process of the nation both biologically and culturally become the lexicon of nationalist speech (e.g., motherland) (Colella, 2021, p. 274). Here, women are represented as the symbols of a nation and the reproducers of culture and identity but are also positioned in opposition to those who attempt to destroy the nation through sexual deviance. In turn, this strengthens heteronormativity in gender roles based on traditional Christian values and stigmatizes those who identify as gender non-conforming (Colella, 2021, p. 281). In short, by not selecting an attribute to the definition of a category, it might further disappear that attributes importance in discussions of that category.

Aside from questions related to the decision-making of the researcher, difficulties defining RWE groups may also be due to active strategies that RWE groups deploy to avoid negative or unwanted attributes. As Jackson and Feldman (2014, p. 1) note, RWE groups have actively sought methods to overcome the label of RWE and corresponding toxic legacies of the Holocaust and the Second World War. A corresponding concern is the strategic use of moderate language by RWE groups to operate as a "kind of Trojan Horse to gain access to the liberal democratic political spectrum" (Jackson & Feldman, 2014, p. 9). The COVID-19 pandemic saw RWE groups taking advantage of the public fear and anxiety by building on existing narratives of racism, xenophobia, and antisemitism. Through conspiracy theories linked to the virus, such as a bioweapon from China or Israel, RWE groups resonated with and propagated these theories to recruit and proliferate their messages online. RWE groups took advantage of this moment in time to integrate populist and extremist ideologies such as anxieties about employment, health, income, and government overreach to more mainstream audiences (Perry et al., 2022, p. 5). Why some groups simply migrate when deplatformed, other RWE groups in Canada actively moderate their public online presence so they do not fall sour of the terms and conditions of digital platforms. As we illustrate in Chapter 3, RWE groups often gravitate toward so-called alternative sites like BitChute and Telegram, precisely because the platforms provide lower levels of content moderation and support the use of free speech more than mainstream platforms like YouTube, Facebook, and Twitter. Though some of the details are not widely known, Facebook has its own list of dangerous organizations and individuals that are banned on its site including several Canadian entities and figures like Gavin McInnes and Faith Goldy (see Biddle, 2021).

Returning to Brubaker (2004), one solution to being complacent with categories of groupism and corresponding attributes is to reflect on the process of group-making projects. In this framing group-making projects may reflect social, cultural, and political projects aimed at establishing or expanding the accepted boundaries of groupness which may also involve processes of exclusion of what does not belong. This starts from the premise that analytical categories of analysis, the boxes in which we categorize groups and other objects of study, are not fixed. As Harvey (2009, p. 232) argues in a more expanded context, they do not "exist outside the processes, flows, and relations that create, sustain, or undermine them". From this approach, we can understand exclusionary group-making projects – be they understood in terms of national purity, Christian values, whiteness, male chauvinism or the like – as the other side of more inclusive forms of group-making projects, with what exclusion and inclusion looking like being specific not only to the interpretations provided by different people and organizations but also subject to change depending on historical and local contexts.

In the context of RWE, and related terms. work has been done to further this end. Within the United States, the development of "whiteness" and "racial purity" associated with RWE has been engaged from a variety of research perspectives and in different historical and regional contexts. "The word *white* refers to a socially constructed and historically fluid category of identity in which people, systems of power, and wealth are invested"; it is neither a biological term or an unstable category, but a neutral descriptor (Belew & Gutiérrez, 2021, p. xi). Ignatiev (1995) and Roediger (1991, 2005) highlight how competing positions in different historical contexts wrestled with the category of whiteness as a group. They examine how and why people began self-identifying as white, showing how it was used by some to elevate their own status vis-a-vis other groups. Though they are themselves white, Ignatiev (1995) shows the historical development of Irish immigrants in the United States as being identified as unwanted racialized foreigners to privilege equals with native Anglo-Saxons. Similarly, Roediger (1991, 2005) highlights how laborers in the United States negotiated the concept of whiteness with white employers to improve positioning in labor disputes. By doing so, white workers could re-inscribe themselves in a moral hierarchy to gain political, economic, and social status within the United States.

Religion can play a significant role in RWE as we have noted about Christian nationalists, Christian Zionists, and the role of religious belief, language, and fervor in mobilization and community building. Some RWE groups such as Church of the Creator, Order of Nine Angels, Tempel ov Blood, the Front Canadian Francais, and Servanthoods are extremist groups with connections to the occult, Odinism, and bricolage of many religions forming one. Religion can also be the catalyst for hate and bigotry, through the creation of the other. Extremists groups can be formed on anti-Islam beliefs and on anti-immigration beliefs, which can marginalize those outside of Christianity.

It is important to note that not all extremist groups are white, with some Manosphere groups such as Men Going Their Own Way (MGTOW) and Incels focused on grievances of manhood rather than religious ethnicity. Immigrants and non-white actors also develop or join their own extremist groups such as the case of Canadians linked to Al Qaeda or ISIS or Sikh extremism. With regard to the latter, there were many militant Sikh separatist groups active in Canada with many promoting the idea of violence in support of an independent state in India. These groups included the Babbar Khalsa (BK), the International Sikh Youth Federation, the Khalistan Liberation Front, and the Bhindranwale Tigers of Khalistan (BTK). A Sikh immigrant to Canada, Talwinder Singh Parmar, created the Canadian chapter of the Babbar Khalsa, which soon became known as the Babbar Khalsa International (BKI). In 2018, BKI and the International Sikh Youth Federation were designated as terrorist entities by the Canadian federal government (Public Safety, 2023). In 1985, a bomb planted in the luggage of an Air India flight (182) initiating from Vancouver exploded over the Atlantic Ocean near Ireland. The bomb had been planted in response to an attack by the Indian government on the Golden Temple, the holiest site for Sikhs. Simultaneously, a bomb planted in the luggage of an Air India flight initiating from Tokyo's Narita airport killed two baggage handlers. The Air India bombing killed 329 passengers, of whom 280 were Canadian, and was the world's most deadly act of aviation terrorism,[1] until the attacks of 9/11 (Roach, 2011. p. 45). Parmar was also implicated in the 1985 Air India bombing and was later killed in India. Many BK groups still remain active in Canada, and there have been several terrorist attacks in Canada against Indian interests by Sikh extremists, including the killing of a prosecution witness in the Air India trial who was murdered in 1988.[2]

Adding complexity to this type of analysis in the Canadian context are the historical dimensions of the "two solitudes" of English and French Canada (See Angus, 1997; Saul, 1998; Taylor, 1993). Despite historic inequalities within Canada, unproblematized categories of whiteness and adjacent terms persist in the literature. For example, Thobani (2000) discusses an alleged policy in Canada to "Keep Canada White" which existed until the 1940s and 1950s while evading the historical constitution of whiteness within a French and English Canada. Unlike the development of the attribute of whiteness in the United States, in Canada racial slurs like "speak white" have been directed at French speakers by Anglo-Canadians that dominated Quebec's political, economic and media industries (Mezei, 1998). While some groups may be inspired by white supremacy, white anglophones and francophones may have very different ideas of what belonging to whiteness looks and sounds like. We define *white supremacy* as a "belief that white people are inherently better than others" (Belew & Gutiérrez, 2021, p. xii). It is also a term to denote systems of inequality that "insure racial disparity of health, income, life, and freedom" (Belew & Gutiérrez, 2021, p. xii). Not all RWE groups have been able to bridge the "two solitudes'" of English and French Canada. A commonality can be found in the Christian "values", tropes of biblical traditional gender roles, interpretations of immorality, and the Christian foundations of the nation.

In this respect, Doosje et al. (2016, p. 79) argue that there are a few defining characteristics of radical groups, one of which being that the group perceives that there is a serious problem in society. Once having perceived the problem, the group is dissatisfied with the manner in which it is being dealt with by institutions. The institutions blamed are predominantly the police and politicians who are understood as not acknowledging or paying attention to the problem or are simply not doing enough to handle the issue. This lack of acknowledgement or action fosters distrust in institutions and an understanding that authorities are not legitimate (Doosje et al., 2016, p. 80). It may also lead to populist leaders responding to the fears, perceived threats and problems. Here too, the media plays a significant role in the spreading of perceived problems and threats. Historically moral panics have been fanned by the role of media expounding and exaggerating the threat or fear narrative to smaller communities, but in the era of the internet and social media, the definition of who and what constitutes ' media" has changed dramatically.

2.2 Far-right and hate influencers

Many journalists, celebrities, and politicians were the original influencers – a designation that can now be applied to online actors who have been able to rise to an influential status and impact political debate in the public sphere. However, influencers as micro-celebrities are now ubiquitous across social media platforms (Carter, 2016; Gurrieri et al., 2023; Riedl et al., 2023). These new actors appear to be self-proclaimed experts on a variety of topics they post most frequently on and often monetize their perceived expertise. Within conspiracy and RWE are actors who blur the lines between politician, pundit, and general citizen (Merino & Kinnvall, 2023 p. 62). These individuals promote a worldview and interpretation of world events through a narrative of fearmongering, perpetual disaster, a political and societal insecurity, and the normalization of far-right discourses. Influencers share ideological representation and identity formation where relationships, discourses, and responses are created and molded (Merino & Kinnvall, 2023, p. 62). The impact of those voices in shaping discourse seeps into conspiracies, extremism, and the perceived need for a political public response on social media platforms.

Politics and promotion are inseparable categories, but in today's digital landscape, influencers often function as ideological intermediaries (Arnesson, 2023), also referred to as "ambassadors of ideology" (Rothut et al., 2023). Influencers may not directly support a political party or politician but *can* influence ideologies by promoting a "lifestyle enabled by specific policies" (Arnesson, 2023, p. 529). While influencers can encourage political engagement and participation (Naderer, 2023), they can also contribute to the spread of harmful or manipulative information that is "anti-democratic or anti-pluralistic" (Rothut et al., 2023, p. 2). This is particularly true for hate influencers who not only influence, but also mobilize publics through hateful ideologies (Stewart et al., 2023).

Hate and far-right influencers are types of *political actors* who advocate for extremist ideologies (Rothut et al., 2023; Stewart et al., 2023). Political influencers endorse social or political causes that can influence politics, hate speech, and conspiracy theories (Goodwin et al., 2023; Riedl et al., 2021; Riedl et al., 2023). Rothut et al. (2023) conceptualize far-right influencers as individual actors who (1) possess a far-right ideology, (2) function as political influencers, and (3) advocate and mobilize extremist ideologies. RWE influencers assume an influential position in communicating political messages to the public through a carefully crafted persona that establishes "credibility, authenticity, and trustworthiness with publics" (Stewart et al., 2023, p. 3).

In platform ecologies, this authenticity is extracted from a static state, functioning as a performative parasocial strategy that aligns with self-presentation techniques (Abidin, 2018; Stewart et al., 2023). These influential actors operate as parasocial opinion leaders, capable of influencing public opinion on far-right politics (Rothut et al., 2023; Stewart et al., 2023). Stemming from early communication research on the kindred concept of "influentials" (Merton, 1949) and "opinion leaders" (Katz et al., 1955), political influencers, including hate influencers, are often studied "through the conceptual prism of opinion leadership" (Riedl et al., 2023, p. 3). These influencers use an "alternative influence network" to "sell" their followers on a far-right ideology (Leidig, 2021). "These far-right influencers effectively merge political content with personal branding techniques in order to gain an audience and, over time, fans" (Leidig, 2021, p. 5).

Stephanie Alice Baker (2022) shows how alt. health influencers use the participatory affordances of social media to spread conspiratorial thinking, misinformation, and far-right extremism. Pete Evans, a wellness influencer and celebrity chef, for instance, established his credibility and following through these other pursuits, before sharing an image of a black sun on Instagram – a neo-Nazi symbol associated with the Christchurch gunman (Baker, 2022). These types of alt. health influencers reveal the vulnerability of the wellness industry (Baker, 2022). Studies show how these "wellness" influencers have slowly moved from one cause to the next: COVID-19 anti-vaccination content to QAnon conspiracies and, more recently, anti-climate narratives (Simmons, 2023). Far-right extremist influencers often anchor into current events and concerns, which can be linked to conspiracy beliefs.

Many far-right influencers and conspiracy influencers in our study assumed the position of a "fake expert". Importantly, information pathologies are able to gain traction when influential fake experts present a sense of manufactured credibility", that often takes up the task of delegitimizing the legitimate (Al-Rawi et al., 2022). Similarly, Trenberth (2011) shows how fake experts are central to the dissemination of conspiratorial arguments supporting climate change denialism. The strategy of assuming the role of a "fake expert" appeared repeatedly in our empirical work, including on Telegram and BitChute, where people without relevant credentials or conclusive empirical data would speak to their followers like "experts" about medical or legal matters.

RWE influencers are influential in the spread of extremism because these actors use hate speech, emotionalization, disinformation, and propaganda as communication tools to influence followers (Al-Rawi, 2021; Lorenzo-Dus & Nouri, 2021; Rothut et al., 2023). RWE influencers use hate speech to incite fear and identity politics, largely as a tool to obfuscate radical ideologies that enable extremists to justify their hate through rationalizations centered around politics or fear (Byman, 2019). This emotional language was particularly visible in our previous work where we observed hate influencers leading White Lives Matter channels frequently engaged in affective narratives like "We declare war against the anti-White system" to fuel emotional contagion among confluent networks situated below the radar (Stewart et al., 2023). On Telegram and BitChute, RWE influencers target particular actors. This often included the support of former President Donald Trump or perceived injustices suffered under "liberals" (generally) or politicians, including Prime Minister Justin Trudeau.

By using mobile chat apps like Telegram, far-right influencers are able to balance visibility and invisibility to *influence* refracted publics who support their ideological views (Stewart et al., 2023). Chat apps like Telegram layer privacy and obfuscation, which makes it easy for influencers to mobilize followers (Stewart et al., 2023). Crystal Abidin (2021, p. 3) defines refracted publics as "publics that are circumvented by users". As vernacular cultures of circumvention strategies pervade refracted publics, hate influencers benefit from being able to mobilize these publics in such a way that communication messages "avoid detection, promote deflection, and facilitate the dissemination of specific messages away from or toward target audiences" (Abidin, 2021, p. 10). A central *dynamic* of refracted publics is the ability for influencers to mobilize these publics through both public and private affordances, allowing an alternation between public and private (Abidin, 2021). Platform features foster algorithmic unpredictability, making public and private spheres no longer stable categories (Abidin, 2021).

Enrique Tarrio ("NobleLead") was one example of a hate influencer who once had over 8,828 subscribers on Telegram. On the latter platform, he described himself as "Chairman of the Notorious ProudBoys Patriot – Super-Villain – Entrepreneur American Supremacist". On January 3, 2021, Tarrio posted to Telegram, "What if we invade it?" One of his followers responded with, "January 6 is D day in America". Hate influencers like Enrique Tarrio and the channel administrators of hate groups on Telegram play a central role in platforming hate (Stewart et al., 2023). The participatory affordances of social media and chat apps like Telegram make it easy for influential far-right actors to propagate hate, extremism, misinformation, and conspiratorial thinking (Baker, 2022; Rothut et al., 2023; Stewart et al., 2023).

Hate influencers are both visible (forward-facing) like Tarrio and invisible (faceless), like the individuals who exert influence on hate group Telegram channels from behind the scenes (Stewart et al., 2023). Importantly, our work on hate influencers shows how these influential actors mobilize publics through a three-part theoretical framework – the hate influencer mobile mobilization model (Stewart et al., 2023). The model entails the process, means, and ends. The first component involves mobile mobilization – the assemblage of diverse people who connect on Telegram channels where parasocial relationships form between hate influencers and channel subscribers. The second stage is the means of mobile mobilization and includes common discourses (fear, othering, victimhood, brotherhood, etc.). Means function as narratives to articulate a collective identity and group memberships through social sorting, including in- and out-groups, generating an "us" versus "them" mentality. The third stage entails the ends – or the end result of mobile mobilization.

Far-right influencers appear at every turn in our work, and they are problematic precisely because they are able to exert influence and social pressure over RWE groups. Importantly, these types of influencing mechanisms can lead followers into deeper forms of extremism. Below, we discuss variances between extremism and terrorism, before outlining the main groupings of RWE groups in Canada.

2.3 Right-wing extremism or terrorism?

In terms of doing an analysis of RWE groups in contemporary Canada, the above reflections situated how we determined the groups included in the book. In the process of making a list of RWE groups in Canada, we discussed where to draw dividing lines between groups that may be right-wing but may not necessarily be extreme. We also debated the lines between far-right extremist groups versus far-right terrorism and how Canada handles the shift from one designation to another. We also avoided including movements like the Yellow Vests or the Convoy Protests here because we wanted to focus on groups only.

Terms like far-right, radical right, extreme right, right-wing terrorism, and far-right terrorism are common terms frequently used interchangeably (Perry et al., 2017). From Aryan Nation gathering weapons and training around issued manifestos to the galvanization of the fringes with the election of America's first Black president Barack Obama to the subsequent enrapture following Donald Trump's surprising success in 2016, far-right rhetoric is now deeply entrenched in the mainstream (Hoffman, 2024). In Canada, the Freedom Convoy movements and the movement of more American style populist rhetoric playing a role in contemporary political campaigns reflect the mainstreaming of far-right rhetoric seeping into Canada. To unpack the murky contours of extremist actors, our work began with an exhaustive examination of all current terrorist entities listed by the Government of Canada (Public Safety Canada, 2023), before cross-referencing the list to various hate group designations and other source types (websites, news, social media, etc.) to confirm national affiliation(s), ideologies, symbols, discourses, proximal locations, and network branches.

In Canada, the criteria for determining a terrorist entity are regulated by Section 83.05 of the *Criminal Code*, which articulates that groups are considered a "listed entity" if they have carried out, attempted to carry out, participated in, or facilitated terrorist activity; or "the entity has knowingly acted on behalf of, at the direction of, or in association with" an entity that meets the first criteria. This process is initiated by the Minister of Public Safety and Emergency Preparedness, who gathers intelligence from organizations like the Canadian Security Intelligence Services, the National Security in Canada and Royal Canadian Mounted Police (RCMP). Public Safety Canada (2023) leads the National Security to ensure the "safety and security of Canadians both at home and abroad". The National Security manages anti-hate initiatives, counter-terrorism activities, cyber security, and more.

These institutions undertake lengthy investigations, only recommending organizations become a "listed entity" if they have satisfied at least one of the criteria above. Importantly, not all terrorist entities are RWE organizations, but regardless, there are legal ramifications for *any* group on the list, including the ability of law enforcement agencies to take action against these groups and its members, including seizing or freezing assets.

Academically, terrorism literature often neglects the far-right, with one consideration being because of the "*success* of Al-Qaeda and related groups in perpetuated large scale attacks and the frequency of those attacks" (Ahmed & Lynch, 2024, p. 200). According to Ahmed and Lynch (2024, p. 200), far-right violence in Canada and the United States is often "more opportunistic" and less organized than large-scale terrorist entities. However, this is not completely accurate as far-right terrorism remains one of the most dangerous security threats in the United States (Walter & Chang, 2021). An official report published in 2021, for example, mentioned that "racially or ethnically motivated violent extremists (RMVEs) and militia violent extremists (MVEs) present the most lethal DVE [domestic violent extremist] threats" in the United States (Committee on Homeland Security, 2021). Similar to other regions, like Europe, "right-wing terrorism and violence cannot be completely separated from far-right" groups or parties (Koehler, 2016, p. 87). Thus, a central question for scholars, students, policymakers, and law enforcement is whether extreme right-wing terrorism displays violence or utilizes "tactical or strategic characteristics that make it harder to detect and counter" (Koehler, 2016, pp. 88–89).

The legal "terrorist" label is seldomly applied to RWE groups as they are often not "taken seriously" because law enforcement agencies rarely monitor the activities of RWE groups (Scrivens & Perry, 2017). While listed entities and RWE actors may share similar ideologies, entailing nationalism, xenophobia, anti-government, anti-immigration, or racist sentiments, the severity of violent actions tends to be the main differentiator between the two. Studies show that "gender constructs and practices can play a key role in influencing and propelling men toward militant-jihadist Islamism and terrorism" (Phelan, 2023, p. 355). Additionally, the concept of "manhood" can be a key driver that sustains "feelings of entitlement, supremacy, respect, and emasculation" (Phelan, 2023, p. 355).

The lone wolf terrorist narrative is also visible in Canada's history. Weeks before killing six Muslims at a mosque in Quebec, lone-wolf terrorist Alexandre Bissonnette was reading the tweets from neo-Nazis and misinformation based conservative news commentators, including Alex Jones and Gavin McInnes. Alexandre Bissonnette also viewed Stefan Molyneux's site a couple of times (Riga, 2018) in addition to numerous other far-right conspiracy theory websites before conducting his attack on a Quebec Mosque that killed 6 people on January 29, 2017. After his arrest at the police station, Bissonnette repeatedly revealed that the attack was "not wrong at all" because he "was convinced that [Muslims] are going to kill my parents, my family" and that he "had to do something" to "save" people and prevent this from happening (Perreaux, 2018).

While there are no legal definitions for RWE groups, "hate group" designations are often made by organizations and research institutions. One of the most prominent North American organizations that issues "extremist" and "hate group" warnings is the Southern Poverty Law Center (SPLC) based in the United States. SPLC (2020) defines "hate groups" as an organization that "based on its official statements or principles, the statements of its leaders, or its activities – has beliefs or practices that attack or malign an entire class of people, typically for their immutable characteristics". This often includes groups that vilify others because of their "race, religion, ethnicity, sexual orientation or gender identity" (SPLS, 2020). SPLC (2020) gathers information and reports from citizens, law enforcement, news media, field sources, and through their own investigations. Additionally, SPLC has an extensive research network to monitor global extremist and hate groups, publishing an annual report that outlines the criteria and ideologies of included groups. Anti-Hate Canada, a federally funded entity, works in conjunction with the SPLC, and provides hate designations for Canadian right-wing groups, too. Other important academic centers and not-for-profit organizations that research hate groups and extremism in Canada include The Canadian Network for Research on Terrorism, Security, and Society, The Mosaic Institute, and the Center for Hate, Bias, and Extremism.

There is no doubt that the different classifications can be confusing due to obvious overlaps, and there are many areas that require further clarification and transparency. Proud Boys is an example of a group whose status transitioned from a far-right hate group to a listed terrorist entity in Canada. Public Safety Minister Bill Blair noted that this decision was influenced by the organization's "pivotal role" in the January 6 Capitol riots in Washington, DC (BBC News, 2021). Blair noted that the designation was implemented due to concerns over a "growing threat of ideologically motivated violent extremism", which clearly fits within the parameters of what constitutes a listed entity in Canada. The classification of the Proud Boys was unprecedented in that Blair announced the department was considering listing the group as a terrorist entity prior to designating them as such. Previous designations were unannounced so that material, posts, websites, and bank accounts could not be deleted or removed. With the Proud Boys, they announced their disbanding in Canada and removed all materials prior to officially being designated as a terrorist entity. New Zealand similarly added Proud Boys to their terrorist list, while in the United States, Proud Boys is still only designated as a hate group. In May 2023, five members of the Proud Boys were found guilty of "seditious conspiracy for their actions before and during the breach of the U.S. Capitol on Jan. 6, 2021" (U.S. Department of Justice, 2023). Still, this raises many questions. For starters, are all Proud Boys chapters the same? How about chapter differences between Canada and the United States?

Terrorist entities and RWE groups both exist in networked structures. These network structures often exist along ideological lines, as is evidenced by Atalante Québec's leader, Raphaël Lévesque, barging into VICE's Montreal newsroom to support other far-right actors/groups. Within these distinct branches, there tends to be variances in radicalization and violence. For example, Blood & Honour is connected to Combat 18, the armed, and much more violent branch of the network. Terrorist organizations and RWE groups both affiliate with other groups in similar ideological alignment, which illustrates the value of mapping out a web of ideologies to uncover current and future linkages. We see this ideological alignment connect associations like Aryan Nations, Blood & Honour, Combat 18, and the Aryan Strikeforce (Barrouquere, 2020), which makes this a logical connection point.

Historical hate networks also propagate current and future hate networks. For example, the KKK can be understood as being largely responsible for the offshoot of many of the radical groups that exist in Canada today. Sons of Odin, for instance, is an example of a Christian identity system known as Odinism that encompasses "white supremacist religious belief systems", similarly asserting that "non-white persons are less than human or not valuable compared to white people" (Belew & Gutiérrez, 2021, p. xv). Historian Allan Bartley argues that while groups like Blood & Honour, The Atomwaffen Division (AWD), La Meute, and Sons of Odin are not formally connected to the KKK, they do "have their origins with the Klan and benefit from that association" (Manasan, 2020). Bartley argues that these new white nationalist and white supremacist groups are "as virulent and as dangerous and as flagrant" as the KKK, creating a "seam of hate in Canadian society" that has never disappeared (Manasan, 2020).

Some groups also have ties to radical groups from Europe and beyond. As groups like Proud Boys and Sons of Odin experience heightened levels of governance or receive terrorist and/or hate group designations, they often disband, rebrand, or join other existing groups. This is precisely how the Edmonton chapter of Soldiers of Odin (SOO) became known as the Wolves of Odin Canada Infidels (WOOCI), and in short form after WOOCI encountered problems, the Canadian Infidels. Similarly, radicalization within these networks often interweaves with gangs and organized crime. Recruitment of military personnel and veterans provide these RWE groups with access to military and weapons training, as well as tactical information for violent acts. Although cases of active Canadian Armed Forces military personnel are relatively low, there have been some incidents such as when five members of the Canadian Armed Forces were suspended for their affiliation to the Proud Boys movement in Canada (CBC, 2017).

It is important to note here that not all listed terrorist entities in Canada have a visible physical presence in the country, nor are all the listed organizations of RWE groups. It is important to recognize that there are also left-wing radical groups listed as terrorist organizations, among others. However, the underlying mechanisms, tenets, and qualities that shape terrorist organizations tend to mimetically replicate with RWE groups in Canada. For example, network branches, overlapping ideologies, community, and an "us" versus "them" framework are critical overlapping areas between terrorist groups and RWE groups.

2.4 RWE groups in Canada

Below, we geographically and ideologically map out recent RWE groups in Canada. Currently, the majority of violent instances from right-wing extremist (RWE) groups occur in Canada's most populated provinces, including Ontario, Quebec, and British Columbia (Parent & Ellis, 2014). These provinces have a significant proportion of visible minorities and historically see a higher concentration of membership to far-right groups (Parent & Ellis, 2014). We analyzed RWE groups in Canada by examining applied designations and scanning digital platforms to uncover far-right activities.

Drawing from our earlier discussions, we recognize that some RWE organizations might actively moderate their self-portrayal in order to claim that they are not an extremist organization or to prevent possible de-platformization. Despite being aware of this, we did find it appropriate to engage in a group-making project that could potentially categorize racist, extremist, and far-right groups with those that actively promote or commit acts of violence. Our criteria for the inclusion of RWE groups in this listing was based upon the groups' mandates and if they committed or called for acts of violence within the country. We used existing literature around RWE groups to design our categorization system that reflects the presence of activity in Canada from around 2015 until about 2022. Drawing primarily from Moslesh (2019), a recent report on RWE groups in Canada (Davey et al., 2020), and recent publications from Perry et al. (2022), our taxonomy of RWE groups in Canada are listed below (see Figure 2.1), mostly relying on the groups' most dominant ideological characteristics.

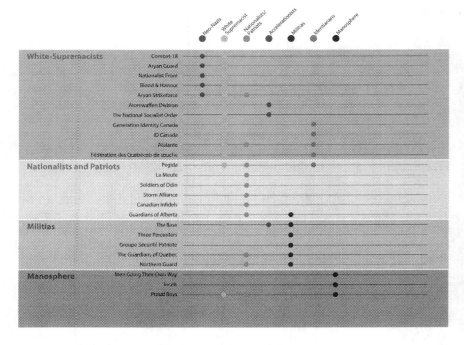

Figure 2.1 Ideological map of RWE groups in Canada*.

* The map is designed by Song Tang.

Figure 2.1 serves as a visual representation of ideological lines that RWE formulate, clearly illustrating the propensity toward white supremacists, nationalists and patriots, militias, and manosphere groups. The ideological map also visualizes the tendency of groups to anchor into one or more ideologies, which is a shared trait among similar, yet disparate groups.

2.4.1 *White supremacists*

A large subset of RWE groups in Canada share white supremacist ideologies – a finding that is consistent with previous work on RWE in Canada (see Perry & Scrivens, 2016). For the purpose of our work, similar to Jakob Guhl and Jacob Davey (2020, p. 13), we define "white supremacy" as the belief that whites are superior to non-whites. This often results in white people believing they have a political or social dominance over non-white people (Guhl & Davey, 2020). "White power movement" or "white supremacist extremist movement" is the "preferred terminology for the broad affiliation of Klansmen, neo-Nazis, sovereign citizens, Three Percenters, posse comitatus members, some skinheads, some militia groups, and similar groups who seek the violent overthrow of the United States through race war" (Belew & Gutiérrez, 2021, p. xiii). Importantly, the "false belief that a conspiracy exists to carry out "white genocide", or to effect a great replacement" of white people is prevalent across the racist far-right, including neo-Nazis to identitarians and nationalists (SPLC, n.d.). The white supremacists category formulates the largest volume of groups, which we describe below by highlighting three major sub-groupings: neo-Nazis, accelerationists, and identitarians.

2.4.1.1 *Neo-Nazis*

Neo-Nazi constitute a variety of groups that often share a love for Adolf Hitler and Nazi Germany and hate Jewish people (and occasionally other minorities such as Muslims, LGBTQ+ communities, and some Christians (SPLC, n.d.)). As mentioned in Chapter 1, at the start of the 21st century, neo-Nazi groups like the KKK, Church of Creator, and skinhead groups like Aryan Guard and Blood & Honour had a presence in Canada, "staging rallies against antiracists, disseminating xenophobic fliers, and engaging" in violent activities (Perry & Scrivens, 2016, p. 820). Neo-Nazi groups include Aryan Guard, Combat-18, and Nationalist Front and a few other ones.

The Aryan Guard is a white supremacist, neo-Nazi group founded in 2006 in Alberta, Canada by Paul Fromm, from the Canadian Association of Free Expression, and Terry Tremaine, the National Socialist Party of Canada leader (Scherr, 2009). It is largely thought to still have groups operating in Canada (Canadian Press, 2021), but it is hard to pinpoint their precise movements as a result of being deplatformed from so many social media sites. The group's spokesperson Kyle McKee, who was also the leader of the Calgary and Edmonton Divisions of the now defunct Blood & Honour and Combat-18 groups (Scherr, 2009), made it more popular. With "White Pride Worldwide" flags in hand, Aryan Guard stormed the steps of

City Hall in Calgary in 2009 (Scherr, 2009). At the time, SPLC wrote that this "hate group" had ties to the American Ku Klux Klan (Scherr, 2009). The Calgary police have noted that the Aryan Guard has also "received ongoing support from Christian Waters, a leader of the Canadian branch of the Brotherhood of Klans Knights of the Ku Klux Klan" (Scherr, 2009). Edmonton Police Sgt. Stephen Camp, co-chair of the Alberta Hate Crime Committee, noted that the Calgary March, while small, caused a lot of anxiety in the community due to the sizable immigrant and minority population, noting about the group, "They're pretty hard-core" (Scherr, 2009). Key ideologies that anchor the AG include white supremacy, white nationalism, neo-Nazism, anti-Islam, and antisemitism.

In relation to Combat-18, also referred to as C-18, 318, and "terror machine", it is a neo-Nazi, fascist group, associated with acts of terrorism and violence, including arson (Lowles, 2021). Combat-18 is the "armed branch" of Blood & Honour (Lowles, 2021). The group originated in the United Kingdom but expanded out to other countries, including Canada and the United States (Lowles, 2021). "The '18' in the name refers to the first and eighth letters of the English alphabet, A and H, for Adolf Hitler" (Counter Extremism, n.d.). Combat-18 was founded by Charlie Sargent and Harold Covington in the early 1990s by the far-right British National Party to keep anti-fascists from attending its events (Ryan, 1998). Charlie Sargent views immigrant communities as the Enemy and uses the term "they" to refer to the state, which they call Zog (Zionist Occupation Government) or the immigrant communities are the Enemy (Ryan, 1998). Sargent once wrote, "I don't vote. What's the point? I'm not gonna play their fucking silly little games" (Ryan, 1998). Combat-18 is also connected to the Aryan Strikeforce, another group that frequently exercised violence. A Vancouver Sun newspaper article by Zak Vescera (2019) article stated after 2012 Blood & Honour had a limited activity in British Columbia (ADL, 2021a). Blood & Honour were prominent in the news in 2019 when the RCMP released a public alert for Kam McLeod and Bryer Schmegelsky, who were murder suspects in northern Manitoba and alleged to have killed three people in British Columbia (Lamoureux & Makuch, 2019). Bryer Schmegelsky posted a photo on Instagram with a gun in his mouth (Lamoureux & Makuch, 2019). Other photographs obtained by the Globe and Mail showed Schmegelsky with a Nazi armband with the Hitler Youth knife inscribed with the German phrase "Blut und Ehre" (Lamoureux & Makuch, 2019). A 2017 RCMP report found the group was active in Alberta, Ontario, and Quebec (Vescera, 2019).

Blood & Honour and Combat-18 are still operational in some parts of the world but are currently in a disbanded status in Canada. Both Blood & Honour, and its armed branch, Combat-18, now both defunct groups in Canada, were associated with Aryan Strikeforce (Barrouquere, 2020), a group that was founded in 2016 by Josh "Hatchet" Steever (ADL, 2006). Aryan Strikeforce's website described the group's goals as to "protect the honour of our women, children and the future of our race and nation" (ADL, 2006). Former President Ronald Pulcher, also known as "Dozer", posted on VK (a Russian social media site) that AS recruits needed to take a blood oath to pledge allegiance to the group (SPLC, 2016). The group engaged in violent behavior, such as assembling in 2016 to make a bomb out of an oxygen bottle that an Aryan Strikeforce member later blew himself up with at a white supremacist rally in the same year. The bomb was intended to target anti-racist demonstrators who were assumed to show up as counter protesters for an event organized by Aryan Strikeforce.

In addition, the Nationalist Front (formerly known as the Aryan Nationalist Alliance) was a branch of the Nationalist Socialist Movement (NSM) (ADL, 2021b). The organization was founded in 2016 at a NSM national meeting that included Klan members, racist skin-heads, and neo-Nazis (ADL, 2022) but got disbanded in 2017. The ideologies embedded into the Nationalist Front include anti-Semitism, creating Federal tyranny, and establishing an ethnostate in North America (ADL, 2022).

2.4.1.2 Accelerationists

The term "accelerationist" describes a variation of white supremacy that assumes an ideological position that attempts to move society beyond capitalism to "build a just economic system" (SPLC, n.d.). Accelerationist factions of the far-right aim to speed up socio-political-ecological collapse, often targeting mass transportation, gas delivery systems, water distribution, and nuclear power plants (Loadenthal, 2022). Accelerationism is "an extreme philosophy that aims to hasten the demise of the current economic and political systems and create a new one, using political violence as a primary mechanism" (Belew & Gutiérrez, 2021, p. xiii). Primary white power accelerationist groups include AWD (see Loadenthal, 2022) whose views are often infused with neo-Nazi ideology.

AWD is a white supremacist, accelerationist group that had "plans to explode power lines and bomb a nuclear power plant" (Loadenthal, 2022, p. 174). The terror group was founded in 2016 by members of the Iron March online forum, offering a good example of how RWE proliferated on digital media (ADL, 2021a). Since then, the organization has infiltrated countries like the United Kingdom, Canada, and Germany (Public Safety Canada, 2023). Atomwaffen, the German word for "atomic weapons" is a listed public terrorist entity in Canada (Public Safety Canada, 2023). The Atomwaffen flag has a black background with four yellow rays stretching from corner-to-corner, with the Waffen insignia shield with a trefoil at the center (ADL, 2021a).

True to the manifesto of most accelerationist groups, Atomwaffen's mission is to produce the total collapse of society, and the organization is allegedly inspired by the serial killer Charles Manson (SPLC, 2021). In 2018, Gabriel Sohier Chaput, a neo-Nazi propagandist from Montreal who went by the pseudonym of "Charles Zeiger", used his position as a "primary publicist" and main contributor for the site Daily Stormer to promote the Atomwaffen (Montpetit, 2018). He was previously a moderator on the Iron March forum (defunct) and was the head editor of the webzine NOOSE (Hankes, 2018) and released the writings of the neo-Nazi James Mason who advocates for cell-base terrorism to pursue racial revolutions (Montpetit, 2018). According to a Pro-Publica report, in early 2018, AWD was banned from YouTube, Discord, and Steam (Thompson & Winston, 2018). Its status as a terrorist organization makes looking for obvious online presence difficult. Daily Stormer no longer has a presence on the open web but does exist on the Dark Web (Biggs, 2017; SPLC Hatewatch Staff, 2019). In 2014, Zeiger posted on Iron March, stating that RWE groups like Attomwaffen were experiencing an "unbelievable popularity surge in Canada", as a result of RWE activity on these kinds of digital websites (Montpetit, 2018). In 2023, an Ottawa man, Patrick Gordon Macdonald, was the first to be charged with terrorism and hate propaganda offences in Canada. Macdonald was charged for making propaganda material for AWD under the alias "Dark Foreigner" (Fraser, 2023).

In terms of its media outreach, Iron March (ironmarch.org) was a fascist website that was connected to approximately 100 hate crimes in 2011, and it was officially shut down in 2020 (Singer-Emery & Bray, 2020), before another website called Iron March Exposed (ironmarch.exposed) appeared to disclose the identities and other social media handles of past users. The Iron March flag is similar to that of Atomwaffen but has orange rays in the background and a symbol of three hands grabbing wrists overtop of a ship wheel and surrounded by a wreath. The decentralized cell-based organization emerged from the online forum Iron March, which was started by a Russian activist and operated from 2011 until being shut down in 2017 (Williams et al., 2021, p. 8). In 2020, its leader, James Mason, circulated a report that Atomwaffen was disbanding and renouncing armed struggle (Makuch, 2020), which can be interpreted as a strategic response to potential legal issues relating to the Canadian authorities' categorization of the group and its members as a threat to society.

When AWD officially disbanded, numerous other splinter groups, with the same goals and ideologies, emerged. The National Socialist Order was one such group that was formed in 2020. According to the Center for International Security and Cooperation, AWD has rebranded itself as the National Socialist Order (CISAC, 2021). While leadership structure may be slightly altered from the original AWD group, it shared many of the same members (Newhouse, 2021). The first pronouncement of the group was to establish "an Aryan, National Socialist world by any means necessary" (Newhouse, 2021).

2.4.1.3 Identitarians

Identitarians focus on assembling within a single identity, often measuring their power by their ability to transform into a majority – a type of counter-eventual becoming. Identitarians include groups like Generation Identity Canada, ID Canada, and Atalante. RWE discourse over the "migrant crisis" enhanced right-wing identitarianism groups and consequently impacted rising hate and attacks by far-right and white supremacist actors (Richards, 2022).

Generation Identity (also referred to as "Generation Identitaire" and "Identitarian Movement") originally emerged in France in 2012 as a far-right youth group (Richards, 2022). The group opposes globalization, wants to stop Islamization, and "Stop and Reverse the Great Replacement" (Richards, 2022, p. 32). Generation Identity uses "media guerilla warfare" tactics to occupy mosques and vandalize cultural sites, disrupt humanitarian efforts to rescue refugees, and block migrants (Richards, 2022). Generation Identity "activists" advocate for the identity/culture of white Europeans from the Great Replacement the group believes derives from immigration or Islamization (Al Jazeera 2018). The group is known for its attacks on young Arabs and visible Nazi salutes in Lille (Al Jazeera, 2018). Far-right Canadian influencer, Lauren Southern, is a major supporter of Generation Identity; her YouTube broadcast of Generation Identity's "Defend Europe: Alps" was viewed 139,056 times by 2019 (Richards, 2022). The syncretic group "attempts to build legitimacy by citing proto and quasi-fascist inspirations", often appropriating left/right-wing political principles that relate to identity (Richards, 2022, p. 20). Currently, the group has factions in many European countries like Italy, Austria, Germany, and the United Kingdom (Al Jazeera, 2018; Richards, 2022). The group built its following by leveraging the affordances of digital media platforms to mobilize tens of thousands of followers (Al Jazeera, 2018). For example, Martin Sellner, a far-right influencer of the Austrian chapter of the group, has more than 100,000 followers on YouTube (Richards, 2022). Sellner, in particular, encourages the sale of Identitarian merchandize, illustrating the commodification of endorsement, despite the discordance it generates with the anti-capitalistic nature of Generation Identity (Richards, 2022).

Inspired by Generation Identity, Generation Identity Canada was created by Tyler Hover and Jonathan McCormack, as a replica of the European group (Smith, 2020). Eventually, another Canadian group emerged calling itself ID Canada (Lamoureux, 2019). As of 2017, the group had a visible presence in some Canadian cities, like Sudbury, where members of the group placed anti-multicultural and anti-immigration messages around the city (Durnan, 2017). Both groups are identitarian, anti-immigrant, anti-Islam, fascist, misogynistic, and promote the conspiracy theory of the great replacement (Anti-Racist, 2018). The groups are known for postering and flier campaigns in large cities across the country (Anti-Racists, 2018). Membership is only open to those who are of European descent and membership groups are based upon region and location (Smith, 2020). The ID Canada mission statement illustrates how members feel they have a birthright, a sense of ownership over the colonization of North America: "We are their descendants. We are the rightful heirs to this nation, not those who come here to reap the benefits of our social assistance, healthcare, education and most importantly – the labours and sacrifices of our forefathers" (ID Canada Mission Statement, as quoted in Derkson, 2022, p. 2). As Derkson (2022, p. 4) observes, the "assertion of white victimhood is a major theme" of ID Canada's website, presenting themselves as the collective "defenders of the downtrodden". Through the exploitation of xenophobia, ID Canada manufactures a shared sense of identity through fear-based tactics (Derkson, 2022).

In relation to Atalante, it was founded in 2016 in Quebec City. The group's founder, Raphaël Lévesque, is the lead singer of the neo-Nazi skinhead band Légitime Violence (Legitimate Violence).[3] *Skinheads* are a white power affiliate, often connected to neo-Nazism or another similar belief system (Belew & Gutiérrez, 2021, p. xv). Atalante promotes direct action to further its critiques of capitalism, communism, and globalization. Their slogan is "action socreferenceé-rence nationale" (social action, favor the nation) (Radio-Canada, 2017). In terms of rhetoric, Atalante draws from neo-Nazi "white genocide" ideologies as well as the *grand replacement* (great replacement) theory (Camus, 2011) popular among RWE francophone groups. Atalante calls for social justice for white Québécois and promotes a program of remigration (forced repatriation) for immigrants (Perron, 2017). To further this end, it advocates for "identity policy for community, sports, cultural and intellectual purposes" (Allchorn, 2021, p. 128) and a "renaissance of the neo-French in Quebec" (Montpetit, 2017). In terms of offline activities, Atalante provides food in underprivileged neighborhoods of Quebec City's but only to people of "Neo-French origin" (Montpetit, 2017). Atalante members have also attacked the offices of journalists in Canada (de l'Église, 2018).

Atalante has established connections to other RWE groups at the national and international level. At the national level, while Atalante is relatively new, core members of Atalante and Fédération des Québécois de souche are the same and have known each other since the late 2000s (Montpetit, 2017). Atalante has co-organized patrols with the Canadian chapter of the Soldiers of Odin (SOO) (Montpetit, 2017) and regularly repost news stories of Atalante Quebec with words of congratulation (Gagnon, 2020, p. 372). Social media records found members of Atalante Québec, Storm Alliance, and Le Front Patriotique du Québec (Patriotic Front of Quebec) all belong to a chat group called Patriotes du Québec (Patriots of Quebec) on the MeWe social media platform, a Facebook clone site, which had members openly planning and advocating for a fake terrorist attack to mobilize the public (Curtis, 2018). At the international level, Atalante has been said to have been modeled after the Italian RWE organization CasaPound (Montpetit, 2017), a group known to direct action in their pursuit for social justice and housing for local people rooted in critiques of globalization (Albanese et al., 2014). In 2017, an Atalante member visited RWE CasaPound in Rome and both co-hosted a lecture in Quebec City by Gabriele Adinolfi, a prominent Italian neo-fascist (Montpetit, 2017). Atalante's Montreal organizer Shawn Beauvais-MacDonald was among other Canadian RWE involved in the 2017 "Unite the Right" Charlottesville rally (Allchorn, 2021, pp. 128–129). In addition, Faith Goldy, a Catholic nationalist, anti-immigrant, and anti-muslim, far-right Canadian political commentator was also in attendance at the Unite the Right Rally. Goldy live-streamed the rally and captured the moment that Heather Heyer was struck and killed by a car driven by a white nationalist. Throughout her livestream, Goldy promoted and praised white racial consciousness (Brigade, 2019). While Lauren Southern (see the Appendix), another far-right Canadian commentator, was not in attendance at the Rally, a leak to the media collective "Unicorn Riot" revealed text messages between Unite the Right organizers discussing having invited Southern to the rally, but had not received a response (Kelley, 2017).

In January 2020, Atalante had 6,725 Facebook, 180 Twitter, and 57 Instagram followers (Allchorn, 2021, p. 129). However, the Atalante Quebec Facebook page has not been accessible since August 2021 (Coutu, 2021). In November 2021, Meta, the parent company for Facebook, Instagram, and WhatsApp formally categorized the group as a dangerous organization (Coutu, 2021). According to Facebook, the initial ban was implemented when members were sharing Nazi concentration camp symbols, including one member posting photos of himself with "Arbeit Macht Frei", the famous slogan brandishing some concentration camps in Hitler's Germany, tattooed on his arm (Coutu, 2021). Atalante's official website (atalantequebec.com) seems to have been taken over by an activist by the name of Abu Zayed.

2.5 Nationalists and patriots

Nationalist groups promote the idea that the movement they are working toward upholding the values, culture, and traditions of the nation-state in which they live. Nationalism presents a perception of belonging to a "national community" (Rydgren, 2018). See Chapter 1 for a more fulsome definition of this concept. We use the term Patriot in this RWE-specific context to denote those who believe in a nation they envision, rather than the one that exists such as the case of the Nationalist RWE groups. This can often turn to nostalgic ideas that may not be a collective memory, but more a critique of modernity reflecting real or perceived injustices or victimhood. Groups within this category include Pegida (also identitarians), La Meute, SOO, Storm Alliance, and Guardians of Alberta.

Pegida (Patriotic Europeans Against the Islamization of the West) is a far-right, fascist, anti-Islamization group from Germany that mobilizes through social media (Hirst, 2015). PEGIDA is a "grassroots ... protest" (Hirst, 2015) whose primary target is Islam (Gonick & Levy, 2017). In early 2015, the PEGIDA presence in Quebec emerged (Perry et al., 2019, p. 102) and its chapter "draws on the same sentiments of the incompatibility of Islam with western values as its European parent group" (Perry & Scrivens, 2015, p. 49). PEGIDA protested in the streets of Montreal in 2015, sending the message to all Canadian Muslims that they are not welcome (Perry & Scrivens, 2016, p. 820). However, in their first March in Quebec, protestors outnumbered PEGIDA that police had to escort PEGIDA outside of the premises (Perry & Scrivens, 2015, p. 76).

The other group is La Meute, also known as "the pack" or "wolf pack", which is a far-right group based in Quebec that is also concerned about the increasing "Islamization" of society (Canadian Press, 2020) and perceived "illegal immigration" (Montpetit, 2017). La Meute was founded in 2015 by two former veterans from the Afghanistan war: Eric Venne (otherwise known as Corvus) and Patrick Beaudry. Group members often wear black shirts with a wolf paw print a badge that "has rapidly become the most visible expression of Quebec's far right" (Montpetit, 2016). One of its goals for social change was allegedly directly inspired by the Coalition Avenir Québec (Coalition for Québec's Future) who won a Québec majority in 2018 (Robichaud, 2018). When La Meute was still active, it had a Facebook page with 43,000 followers, and members were encouraged to "exchange calls to boycott halal products, circulated petitions against government policies that foster multiculturalism and post stories from little-known publications about the influence of the Muslim Brotherhood in Quebec" (Montpetit, 2016). In their manifesto, La Meute proposes that political adversaries should be labelled terrorists and that "first-generation immigrants" should be stripped of their citizenship and deported if found guilty of acts of treason (La Meute, 2018). La Meute is not a listed terrorist entity in Canada.

In 2018, La Meute released their manifesto and carried out high-visibility direct action during the provincial election campaign. "A manifesto is a document laying out a political ideology, often to explain or incite violence" (Belew & Gutiérrez, 2021, p. xv). According to Nadeau (2021, p. 16), the group was one of the most visible and active groups in Quebec, with the largest membership and the best structured RWE group in the province, but it shrank by 2020 due to internal fighting. La Meute was careful in the moderation of their public Facebook page where their administrators had disabled comments on all of their posts to ensure, they had said, no instances of racism, xenophobia, sexism, or homophobia (Rutherford, 2020, p. 69). While La Meute had a public page, they also had a "secret" Facebook page where members had to be vetted to join, a move that has been characterized as being more radical (Rutherford, 2020, p. 69). Their Facebook "secret" page claimed (a much disputed) 40,000 members in 2016 (Radio-Canada, 2016; Rutherford, 2020, p. 69). As of January 15, 2020, the La Meute Publique Facebook presence had over 16,000 members and remained active while The La Meute "secret" group, created in late 2015, had over 24,000 members.

Another group that is similar to La Meute is the SOO, also known as Sons of Odin. This is a far-right, anti-refugee, Islamophobic group that emerged in Finland in 2015, before infiltrating branches into Canada and the United States less than a year later (ADL, 2016). SOO emerged as a result of the "ongoing refugee crisis in Europe" (ADL, 2016). It is known as an anti-government and "anti-refugee vigilante" "Patriot" group described by the Anti-Defamation League as the "most significant coalition of extremists ... since the early 1990s". SOO Quebec have publicly expressed their support to the neo-Nazi group, Légitime Violence (Gagnon, 2020). In 2017, the Canadian chapter of SOO detached itself from the original group (Biber, 2016), stating: "We are here to help and protect the people of our great country, not to adhere to some racist, unorganized, reckless wanna be thug collaboration" (Lamoureux, 2017).

In 2018, the Edmonton chapter of SOO rebranded as the WOOCI, also known in short form as the Canadian Infidels. The Canadian Infidels are a far-right hate group in Canada with a heavy emphasis on anti-Islamophobia (Lamoureux, 2019). The group emerged out of the closure of the Edmonton chapter of the SOO (Lamoureux, 2019). In 2019, the group "stalked out and entered Canada's oldest mosque" (Lamoureux, 2019). The alleged founder, Tyson Hunt, alongside another member of the Canadian Infidels entered an Edmonton mosque where they proceeded to provoke worshipers, prompting a police investigation (Moslesh, 2019). At one point, an Infidel-affiliated man posted on Facebook: "We're freedom fighters, we believe in freedom of speech so we may not agree with what you believe in or what you have to say but we appreciate the fact that you come to our country Canada and have those rights" (Lamoureux, 2019).

As for Storm Alliance, it was created by former members of the Quebec chapter of the SOO (Tasker, 2017). The founder and leader of Storm Alliance, Dave Tregget, was reported saying that he left SOO because of its overt racism (Tasker, 2017). On their bilingual Facebook page (Storm Alliance W2A support), Storm Alliance describes the sole mission of the organization "to preserve the rights of the people and Canadian culture [through] charitable work, vigilant citizens and activism in Canadian communities". There is no official government classification for this group. While known to be based in Quebec, it is described as a mostly online organization having some presence in Ontario (Gonick & Levy, 2017; Perry & Scrivens, 2016). Storm Alliance is known to have connections with La Meute as the two periodically held joint protests at Roxham Road and St-Bernard-de-Lacolle, Quebec, to criticize Canada's decision to take refugees arriving via the United States (Macdonald & Ayres, 2020).

According to a 2020 report from a Quebec-based antifascist group, Storm Alliance ceased to be a major player in Quebec's extreme far right scene after the departure of founder Dave Tregget in 2018 (Montréal Antifasciste, 2020). Tregget also renounced the use of social media for an indeterminate amount of time (Côté, 2018). It has been reported that Tregget left the group after reports of sexual harassment that brought criticism within Storm Alliance (Côté, 2018). As of January 15, 2020, while Dave Tregget, also known as Dave Treg, is no longer an admin, he still has a pinned post on the main Storm Alliance Facebook page (Storm Alliance W2A support) which has 1247 members; another group claiming to be a Storm Alliance information page which is primarily in French (Storm Alliance Infos) and had 568 followers, as of January 2021.

Finally, the Guardians of Alberta was formed in 2017 as a breakaway faction from the SOO (Montpetit, 2017). After the split, the Guardians of Alberta re-oriented their activities to focus on local community assistance rather than continuing to do street patrols (Archambault & Veilleux-Lepage, 2019, pp. 275–276). Its founder, who defines himself in terms of having black and native American heritage, has been quoted as explicitly attributing the split to "the racist overtones" of the Canadian chapter of the SOO "and its ties to neo-Nazi organizations" (As cited in Archambault & Veilleux-Lepage, 2019, p. 276). Despite this claim, it has been argued that the Guardians of Alberta's social media fit within an RWE framework (Archambault & Veilleux-Lepage, 2019, pp. 275–276). As of February 9, 2022, the Twitter account (@goaleth) had 21 followers and inactive with the last post occurring in 2017.

2.6 Militias

Militia groups mistrust federal authority, have a fear of foreign influence, and believe that there is a need to have a paramilitary for self-defense (Robinson et al., 2023. p. 76). These groups often form local clusters that usually form small, local paramilitary groups, with a designated leader, formal membership, and in some cases hierarchical organizational structures. National forms of militia groups have a national leadership that denotes the general ideological and strategic direction of the overall group, but individual chapters are independent and have their own activities (Robinson et al., 2023. p. 78). Groups like The Base, Three Percenters, the Northern Guard, Les Gardiens du Québec, Groupe Sécurité Patriote are situated in militia category.

In relation to The Base,[4] it is a militant accelerationist group that relies on the use of "armed rightwing militias" (Boucher & Young, 2023, p. 146) – what SPLC describes as "accelerationist terror". As a wing of the white power movement, accelerationist groups like The Base also espouse white nationalist, neo-Nazi ideologies. The Base first appeared in 2018, primarily within the United States (ADL, 2021a). "The group espouses nihilistic and accelerationist rhetoric – an ideology embraced by white supremacists who have determined that a societal collapse" is essential (ADL, 2021a). The Base is a group of survivalists who resort to violence and self-defense to overthrow existing social and political order (ADL, 2021a). The members view non-white people as enemies of the white race and believe there is an impending race war that will be started by "non-European races" (ADL, 2021a). In February 2021, The Base was added to the Canadian terrorist entity list (Smith, 2020; Public Safety Canada, 2023).

The second group in this category is The Three Percenters (also referred to as 3 Percenters, %ers, and III%ers), which is a far-right militia that evokes ideologies of racist extremism, white nationalism/supremacy, anti-government extremism, nativist extremism, anti-abortion extremism, and male supremacy (Beutel & Johnson, 2021). There are different groups often clustered within the same extremist ideology, and they are notoriously anti-government, holding a high resistance to governments in Canada and the United States. The %ers were founded in 2008 in response to President Barack Obama's election, and concern about government interferences related to issues like gun control. There have been reports of Three Percenters at events in cities like Calgary and Toronto (Lamoureux, 2017). The organization has been connected to the January 6 attack on Capitol Hill, which was largely mobilized by Donald Trump's supporters (Feur & Rosenberg, 2021). During the 2021 Canadian election, Maxime Bernier's campaign phrase, "When tyranny becomes law, revolution becomes our duty", raised some concern that "some far-right extremist groups like the Three Percenters" would perceive it as an endorsement (Thompson, 2021). According to Balleck (2019), the now defunct %ers website formerly declared:

> The Three Percenter movement started shortly after the attack on the world trade centers. The movement has continued to gain momentum as our federal government grows more powerful. The states are losing control, federal judges are overruling the people, liberals and democrats are determined to disarm citizens, and the political climate is aggressive and leaning towards socialism. Our founding fathers warned us about this with their intentional laws written into the constitution and the bill of rights. Three Percenters are ex and current military, police, and trained civilians that will stand up and fight if our rights are infringed in any way.
>
> (Three Percenters Club)

A splinter group from the SOO, they rebranded themselves as the Northern Guard in 2019 (Boonstra et al., 2019). Founded by Nick Gallant and Ed Jamnisek, this militant group is located in the east coast. The group is an organized "American-style militia" with anti-Islamic ideologies. With a strong online presence, the group has been recently associated with anti LGBTQ2SA postings (Canada Anti-Hate, 2020).

Finally, Les Gardiens du Québec (The Guardians of Quebec), hereinafter referred to as LGDQ, is a small militant group organized around the Bécancour/Trois-Rivières region of Quebec. According to a Quebec-based anti-fascist organization, the group is a splinter group from La Meute and some vocal members of the Gilets jaunes who later joined the LGDQ (Montréal Antifasciste, 2020). With connections to Storm Alliance, the LGDQ became a major organizing force within the Vague bleu (Blue Wave) movement. The group was seen protesting the false rumor that the Mount Royal cross in Montreal was to be removed (Ouatik, 2019). A Montreal-based anti-fascist organization has reported ongoing conflicts between the LGDQ and the Groupe Sécurité Patriote which flared up with physical confrontations during a demonstration in Saint-Bernard-de-Lacolle, Québec (Montréal Antifasciste, 2020). Their Facebook group page explains that they are against the United Nations and religion, in favor of laicity in government and in education. They advocate for direct action in order to further their ends. They have a private Facebook group (Les Gardiens Du Québec) which, as of February 5, 2022, has 75 total members.

2.7 Manosphere

The last broad category in our mapping of RWE includes men's extremist groups which we refer to here as Manosphere. Male supremacy is a "hateful ideology rooted in the belief of the innate superiority of cisgender men and their right to subjugate women, trans men, and nonbinary people" (SPLC, n.d.). Emblematic of hegemonic masculinity, this "pattern of practice" allowed the dominance of men over women (Connell et al., p. 832). These practices established hierarchies with other forms of (nonhegemonic) masculinities and played a role in defining the "most honored" way to be a man (Carian et al., 2023). Conceptualizations of gender hierarchies are commonplace in RWE discourse, with views that are largely conservative, seeking to "keep men and women in their respective places" (White, 2022, p. 3). Importantly, the far-right generally expects their women to conform and comply with sexist and racist norms, including never dating outside their culture or race (White, 2022). These narratives often present white women as vulnerable, feeble, and in need of protection from "dangerous non-white men" (White, 2022, p. 3). As an anti-feminist, backlash movement, the dominant group position is *"straight, white* men" (Carian, 2022, p. 31). As a heteronormative, white supremacist movement, the term "white" is often used in discussion boards by these group members (Carian, 2022).

It is important first to offer a brief historical background on these groups. In 1963, Lesley Gore released a song called, "You Don't Own Me" that was taken up as an "anthem for women" – a song that has resurfaced throughout history such as when the *Saturday Night Live* sang the song with actress Jessica Chastain the night of the 2018 Women's March (Ulaby, 2019). In the 1960s and 1970s, the women's movement made "radical" claims about the place of women in society (Belew, 2018). Stemming from the second wave of feminism, one of the oldest groups opposed to gender hierarchies is the Men's Right Movement (MRM) (Perlinger et al., 2023). The MRM emerged in the 1970s as a response to the men's liberation movement (Carian, 2022; Messer, 1998). These men's liberation groups narrowly defined "sex roles" and outlined the obligations that men and women *should* follow (Carian, 2022). Emily Carian (2022, p. 31) argues the MRM is typically anchored around the belief that "feminism oppresses men and privileges women". Importantly, especially in the 1960s and 1970s, notions about women, sexuality, and birth were deeply entrenched with racial ideology (Belew, 2018). Mainstream ideology during this time perpetuated the belief that to "propagate a white race, white women had to bear white children" (Belew, 2018, p. 159). In the 1960s and 1970s, the Civil Rights Movement and Women's Rights movements were seeking equality and challenging the status quo of white men in society. Second wave feminism was predominantly concerned with the rights of white women, often articulating the position of privilege; here too the response of the men's groups reflected a white narrative and response. These early men's rights movement groups were "effective at describing the costs of masculinity" (Carian, 2022, p. 32). An early example of one of these groups was The Promise Keepers, an evangelical movement that "emphasized a return to male dominance in families" (Rafail & Freitas, 2019, p. 1).

Men's rights groups often express *feeling* "hated", "like an enemy", or "bullied" by feminists, leading to the impression that "feminism demonizes *men*" (Carian, 2022, p. 36). In *Good Guys, Bad Guys: The Perils of Men's Gender* Activism, Emily K. Carian discusses how men's rights movement activists see feminism as problematic and actually believe that it is men who are disadvantaged. Despite piles of evidence that women are systematically disadvantaged, these men come to believe that the world is actually stacked against men. In some cases, these feelings resulted in violent actions. For example, in 1989, Marc Lepine entered a Montreal engineering school, killing 14 women and injuring another 14. Before the attack, he blamed feminists for ruining his life (Lindeman, 2019). According to his rationale for the attack, he was not just targeting individual female engineering students but women who were replacing men in academia. Hatred of women would give rise to the online involuntary celibate (Incel) community in the early 21st century.

The men's liberation movement countered second wave feminism, arguing that women were held captive in the private sphere of the home by arguing that men were excluded from the private sphere, merely acting as robotic workers at the behest of family and women. As the women's movement began to critique men's behaviors through bringing awareness to rape, sexual harassment, and domestic violence, the men's liberation movement distanced themselves and focused on gender discrimination toward men, in areas of military service where men were perceived as expendable, and women were not held to the same requirements (Kimmel, 2017, p. 104).

As feminist, anti-racist, and anti-heterosexual narratives sit in contradistinction to "the normative invisibility of masculinity, whiteness, and straightness", the MRM has led to a collective identity where they, as a community, feel victimized and have developed as a sense of "we" through these shared interests and grievances (Carian, 2022, p. 39). The shared collective identity of MRM often objectifies violent fantasies toward women. MRM have since splintered into various anti-feminist men's right activists (MRAs) (Perlinger et al., 2023). MRAs position men as the victims of discrimination in the political, social, economic spheres of society due to feminism. This change in their status was considered the "wimpification of American Manhood", and to gain their manhood back, they needed to rise up and fight for their rights (Kimmel, 2017. p 102). Some of this ire was created by the idea that men were being discriminated against in the courts, the perceived special treatment women were receiving in areas such as domestic violence and family life, and the increase of women in educational systems (Kimmel, 2017, p. 102). The most influential figure in MRA groups is Paul Elam who runs the "A Voice for Men" website where contributors use violent rhetoric and support father's rights, antiabortion laws, and tackle the epidemic of "false rape claims" (Perlinger et al., 2023, p. 2).

In the 1980s and 1990s, in *Angry White Men*, Michael Kimmel (2017) describes the metamorphosis into a celebration of masculinity and a strong desire to counter women's rights movements fighting for equality, empowerment, and feminism. The MRM only intensified as women "gained ground in the workplace and family structures loosened" (SPLC, n.d.). In the *Myth of Male Power*, Warren Farrell (1993) declared "men were as oppressed as women, if not more", and has become a "seminal text" for the men's rights movement (SPLC, n.d.). Farrell argued that women had become too powerful, and therefore dangerous, as a result of holding sexual power over men and their ability to trigger a man's demise through accusations of sexual harassment or assault (SPLC, n.d.). In "Introducing the Pseudopenis, or Why Female Hyenas Are Feminist as Fuck", Kaitlyn Tierney (2015) argues the *penis means power*, and the "dominance of dicks" is an "unavoidable consequence of Big Patriarchy keeping women down". *Patriarchy* is not simply sexism, but a particular structure – a social arrangement – that favors male-gendered power in both small-scale contexts like family or gangs and large-scale institutional contexts such as the military, police, religion, or state (Ortner, 2022). Importantly, instances of extreme misogyny are supported by both men and women (Perliger et al., 2022). Misogyny in the manosphere often relates to the theory of ambivalent sexism, which asserts there are two types of sexism: (1) *hostile sexism* where aggressive misogyny situates women as "controlling, manipulative and subhuman", and (2) *benevolent sexism* that endorse gender roles and asserts that women need protection from men (Halpin et al., 2023, p. 4; see also Glick & Fiske, 2018). Male supported misogyny often draws cultural references from *The Matrix*, where the "Red Pill" has become a "cultural motif" in the manosphere to represent the need for men to wake up to "feminism's misandry and brainwashing".

Many MRMs and MRAs are supported by #Trad culture and TradCon (traditional Christian conservatives), where people who participate want to return to "traditional" gender roles that situate men as patriarchs and strong leaders (Mattheis, 2021). Trad-Con supports subservient women and patriarchal societal structures, converging the ideal of being redpilled with Bible study, encouraging men to never marry a woman over the age of 30. #Trad culture refers specifically to women who support these traditional conservative Christian values, and support the promotion of women as "submissive helpmeets", reproducing whiteness through the mobilization of (white) femininity (Mattheis, 2021, p. 93). The term "helpmeet" is from Genesis 2:18 and is a term used to support Christian complementarianism, based on biblical manhood and womanhood, where men and women were created by God as equals but given different roles and responsibilities that complement each other. Ashley A. Mattheis (2021, p. 92) argues #trad culture in online environments often operates as a "bridge between normative, extreme white supremacists, and neo-fascist cultures". Within the traditional culture are influential #Tradwives who use social media to promote their submissive lifestyle. Some #Tradwives also promote extremism and conspiratorial convergence. On the surface, tradwives promote a lifestyle purely within the private sphere and denounce feminism as the oppression of women who hold traditional gender roles. In between posts of homekeeping tips, 1950s fashion, and childcare, are racist, anti-immigration, suggested violence against liberals, and shaming white people who criticize their own race or support anti-racism posts (Cooksey, 2021).

Social media platforms have also become essential to the rise and mobilization of Manosphere groups, drastically expanding their reach – a "dense network of blogs, social media accounts, and online communities" (Rafail & Freitas, 2019). In general, Web 2.0 ushered in an era of a "particularly toxic brand of antifeminism" (Ging, 2019a, p. 638). An example of this is when Andrew Anglin posted a thread on *The Daily Stormer* in 2021 titled, "How to Kill Your Wife on a Cruise: Dump Her Off the Side and You Slide", where he wrote: "Many men want to murder their filthy whore wives to protect their children. In fact, calling this 'murder' is wrong, as it is actually an act of self-defense.... death is much better than divorce" (SPLC, n.d.). Red Pill-related subreddits support antifeminism and defend rape culture (Ging, 2019a). Indeed, the technical affordances of social media have "radically increased the flow of antifeminist ideas and information across groups, platforms, and geographical boundaries" (Ging, 2019a, p. 645).

Platform algorithms play a central role in the spread of hate, the growth of far-right content, and the manosphere. For example, one study found that Incel-related videos on YouTube are recommended to users through their algorithm, even if they watch non-Incel-related content (Papadamou et al., 2021). Far-right groups use an evolving set of techniques to exploit the algorithmic feeds of mainstream platforms such as Facebook, Twitter, and YouTube (Schmitt et al., 2018). By continuously recommending user's channels that feature extremist content, it can draw them further into the pipeline of radicalization (Schmitt et al., 2018). Recently, the *digital manosphere* has been taken up by groups like MGTOW, Incels, and the Proud Boys (see Ging, 2019a; Perlinger et al., 2023). These groups use a precise lexicon "to describe women, sex, and other men" and are "explicit in their rejection of feminism which they believe has come to dominate society at the expense of men" (Davey et al., 2020).

The first group described here is known as MGTOW which acts like a political movement similar to the MRM and the men's liberation movement of the 1970s (Perlinger et al., 2023). The group believes that society has been built to benefit women, and this has been supported by the systemic tools of laws and policies to extract resources from men. In particular, MGTOW argues society is "gynocentric" and dominated by female perspectives and interests (Lin, 2017; Perlinger et al., 2023). In this viewpoint, men are understood as the victims, leaving MGTOW members to call for a separation from society between men and women. They reject traditional roles of men as husbands, fathers, and providers and refuse any sexual or emotional interactions with women to ensure they are not exploited (Han & Yin, 2023, p. 1931). In contrast to other manosphere communities, like incels, MGTOW members believe that a "total avoidance of women can contribute to perceptions of individual worth and empowerment of men" (Perlinger et al., 2023, p. 4). Many of these men "stop pursuing romantic relationships", focusing on "individualistic, self-empowering actions" (Jones et al., 2020, p. 1904; see also Lin, 2017).

In addition, MGTOW is often viewed as harmless because of their avoidance of women, but in reality, these "communities spread one of the highest volumes of violent misogynistic" content on platforms like Reddit and Twitter (Perlinger et al., 2023, p. 3). Members construct a form of *woman-obsessed separatism*, and their forum discussions often situate women as "cunts", "bitches", "whores", "hoes", and "skanks" (Jones et al., 2020, p. 1915). Group ideology dictates that a "real man" is defined as a human born with XY chromosomes and often use oppressive gender stereotypes to reclaim their own sovereignty (Jones et al., 2020). Importantly, the narratives of this group are anchored in "deeply misogynistic ideology that propagates beliefs of the toxic aspects of masculinity" (Jones et al., 2020, p. 1917).

The second group in the Manosphere category is called Incels, consisting of members of an online subculture which originated in Canada (Taylor, 2018), with the first "incel" community tracing back to an internet discussion forum in the 1990s (Carian et al., 2023). The term "Incel" was initially coined in 1993 by a Canadian university student by the name of Alana. In 1997, before the days of platforms like Facebook, Tinder, and MySpace, a Toronto woman named Alana developed a website called "Alana's Involuntary Celibacy Project" (Taylor, 2018; Hoffman et al., 2020; Zimmer, 2018). The bisexual woman noted that she created the forum for "all 'involuntarily celebate' people" (Carian et al., 2023, p. 3; Griffin, 2021). The forum became a place for men and women to discuss difficulties establishing romantic relationships. While not entirely free of negativity, forum participants were largely supportive and offered advice to other members, banning "men who expressed violent or hateful content" (Carian et al., 2023, p. 3). Some of these "banned" members went on to create their own forums where violence and hate speech were permitted (Carian et al., 2023; Kelly, 2021).

In 2003, another message board called "Love Shy" was founded as a space for introverts who felt lonely and rejected (Baker, 2016). However, over time, these groups migrated to new areas online such as 4chan and Reddit, developing an increasingly hostile community that advocates for violence against women

(Hoffman et al., 2020). On 4chan, these "betafags" and "incels" defend their unfettered misogyny and racism, routinely applauding the actions of Isla Vista killer Elliot Rodger (Ging, 2019a). Jensen (2020) argues that the drive toward these communities is rooted in loneliness, fueling toxic masculinist beliefs.[5]

This band of more hateful and violent incels often comprises a group of straight men who have developed a violent political ideology toward young, attractive women who refuse to have sex with them (Tolentino, 2018). Incels denigrate all women, but "Women of Color are doubly denigrated" (Halpin et al., 2023, p. 2). Additionally, incels have racialized masculine hierarchies where they see the "Stacys and Beckys" of the world as being reserved for the "Chads" (the most attractive white men) (Halpin et al, 2023). Incels have been described as being "diabolically misogynistic" white supremacists, whose core self-definition draws from them being "unattractive and socially inept" (Tolentino, 2018). A recent study by Halpin et al. (2023) found that 83.3% of the incel threads and 81.2% of the posts they analyzed contained at least one misogynistic term, with members 2.4 times more likely to use misogynist terms than neutral terms for women. A post from an Incel message board stated, "Society has become a place for worship of females and it's so fucking wrong, they're not Gods they are just a fucking cum-dumpster" (Tolentino, 2018). The most notable instance of Incel violence is the Toronto, Ontario van attack on April 23, 2018, by Alex Minassian that killed ten people and injured 16. Prior to the attack, Minassian wrote on Facebook, "The Incel Rebellion has already begun" (Wendling, 2018). In March 2021, Minassian was found guilty of ten counts of first degree murder (Westoll, 2021).

Involuntary celibates, or Incels, blame women for their lack of relationships, social status, and loneliness. Incels are not homogenous in race and do not always focus on their grievances of loneliness and relationship misfortunes. They believe that women owe them sex and that feminism has destroyed their inherent right to sex. Feminism is the cause of many of the issues faced by incels and society as a whole including the changing of gender norms and traditional roles, the perceived marginalization of white men, and in response Incels call for a return of historical hierarchy and patriarchal power systems (Miller et al., 2022, p 135). Incels can react violently and articulate their failures in developing relations and call for a war against women as an act of revenge and to restore the patriarchal hierarchy of earlier eras (Han et al., 2023, p 1934). Incels see themselves as victims of *lookism* – a type of "prejudice and discrimination that orients to physical attractiveness" (Halpin et al., 2023).

The last group discussed here is called the Proud Boys. In addition to being part of the manosphere category, this group is also a far-right, neo-fascist organization that was founded during the 2016 presidential election. Proud Boys was founded by Gavin McInnes, the co-founder of VICE (SPLC, 2021). McInnes was bought out of Vice in 2008 when the media organization merged with Viacom because he was considered a "liability" (Kutner, 2022). McInnes (2013) published a book called *The Death of Cool* and a memoir, where he has provided an unfiltered and unapologetic stance that illuminates his "ethnonationalist and racist views" (Kutner, 2022, p. 2). By the time McInnes formed the Proud Boys in 2016, he was on an indefinite leave at the advertising agency, Rooster, for publishing a transphobic article at Thought Catalog (Kutner, 2022). While McInnes is longer connected with VICE, he still regularly spews hate on a podcast titled Get Off My Lawn (2021). McInnes once said the Proud Boys were built for violence, and Donald Trump propped the ground up, saying "Proud Boys, stand back and stand by. But I'll tell you what, somebody has to do something about antifa and the left" (Beers, 2020).

Kitts describes Proud Boys as a "hate group whose message of white male chauvinism is infused with religious and nationalist symbols". The group is a pro-West fraternal organization with a clear anti-feminist agenda (Perlinger et al., 2023; Stewart et al., 2023). Proud Boys promotes anti-masturbation, or no-fap, in an effort to dedicate the betterment of themselves by not masturbating or watching pornography; the group states that the no fap rule is also a conscious effort to procreate for the West (Travis, 2023, p. 608).

In general, the Proud Boys group often uses memes on social media to position organizations like the KKK and Nazis as hate groups as a way to distance themselves from them while simultaneously spreading racist messages. In 2018, five members of the Canadian Armed Forces were suspended for disrupting an Indigenous protest and their apparent connection was to the Proud Boys (CBC, 2017). In 2021, the Canadian branch of Proud Boys dissolved, claiming they were never a violent, white supremacist group in Canada (Reuters, 2021); however, as Barbara Perry argues, the Proud Boys only disbanded in name, the "real die-hards will continue" (Paling, 2021).

To conclude, the grouping in this chapter is not meant to provide an exhaustive examination of all the recent RWE groups in Canada. Instead, it is provided as a practical summary to understand the individual group descriptions in relation to their broader ideological classification which can change overtime. It is important to mention here that our team initially considered including separate categories for anti-Islamophobia and anti-immigration groups; however, upon further reflection, we concluded that there are too many extremist groups that embed these ideas into the infrastructure of the community to create distinct taxonomies. Subjects like anti-immigration and anti-Islamophobia (among other topics) were so pervasive that we could not consider them to be an umbrella ideology to differentiate amongst groups. As a result, these distinct topics were removed from the map. There are also several cross-over groups, an aspect that has been visualized above.

Notes

1 After the terrorist act, the Canadian government and intelligence agencies began years of investigation into the readiness of Canada to prevent attacks in the future. One outcome of this investigation was the Kanishka Project. In 2011, a 10 million CAD initiative invested the money into research on terrorism and counter-terrorism over five years (Public Safety, 2023).
2 Canada has one of the largest concentrations of Sikhs outside of India with Sikhs representing 2.1% of Canada's population (Mehra & Clarke, 2023). Sikh Nationalism and the call for an independent state in India, Khalistan, by the Sikh diaspora in Canada has led to diplomatic tensions between Canada and India. Since the 1980s, there has been an

increase in Sikh nationalism within the diaspora in Canada that became more involved in the Khalistan movement. More recently, India has accused Canada of not limiting the activities of Sikh nationalists, including fundraising, and recruitment of supporters (Shahed, 2019). In 2023, Prime Minister Justin Trudeau announced that his government had attained credible information from the Five Eyes partners that the Indian government had been involved in the murder of Hardeep Singh Nijjar in British Columbia. Nijjar had been active in Sikh independence in Canada and was accused by India of being the leader of the Khalistan Tiger Force (KTF), a group that had been designated a terrorist group in India. However, the Indian government claimed not to have been involved in the murder and in retaliation for Canada's accusation suspended visa services for Canadians and removed many of its diplomats (Mehra & Clarke, 2023).

3 Légitime Violence, anti-communist skinhead punk band, was Formed in 2009 in Quebec. Within Quebec's larger skinhead community, they form part of its extremist and violent segment (Tanner & Campana, 2014). In terms of international ties, it has been reported that they have played in a neo-Nazi music festival in France and alleged that they performed in a commemorative concert in Italy for the 75th anniversary of the liberation of Mussolini by Hitler's Germany (Teisceira-Lessard, 2013).

4 Incidentally, this is the meaning in Arabic for the name of the terrorist group, Al Qaeda.

5 *Toxic masculinity* is a term that was coined in the 1990s to understand representations of masculinity (Haider, 2016; Jones et al., 2020). As a central term in popular "post-feminist" vernacular, toxic masculinity treats "sexism as a character flaw of *some* men" and has contributed to shaping conversations around Trumpism and the #MeToo movement (Harrington, 2021, p. 346).

References

Abidin, C. (2018). *Internet celebrity: Understanding fame online*. Emerald Publishing Limited.

Abidin, C. (2021). From "networked publics" to "refracted publics": A companion framework for researching "below the radar" studies. *Social Media+ Society*, 7(1), 2056305120984458.

ADL. (2006, June 16). Racist skinhead threatens students at California high school. Retrieved from https://www.adl.org/news/article/racist-skin-head-threatens-students-at-california-high-school

ADL. (2016). ADL report warns soldiers of odin extremist group is rapidly gaining strength in the U.S. *Anti-Defamation League*. https://sandiego.adl.org/news/adl-report-warns-soldiers-of-odin-extremist-group-is-rapidly-gaining-strength-in-the-u-s/

ADL. (2021a). The base. *ADL*. https://www.adl.org/resources/backgrounders

ADL. (2021b). *Nationalist Front (formerly known as the Aryan Nationalist Alliance)*. https://www.adl.org/resources/backgrounder/nationalist-front-formerly-known-aryan-nationalist-alliance

Ahmed, Y., & Lynch, O. (2024). Terrorism studies and the far right–the state of play. *Studies in Conflict & Terrorism*, 47(2), 199–219.

Albanese, M., Bulli, G., Castelli Gattinara, P., & Froio, C. (2014). Fascisti di un altro millennio? Crisi e partecipazione in Casa Pound Italia. *Bonanno Editore*.

Al Jazeera. (2018, December 10). What is Generation Identity? [Online]. https://www.aljazeera.com/news/2018/12/10/what-is-generation-identity

Allchorn, W. (2021). *Moving beyond islamist extremism: Assessing counter narrative responses to the global far right*. ibidem Press.

Al-Rawi, A. (2021). Telegramming hate: Far right themes on the dark social media. *Canadian Journal of Communication*, 46(4), 31–pp.

Al-Rawi, A., Stewart, N. K., Celestini, C., & Worku, N. (2022). Delegitimizing the legitimate: Dark social movements on Telegram. *Global Media Journal*, *14*(1), 28–47.
Angus, I. (1997). *A border within: National identity, cultural plurality, and wilderness*. Montreal: McGill-Queens University Press.
Anti-Defamation League. (2016, September 16). BitChute: A hotbed of hate. https://www.adl.org/blog/bitchute-a-hotbed-of-hate
Anti-Racist Canada. (2018, January 7). Likely generation identity Canada leader revealed. Retrieved from https://anti-racistcanada.blogspot.com/2018/01/likely-generation-identity-canada.html
Archambault, E., & Veilleux-Lepage, Y. (2019). The soldiers of Odin in Canada: The failure of a transnational ideology. In M. Mares & T. Bjørgo (Eds.), *Vigilantism against migrants and minorities* (pp. 272–285). New York: Routledge.
Arnesson, J. (2023). Influencers as ideological intermediaries: Promotional politics and authenticity labour in influencer collaborations. *Media, Culture & Society*, *45*(3), 528–544.
Baker, P. (2016, February 29). What happens to men who can't have sex. *ELLE*. https://www.elle.com/life-love/sex-relationships/a33782/involuntary-celibacy/
Baker, S. A. (2022). Alt. Health Influencers: How wellness culture and web culture have been weaponised to promote conspiracy theories and far-right extremism during the COVID-19 pandemic. *European Journal of Cultural Studies*, *25*(1), 3–24.
Balleck, B. J. (2019). *Hate groups and extremist organizations in America: An encyclopedia*. New York: ABC-CLIO.
Barrouquere, B. (2020, July 20). Aryan strikeforce leader gets 20 years in prison as Neo-Nazi gang. Southern Poverty Law Center. https://www.splcenter.org/hatewatch/2020/07/20/aryan-strikeforce-leader-gets-20-years-prison-neo-nazi-gang-falters
BBC News (2021, February 3). Proud Boys: Canada labels far-right group a terrorist entity. https://www.bbc.com/news/world-us-canada-55923485
Beers, D. (2020, October 1). Gavin McInnes said his proud boys were built for violence. Now Trump is sending them signals. *The Tyee*. https://thetyee.ca/News/2020/10/01/Gavin-McInnes-Proud-Boys-Violence/
Belew, K. (2018). *Bring the war home: The white power movement and paramilitary America*. Harvard University Press.
Belew, K., & Gutiérrez, R. A. (Eds.). (2021). *A field guide to white supremacy*. University of California Press.
Beutel, J. A., & Johnson, D. (2021). *The Three Percenters: A look inside an anti-government militia*. Washington: New Lines Institute for Strategy and Policy.
Biber, B. (2016, September 14). Soldiers of Odin Canada says group not the same as what's going on overseas. *CBC News*. https://www.cbc.ca/news/canada/saskatoon/soldiers-of-odin-canada-community-group-watch-1.3761178
Biddle, S. (2021, October 12). Revealed: Facebook's secret blacklist of "dangerous individuals and organizations". *The Intercept*. Retrieved from https://theintercept.com/2021/10/12/facebook-secret-blacklist-dangerous/
Biggs, J. (2017, August 24). DailyStormer has officially retreated to the dark web. *TechCrunch*. https://techcrunch.com/2017/08/24/daily-stormer-has-officially-retreated-to-the-dark-web/
Boonstra, O., & the Canadian Anti-Hate Network. (July 29, 2019). Hate groups find foothold on East Coast. *AntiHate.ca*. https://www.antihate.ca/hate_groups_find_foothold_on_east_coast
Boucher, G., & Young, H. (2023). Digital books and the far right. *Continuum*, *37*(1), 140–152.

Brigade Initiative Team. (2019, March 9) Factsheet: Faith Goldy. https://bridge.georgetown.edu/research/factsheet-faith-goldy/

Brubaker, R. (2004). *Ethnicity without groups*. Cambridge: Harvard University Press.

Byman, D. (2019). *Road warriors: Foreign fighters in the armies of jihad*. Oxford: Oxford University Press.

Camus, R. (2011). Le Grand remplacement.

Canada Anti-Hate. (2020, February 26). State of Hate: Canada 2020. https://www.antihate.ca/state_of_hate_canada_2020

Canadian Press. (2020, January 26). 'There are many degrees of hate': Quebec blogger takes on far right. *Lethbridge News Now*. https://lethbridgenewsnow.com/2020/01/26/there-are-many-de-grees-of-hate-quebec-blogger-takes-on-far-right/

Canadian Press. (2021, June 25,) Two more extreme right-wing groups join Proud Boys on Canada's terror list. *City News - Kitchener*. https://kitchener.citynews.ca/national-news/two-more-extreme-right-wing-groups-join-proud-boys-on-canadas-terror-list-3906877

Carian, E. (2022). "No seat at the party": Mobilizing White masculinity in the men's rights movement. *Sociological Focus*, 55(1), 27–47.

Carian, E. K., DiBranco, A., & Kelly, M. (2023). Intervening in problematic research approaches to incel violence. *Men and Masculinities*, 0(0). https://doi.org/10.1177/1097184X231200825

Carter, D. (2016). Hustle and brand: The sociotechnical shaping of influence. *Social Media+Society*, 2(3), 2056305116666305

Carter, E. (2005). *The extreme right in Western Europe: Success or failure?* Manchester University Press.

Carter, E. (2018). Right-wing extremism/radicalism: Reconstructing the concept. *Journal of Political Ideologies*, 23(2), 157–182. https://doi-org.libproxy.txstate.edu/10.1080/13569317.2018.1451227

CBC News. (2017, July 6). Who are the proud boys? https://www.cbc.ca/player/play/984404035633

Cicourel, A. V. (1964). *Method and measurement in sociology*. United States of America: The Free Press.

CISAC. (2021, February). Mapping militant organizations. "Atomwaffen division/national socialist order". [Stanford]. *Center for International Security and Cooperation*. https://cisac.fsi.stanford.edu/mappingmilitants/profiles/atomwaffen-division

Colella, D. (2021). Femonationalism and anti-gender backlash: the instrumental use of gender equality in the nationalist discourse of the Fratelli d'Italia party. *Gender & Development*, 29(2–3), 269–289.

Committee on Homeland Security. (2021). *Subcommittee on Intelligence and Counterterrorism- House of Representatives*. https://www.govinfo.gov/content/pkg/CHRG-117hhrg44824/html/CHRG-117hhrg44824.htm

Cooksey, M. (2021). Why are Gen Z girls attracted to the tradwife lifestyle? *Political Research Associates*. https://politicalresearch.org/2021/07/29/why-are-gen-z-girls-attracted-tradwife-lifestyle

Côté, S. (2018, January 25). Le groupe identitaire Storm Alliance perd son chef: Il part dans la tourmente. *Le Journal De Quebec*. https://www.journaldequebec.com/2018/01/25/le-groupe-identitaire-storm-alliance-perd-son-chef

Counter Extremism Project. (n.d.). Combat 18. https://www.counterextremism.com/supremacy/combat-18

Coutu, S. (2021, November 10). Facebook désigne Atalante Québec comme une organisation dangereuse. *Radio-Canada*. https://ici.radio-canada.ca/nouvelle/1838750/facebook-designe-atalan-te-quebec-organisation-dangereuse-banni

Curtis, C. (2018, November 26). Far-right group spoke of staging "fake" terrorist attack in Quebec. *Montreal Gazette*. https://montrealgazette.com/news/local-news/far-right-group-spoke-of-staging-fake-terrorist-attack-in-quebec

Davey, J., Hart, M., Guerin, C., & Birdwell, J. (2020). An online environmental scan of right-wing extremism in Canada. *Institute for Strategic Dialogue*, 21. www.isdglobal.org/wp-content/uploads/2020/06/An-Online-Environmental-Scan-of-Right-wing-Extremism-in-Canada-ISD.pdf

de l'Église, J. (2018, June 19). Leader of far-right group arrested for invasion of VICE office. *VICE News*. Retrieved from https://www.vice.com/en/article/pav87z/leader-of-far-right-group-arrested-for-invasion-of-vice-office

Derkson, J. (2022). Not racist, but…: ID Canada and the mainstream marketing of fringe ideas. *USURJ: University of Saskatchewan Undergraduate Research Journal*, 8(1), 1–9.

Doosje, B., Moghaddam, F. M., Kruglanski, A. W., De Wolf, A., Mann, L., & Feddes, A. R. (2016). Terrorism, radicalization and de-radicalization. *Current Opinion in Psychology*, 11, 79–84.

Durnan, M. (October 27, 2017). Generation Identity: Posters for group with anti-multicultural, anti-immigration message appearing around Sudbury. *Sudbury News*. https://www.sudbury.com/local-news/generation-identity-posters-for-group-with-anti-multicultural-anti-immigration-group-appearing-around-sudbury-751056

Eatwell, R. (2000). The rebirth of the 'extreme right' in Western Europe? *Parliamentary Affairs*, 53(3), 407–425.

Farrell, W. (1993). *The myth of male power: Why men are the disposable sex*. Simon & Schuster.

Feur, A. & Rosenberg, M. (2021, June 10). 6 men said to be tied to three percenters movement are charged in Capitol riot. *The New York Times*. https://www.nytimes.com/2021/06/10/us/politics/three-percenter-capitol-riot.htm

Fraser, D. (2023, July 5). Ottawa man first to face terrorism, hate charges linked to far-right propaganda. *CTV News*. https://ottawa.ctvnews.ca/ottawa-man-first-to-face-terrorism-hate-charges-linked-to-far-right-propaganda-1.6467990

Gagnon, A. (2020). Far-right framing processes on social media: The case of the Canadian and Quebec chapters of soldiers of Odin. *Canadian Sociological Association/La Société Canadienne de Sociologie*, 57(3), 356–378 https://doi.org/10.1111/cars.12291

Ging, D. (2019a). Alphas, betas, and incels: Theorizing the masculinities of the manosphere. *Men and Masculinities*, 22(4), 638–657. https://doi.org/10.1177/1097184X17706401

Ging, D. (2019b). Bros v. Hos: Postfeminism, anti-feminism and the toxic turn in digital gender politics. In D. Ging, & E. Siapera (Eds.), *Gender hate online: Understanding the New Anti-feminism* (pp. 45–67). Palgrave Macmillan: Springer.

Glick, P., & Fiske, S. T. (2018). The ambivalent sexism inventory: Differentiating hostile and benevolent sexism. In *Social cognition* (pp. 116–160). London: Routledge.

Gonick, C., & Levy, A. (2017). Barbara Perry on the far right in Canada. *Canadian Dimension*, 54(4), 13–21.

Goodwin, A., Joseff, K., Riedl, M. J., Lukito, J., & Woolley, S. (2023). Political relational influencers: The mobilization of social media influencers in the political arena. *International Journal of Communication*, 17, 21.

Gregor, A. J. (2006). *The search for neofascism: The use and abuse of social science*. Cambridge: Cambridge University Press.

Griffin, J. (August 13, 2021). Incels: Inside a dark world of online hate. *BBC News*. https://www.bbc.com/news/blogs-trending-44053828

Guhl, J., & Davey, J. (2020). A safe space to hate: White supremacist mobilisation on Telegram. *ISD Global*. https://www.isdglobal.org/isd-publications/a-safe-space-to-hate-white-supremacist-mobilisation-on-telegram/

Gurrieri, L., Drenten, J., & Abidin, C. (2023). Symbiosis or parasitism? A framework for advancing interdisciplinary and socio-cultural perspectives in influencer marketing. *Journal of Marketing Management, 39*(11–12), 911–932.

Haider, S. (2016). The shooting in Orlando, terrorism or toxic masculinity (or both?). *Men and Masculinities, 19*(5), 555–565.

Halpin, M., Richard, N., Preston, K., Gosse, M., & Maguire, F. (2023). Men who hate women: The misogyny of involuntarily celibate men. *New Media & Society, 0*(0). https://doi.org/10.1177/14614448231176777

Han, X., & Yin, C. (2023). Mapping the manosphere. Categorization of reactionary masculinity discourses in digital environment. *Feminist Media Studies, 23*(5), 1923–1940.

Hankes, K. (2018). Prolific neo-Nazi propagandist "Zeiger" outed as Montreal-based Gabriel Sohier Chaput. *SPLC Southern Poverty Law Center*. https://www.splcenter.org/hatewatch/2018/05/04/prolific-neo-nazi-propagandist-zeiger-outed-montreal-based-gabriel-sohier-chaput

Harrington, C. (2021). What is "toxic masculinity" and why does it matter? *Men and Masculinities, 24*(2), 345–352.

Harvey, D. (2009). *Cosmopolitanism and the geographies of freedom*. Columbia University Press.

Hirst, M. (2015, January 13). Germany protests: What is Pegida movement? 60 seconds. *BBC News*. https://www.bbc.com/news/av/world-europe-30713898

Hoffman, B. (2024). *God, guns, and sedition: Far-right terrorism in America* (J. Ware (Ed.)). Columbia University Press.

Hoffman, B., Ware, J., & Shapiro, E. (2020). Assessing the threat of incel violence. *Studies in Conflict and Terrorism, 43*(7), 565–587. https://doi.org/10.1080/1057610X.2020.1751459

Husbands, C. T. (1981). Contemporary right-wing extremism in Western European democracies: A review article. *European Journal of Political Research, 9*(1), 75–99.

Ignatiev, N. (1995). *How the Irish Became White*. London: Routledge.

Jackson, P., & Feldman, M. (2014). Introduction. In M. Feldman & P. Jackson (Eds.), *Doublespeak: The rhetoric of the far right since 1945*. ibidem–Verlag.

Jensen, N. (2020). *Understanding and addressing "The Incel Rebellion"*. The Pub: MPPGA Student Media. https://www.pubpoli.com/pubpoli-journal/2020/9/17/understanding-and-addressing-the-incel-rebellion

Jones, C., Trott, V., & Wright, S. (2020). Sluts and soyboys: MGTOW and the production of misogynistic online harassment. *New Media & Society, 22*(10), 1903–1921.

Katz, E., Lazarsfeld, P. F., & Roper, E. (1955). *Personal influence: The part played by people in the flow of mass communications*. London: Routledge.

Kelley, B. Joel. (2017, November 07). Lauren southern: The alt-right's Canadian dog whistler. *SPLC*. https://www.splcenter.org/hatewatch/2017/11/07/lauren-southern-alt-right%E2%80%99s-canadian-dog-whistler

Kelly, M. (2021). The mainstream pill: How media and academia help incels rebrand. *Political Research Associates*, July 1. Retrieved from https://www.politicalresearch.org/2021/07/01/mainstream-pill

Kimmel, M. (2017). *Angry white men: American masculinity at the end of an era*. Hachette, UK.

Koehler, D. (2016). Right-wing extremism and terrorism in Europe. *Prism, 6*(2), 84–105.

Kutner, S. (2022). *Swiping right: The allure of hyper masculinity and cryptofascism for men who join the Proud Boys*. International Centre for Counter-Terrorism.

La Meute. (2018). Manifeste De La Meute. *La Meute*.

Lamoureux, M. (2017, January 5). Soldiers of Odin Canada splinters over allegiance to 'Racist' Finnish group. *Vice*. Retrieved from https://www.vice.com/en/article/soldiers-of-odin-canada-splinters-over-allegiance-to-anti-immigration/

Lamoureux, M. (2017, September 5). Justin Trudeau's Neo-Nazi run-in highlights security risk. *Vice*. https://www.vice.com/en/article/justin-trudeaus-neo-nazi-run-in-highlights-security-risk/

Lamoureux, M. (2019, January 28). Far-right group called Canadian infidels staked out Edmonton mosque. *Vice*. https://www.vice.com/en/article/panbpb/far-right-group-called-canadian-infidels-staked-out-edmonton-mosque

Lamoureux, M. (2019, March 27). Christchurch shooting suspect donated to a far-right group active in Canada. *Vice*. https://www.vice.com/en/article/vbwaq9/christchurch-shooting-suspect-donated-to-a-far-right-group-active-in-canada

Lamoureux, M. (2019, July 23). Far-right group tries to run for office, discovers that means outing themselves. *Vice*. https://www.vice.com/en/article/8xzzma/far-right-canadian-nationalist-party-led-by-travis-patron-faces-doxxing-threat

Lamoureux, M., & Makuch, B. (2019, July 25). Dark portrait emerging of teenage BC murder suspect. *Vice*. https://www.vice.com/en/article/ywyyyb/dark-portrait-emerging-of-teenage-bc-murder-suspect-bryer-schmegelsky

Leidig, E. (2021). From love jihad to grooming gangs: Tracing flows of the hypersexual Muslim male through far-right female influencers. *Religions, 12*(12), 1083.

Lin, J. L. (2017). Antifeminism online MGTOW (men going their own way): Ethnographic perspectives across global online and offline spaces.

Lindeman, T. (2019, December 4). 'Hate is infectious': How the 1989 mass shooting of 14 women echoes today. *The Guardian*. https://www.theguardian.com/world/2019/dec/04/mass-shooting-1989-montreal-14-women-killed

Loadenthal, M. (2022). Feral fascists and deep green guerrillas: Infrastructural attack and accelerationist terror. *Critical Studies on Terrorism, 15*(1), 169–208. https://doi-org.libproxy.txstate.edu/10.1080/17539153.2022.2031129

Lorenzo-Dus, N., & Nouri, L. (2021). The discourse of the US alt-right online–a case study of the traditionalist worker party blog. *Critical Discourse Studies, 18*(4), 410–428.

Lowles, N. (2001, November 25). BBC News | PANORAMA | Ex-Combat 18 man speaks out. *BBC News*. https://news.bbc.co.uk/2/hi/programmes/panorama/1672100.stm

Macdonald, L., & Ayres, J. (2020). The safe third country agreement must end much is at stake in Canada's appeal of a court ruling against a harmful refugee pact with the United States. *Canadian Centre for Policy Alternatives*. https://www.policyalternatives.ca/publications/monitor/safe-third-country-agreement-must-end

Makuch, B. (2020, March 14). Audio recording claims neo-terror group is disbanding. *Vice*. https://www.vice.com/en/article/qjdnam/audio-recording-claims-neo-nazi-terror-group-is-disbanding

Manasan, A. (2020, November 28). The rise of the Ku Klux Klan in Canada and why its lasting impact still matters. *CBC - The Sunday Magazine*. https://www.cbc.ca/radio/sunday/the-sunday-magazine-for-november-22-2020-1.5807350/the-rise-of-the-ku-klux-klan-in-canada-and-why-its-lasting-impact-still-matters-1.5807353

Mattheis, A. A. (2021). # TradCulture: Reproducing whiteness and neo-fascism through gendered discourse online. In S. Hunter & C. Van der Westhuizen (Eds.), *Routledge Handbook of Critical Studies in Whiteness* (pp. 91–101). London: Routledge.

McInnes, G. (2021). Get off my lawn [Podcast].

McInnes, G. (2013). *The death of cool: From teenage rebellion to the hangover of adulthood*. Simon and Schuster.

Mehra, T., & C. P. Clarke. (October 17, 2023). The India-Canada rift: Sikh extremism and rise of Transnational repression? *International Centre for Counter-Terrorism*. https://www.icct.nl/publication/india-canada-rift-sikh-extremism-and-rise-transnational-repression

Merino, P., & Kinnvall, C. (2023). Governing emotions: Hybrid media, ontological insecurity and the normalisation of far-right fantasies. *Alternatives*, *48*(1), 54–73.

Merton, R. K. (1949). Patterns of influence: A study of interpersonal influence and of communications behavior in a local community. In P. F. Lazarsfeld & F. N. Stanton (Eds.), *Communication research, 1948–49* (pp. 180–209). Harper & Row.

Messer, M. A. (1998). The limits of "the male sex role": An analysis of the men's liberation and men's rights movements' discourse. *Gender & Society*, *12*(3), 255–276. https://doi.org/10.1177/0891243298012003002

Mezei, K. (1998). Bilingualism and translation in/of Michèle Lalonde's speak White. *The Translator*, *4*(2), 229–247. https://doi.org/10.1080/13556509.1998.10799021

Miller, E., A. Yates, E., & Kane, S. (2022). Check all that apply: Challenges in tracking ideological movements that motivate right-wing terrorism. In *Right-wing extremism in Canada and the United States* (pp. 119–151). Cham: Springer International Publishing.

Montpetit, J. (2016, December 4). Inside Quebec's far right: A secretive online group steps into the real world. *CBC News*. https://www.cbc.ca/news/canada/montreal/quebec-far-right-la-meute-1.3876225

Montpetit, J. (2017, January 8). Inside Quebec's far right: Radical groups push extreme message. *CBC News*. https://www.cbc.ca/news/canada/montreal/inside-quebec-far-right-alt-right-1.3919964

Montpetit, J. (2017, May 2). Canadian branch of far-right group fragments amid infighting. *CBC News*. https://www.cbc.ca/news/canada/montreal/canadian-branch-of-far-right-group-fragments-amid-infighting-1.4095498

Montpetit, J. (2017, August 20). Far-right group claims PR victory after duelling protests in Quebec City. *CBC News*. https:// www.cbc.ca/news/canada/montreal/quebec-far-right-la-meute-1.4254792

Montpetit, J. (2018, May 5). Montreal neo-Nazi, outed this week, was lead cheerleader for deadly U.S. cell. *CBC News*. https://www.cbc.ca/news/canada/montreal/montreal-neo-nazi-outed-this-week-was-lead-cheerleader-for-deadly-u-s-cell-1.4648990

Montréal Antifasciste. (2020, May 9). 2019 In review. *Montréal Antifasciste Info*. https://montreal-antifasciste.info/en/2020/05/09/2019-in-review/

Moslesh, O. (2019, April 23). Alberta home to disproportionate number of extremists groups, report says. *The Star*. https://www.thestar.com/edmonton/2019/04/23/alberta-home-to-disproportionate-number-of-extremist-groups-report-says.html

Mudde, C. (1995), 'Right-wing extremism analyzed: A comparative analysis of the ideologies of three alleged right-wing extremist parties (NPD, NDP, CP'86)', *European Journal of Political Research*, *27*(2): 203–24.

Nadeau, F. (2021). Rupture ou continuité? La matrice idéologique de l'extrême droite québécoise. In D. Helly (Ed.), *Rupture ou continuité? La matrice idéologique de l'extrême droite québécoise* (pp. 89–142). Marquis (Classiques des sciences sociales).

Naderer, B. (2023). Influencers as political agents? The potential of an unlikely source to motivate political action. *Communications*, *48*(1), 93–111.

Newhouse, A. (2021, June). The threat is the network: The multi-node structure of neo-fascist accelerationism. *Anarchist Federation*. https://www.anarchistfederation.net/the-threat-is-the-network-the-multi-node-structure-of-neo-fascist-accelerationism/

Ortner, S. B. (2022). Patriarchy. *Feminist Anthropology*, 3(2), 307–314. https://doi-org.libproxy.txstate.edu/10.1002/fea2.12081

Ouatik, B. (2019, November 7). Pourquoi des internautes ont cru que la croix du mont Royal serait retirée. *CBC Radio-Canada*. https://ici.radio-canada.ca/nouvelle/1379195/rumeur-demantelement-croix-mont-royal-mcgill-montreal

Paling, E. (2021, May 2). Proud Boys Canada may have disbanded 'in name only,' researchers warn. *CBC News*. https://www.cbc.ca/news/politics/proud-boys-canada-dissolves-1.6011282

Papadamou, K., Zannettou, S., Blackburn, J., De Cristofaro, E., Stringhini, G., & Sirivianos, M. (2021). "How over is it?" Understanding the incel community on YouTube. *Proceedings of the ACM on Human-Computer Interaction*, 5(CSCW2), 1–25.

Parent, R., & Ellis, J. (2014). Right-wing extremism in Canada. *Canadian Network for Research on Terrorism, Security and Society*, 14(3), 1–44.

Perliger, A., Stevens, C., & Leidig, E. (2022). *Mapping the ideological landscape of extreme misogyny*. International Centre for Counter-Terrorism.

Perlinger, J., Gisch, H., Ehrenthal, J. C., Montag, C., & Kretschmar, T. (2023). Structural impairment and conflict load as vulnerability factors for burnout–A cross-sectional study from the German working population. *Frontiers in Psychology*, 13, 1000572.

Perreaux, L. (2018, April 13). Quebec mosque shooter told police he was motivated by Canada's immigration policies. *The Globe and Mail*. Retrieved from https://www.theglobeandmail.com/canada/article-mosque-shooter-told-police-he-was-motivated-by-canadas-immigration/

Perron, L.-S. (2017, August 15). L'extrême droite québécoise se mobilise. *La Presse*. https://www.lapresse.ca/actualites/201708/14/01-5124595-lextreme-droite-quebecoise-se-mobilise.php

Perry, B., & Scrivens, R. (2015). *Right-wing extremism in Canada: An environmental scan*. Ottawa, ON: Public Safety Canada.

Perry, B., & Scrivens, R. (2016). Uneasy alliances: A look at the right-wing extremist movement in Canada. *Studies in Conflict & Terrorism*, 39(9), 819–841.

Perry, B., Mirrlees, T., & Scrivens, R. (2017). The dangers of porous borders: The "Trump Effect" in Canada. *Journal Hate Studies*, 14, 53.

Perry, B., & Scrivens, R. (2019). *Right-wing extremism in Canada*. Springer Nature.

Perry, B., Gruenewald, J., & Scrivens, R. (2022). *Right-wing extremism in Canada and the United States*. Cham: Springer International Publishing.

Phelan, A. (2023). Special issue introduction for terrorism, gender and women: Toward an integrated research agenda. *Studies in Conflict & Terrorism*, 46(4), 353–361.

Public Safety Canada (2023). Remembering Air India Flight 182. *Government of Canada*. https://www.publicsafety.gc.ca/cnt/ntnl-scrt/cntr-trrrsm/r-nd-flght-182/index-en.aspx

Radio-Canada. (2016, December). 43 000 membres pour le groupe d'extrême droite la Meute. https://ici.radio-canada.ca/nouvelle/1004095/43-000-membres-pour-le-groupe-dextreme-droite-la-meute

Radio-Canada. (2017, août). Mobilisation à Québec contre l'« immigration illégale » https://ici.radio-canada.ca/nouvelle/1050424/mobilisation-groupes-extreme-droite-quebec-immigration-illegale-la-meute-atalante

Rafail, P., & Freitas, I. (2019). Grievance articulation and community reactions in the men's rights movement online. *Social Media + Society*, 5(2), 2056305119841387.

Reuters (2021, May 2). Proud Boys Canada dissolves itself, says it was never a 'white supremacy' group. *Reuters*. https://www.reuters.com/world/americas/proud-boys-canada-dissolves-itself-says-it-was-never-white-supremacy-group-2021-05-02/

Richards, I. (2022). A philosophical and historical analysis of "generation identity": Fascism, online media, and the European new right. *Terrorism and Political Violence*, *34*(1), 28–47.

Riedl, M., Schwemmer, C., Ziewiecki, S., & Ross, L. M. (2021). The rise of political influencers—Perspectives on a trend towards meaningful content. *Frontiers in Communication*, *6*, 752656.

Riedl, M. J., Lukito, J., & Woolley, S. C. (2023). Political influencers on social media: An introduction. *Social Media+ Society*, *9*(2), 20563051231177938.

Riga, A. (2018, April 17). Quebec mosque killer confided he wished he had shot more people, court told. *Montreal Gazette*. Retrieved from https://montrealgazette.com/news/local-news/quebec-mosque-shooter-alexandre-bissonnette-trawled-trumps-twitter-feed

Roach, K. (2011). The Air India Report and the regulation of charities and terrorism financing. *University of Toronto Law Journal*, *61*(1), 45–57.

Roberts, G. K. (1994). Extremism in Germany: Sparrows or avalanche? *European Journal of Political Research*, *25*(4), 470–489.

Robichaud, O. (2018, September 13). Le Groupe Identitaire La Meute Insiste Qu'Il s'Inspire De La CAQ. *Huffington Post Quebec*. https://quebec.huffingtonpost.ca/2018/09/13/la-meute-caq-elections_a_23526065/

Robinson, K., Malone, I., & Crenshaw, M. (2023). Countering far-right anti-government extremism in the United States. *Perspectives on Terrorism*, *17*(1), 73–87. https://www.jstor.org/stable/27209219

Roediger, D. R. (1991). *The wages of Whiteness: Race and the making of the American working class: The role of race divisions in the formation of the 19th century US working class*. Verso.

Roediger, D. R. (2005). *Working toward Whiteness: How America's immigrants became White*. Basic Books.

Rothut, S., Schulze, H., Hohner, J., & Rieger, D. (2023). Ambassadors of ideology: A conceptualization and computational investigation of far-right influencers, their networking structures, and communication practices. *New Media & Society*, 14614448231164409.

Rutherford, S. (2020). Wolfish White nationalisms? Lycanthropic longing on the alt-right. *Journal of Intercultural Studies*, *41*(1), 60–76. https://doi.org/10.1080/07256868.2020.1704227

Ryan, N. (1998, February 1). Combat 18: Memoirs of a street-fighting man. *The Independent*. https://www.independent.co.uk/arts-entertainment/combat-18-memoirs-of-a-street-fighting-man-1142204.html

Rydgren, J. (2018). *The Oxford handbook of the radical right*. Oxford: Oxford University Press.

Saul, J. R. (1998). *Reflections of a Siamese Twin: Canada at the beginning of the twenty first century*. Penguin Canada.

Scherr, S. (2009, May 29). Aryan guard marches on calgary. *Southern Poverty Law Center*. https://www.splcenter.org/fighting-hate/intelligence-report/2009/aryan-guard-marches-calgary

Schmitt, J. B., Rieger, D., Rutkowski, O., & Ernst, J. (2018). Counter-messages as prevention or promotion of extremism?! The potential role of YouTube. *Journal of Communication*, *68*(4), 780–808. https://doi.org/10.1093/joc/jqy029

Scrivens, R., & Perry, B. (2017). Resisting the right: Countering right-wing extremism in Canada. *Canadian Journal of Criminology and criminal justice*, *59*(4), 534–558.

Shahed, K. (2019). Sikh Diaspora nationalism in Canada. *Studies in Ethnicity and Nationalism*, *19*(3), 325–345. https://doi.org/10.1111/sena.12307

Simmons, C. (2023, November 15). 'Conspirituality' and climate: How wellness and new age influencers are serving anti-climate narratives to their audiences. *ISD*. https://www.isdglobal.org/digital_dispatches/conspirituality-and-climate-how-wellness-and-new-age-influencers-are-serving-anti-climate-narratives-to-their-audiences/

Singer-Emery, J., & Bray III, R. (2020). The iron march data dump provides a window into how white supremacists communicate and recruit. *Lawfare*, February, 27.

Smith, P. (2020, December 15). Inside one of Canada's longest active alt-right organizations. *Canadian Anti-Hate Network*. Retrieved from https://www.antihate.ca/inside_id_canada_longest_active_alt_right_organizations

SPLC (2020, March 18). Methodology: How hate groups are identified and categorized. *Southern Poverty Law Center*. Retrieved from https://www.splcenter.org/news/2020/03/18/methodology-how-hate-groups-are-identified-and-categorized

SPLC. (n.d.). White lives matter. *Southern Poverty Law Center*. Retrieved from https://www.splcenter.org/fighting-hate/extremist-files/group/white-lives-matter

SPLC. (n.d.). Proud boys. *Southern Poverty Law Center*. https://www.splcenter.org/fighting-hate/extremist-files/group/proud-boys

SPLC Hatewatch Staff. (2019, September 18). Daily stormer website goes dark amid chaos. *Southern Poverty Law Center*. Retrieved from https://www.splcenter.org/hatewatch/2019/09/18/daily-stormer-website-goes-dark-amid-chaos

Stewart, N. K., Al-Rawi, A., Celestini, C., & Worku, N. (2023). Hate influencers' mediation of hate on telegram: "We declare war against the anti-white system". *Social Media + Society*, 9(2), 20563051231177915.

Strong-Boag, V. (1996). *Independent women, problematic men: First-and second-wave anti-feminism in Canada from Goldwin Smith to Betty Steele*. Histoire Sociale/Social History.

Tanner, S., & Campana, A. (2014). The Process of Radicalization: Right Wing Skinheads in Quebec (No. 14-07). *Canadian Network for Research on Terrorism, Security and Society*.

Tasker, J. P. (2017, September 30). Far-right, anti-fascist protesters temporarily shut Quebec border crossing. *CBC News*. www.cbc.ca/news/politics/far-right-antifa-clash-across-canada-1.4315053

Taylor, C. (1993). *Reconciling the solitudes essays on Canadian federalism and nationalism*. Montreal: McGill-Queens University Press.

Taylor, J. (2018, August 30). The woman who founded the 'incel' movement. *BBC Radio 5*. https://www.bbc.com/news/world-us-canada-45284455

Teisceira-Lessard, P. (2013). Pastagate": La présidente de l'OQLF démissionne. 08.03.2013.

Thobani, S. (2000). Closing ranks: Racism and sexism in Canada's immigration policy. *Race & Class*, 42(1), 35–55. https://doi.org/10.1177/030639600128968009

Thompson, A. C., & Winston, A. (2018, March 6). Atomwaffen, extremist group whose members have been charged in five murders, loses some of its platforms. *ProPublica*. https://www.propublica.org/article/atomwaffen-extremist-group-whose-members-have-been-charged-in-five-murders-loses-some-of-its-platforms

Thompson, J. (2021, June 30). Examining extremism: The Boogaloo movement. CSIS: Center for Strategic & International Studies. https://www.csis.org/blogs/examining-extremism/examining-extremism-boogaloo-movement

Tierney, K. (2015, July 6). Introducing the pseudopenis, or why female hyenas are feminist as fuck. *Jezebel*. https://www.jezebel.com/introducing-the-pseudopenis-or-why-female-hyenas-are-f-1714981846#:~:text=But%20amazingly%2C%20in%20the%20case,essentially%20a%20very%20enlarged%20clitoris

Tolentino, J. (2018, May 15). The race of the incels. *The New Yorker*.

Travis, C. K. (2023). Nostalgia, hypermasculinity, and the American far right: What ever happened to being proud of your boy? *New Political Science*, *45*(4), 591–612.

Trenberth, K. (2011). The five types of climate change denial argument. *University of Colarado*. https://sciencepolicy.colorado.edu/students/envs_4800/washington_2011_ch3.pdf

U.S. Department of Justice (2023, May 4). Press release: Jury convicts four leaders of the proud boys of seditious conspiracy related to U.S. Capitol Breach. *Office of Public Affairs*. https://www.justice.gov/opa/pr/jury-convicts-four-leaders-proud-boys-seditious-conspiracy-related-us-capitol-breach

Ulaby, N. (2019, June 16). 'You don't own me,' a feminist anthem with civil rights roots, is all about empathy. *NPR*. https://www.npr.org/2019/06/26/735819094/lesley-gore-you-dont-own-me-american-anthem

Vescera, Z. (2019, July 9). Vancouver organization offers new look at first far-right group on Canada's terror list. https://vancouversun.com/news/local-news/vancouver-organization-offers-new-look-at-first-far-right-group-on-canadas-terror-list

Walter, J., & Chang, A. (2021, September 8). Far-right terror poses bigger threat to the US than Islamist extremism post-9/11. *The Guardian*. https://www.theguardian.com/us-news/2021/sep/08/post-911-domestic-terror

Wendling, B. M. (2018, April 24). Toronto van attack: What is an 'incel'? *BBC News*. https://www.bbc.com/news/blogs-trending-43881931

Westoll, N. (2021, March 3). Alek Minassian found guilty of 10 counts of 1st-degree murder after 2018 Toronto van attack. *Global News*. https://globalnews.ca/news/7672444/alek-minassian-trial-verdict-toronto-van-attack/

White, J. (2022). Finding the right mix: re-evaluating the road to gender-equality in countering violent extremism programming. *Critical Studies on Terrorism*, *15*(3), 585–609. https://doi-org.libproxy.txstate.edu/10.1080/17539153.2022.2036423

Williams, H. J., Evans, A. T., Ryan, J., Mueller, E. E., & Downing, B. (2021). The online extremist ecosystem: Its evolution and a framework for separating extreme from mainstream. *RAND Corporation*. https://www.rand.org/pubs/perspectives/PEA1458-1.html

Zimmer, B. (2018, May 8). How 'Incel' Got Hijacked. *POLITICO Magazine*. https://www.politico.com/magazine/story/2018/05/08/intel-involuntary-celibate-movement-218324/

3 RWE sites

3.1 Introduction

Alternative social media channels provide appropriate venues for communicating conspiracies as well as an encrypted way to exchange ideas (Urman & Katz, 2020). In this chapter, we focused on the analysis of BitChute and Telegram because they are two platforms that we reviewed extensively and applied our operationalization of conspiracy theories. While our analysis did cross platforms (see the Appendix), it was too time-consuming to conduct a manual analysis on all of the datasets. Besides, our goal was to understand whether the operationalization of conspiracy theories was possible, which we think is illustrated (with some minor changes) by our work on BitChute and Telegram below.

This section contextualizes alternative social media sites within the dark platform ecosystem. As mentioned earlier, our study focuses on conspiratorial topics like the Great Reset, the Great Awakening, the United Nations, technology, China, Deep State, COVID-19, Islamophobia, and New World Order (NWO).

Content liberation is connected to content moderation. The primary difference between alternative versus mainstream platforms is that there is less regulation and moderation, which allows conspiracy theories to circulate more freely (Zeng & Schäfer, 2021, p. 1). Dark platforms focus on free informational flows, rather than expanding or enforcing policies around content moderation (Zeng & Schäfer, 2021). These alternative dark platforms are not under the same pressure to police content moderation the way prominent technology companies are. Another aspect of content liberation on alternative social media sites is how entwined it is with platform capitalism. For example, Alex Jones was not only deplatformed on sites like YouTube but also by the Google and Apple app stores (Zeng & Schäfer, 2021). When the microblogging service, Gab, was deplatformed by Visa and PayPal, the platform responded by allowing users to donate money to content creators with Bitcoin (Zeng & Schäfer, 2021). These examples underscore the intensification of commodity mechanisms (van Dijck et al., 2018) and platform capitalism (Srnicek, 2017). The entanglement between deplatformization and platform capitalism is a result of the user-driven nature of platforms (Srnicek, 2017). Importantly, platforms are a centralized, economic mode of cultural production (Nieborg & Poell, 2018). As a result, deplatforming has resulted in the unfolding of a "parallel darker ecosystem of content distribution and monetization"

DOI: 10.4324/9781003502173-4

(Zeng & Schäfer, 2021, p. 3). Alternative social media site users are mostly engaged in participation that is characterized by bad content that is negative or conspiratorial in nature. We borrow below the concept of dark participation from the field of journalism studies because we believe that it fits the framework of our study.

Indeed, modern information networks – like the ones on Telegram and BitChute – allow coordinated campaigns to disseminate conspiracies (Pereira et al., 2020). Without these networks, such reach may be impossible: "[S]ocial media has provided both conspiracies and conspiracy theories with fertile new grounds on which to hatch" (Gabriel, 2017, p. 218). Telegram's mobile messaging application has social media features that are routinely adopted by social movements, including RWE, who use it to organize and "disseminate racist and violent ideology" (Baumgartner et al., 2020, p. 840). Unlike the dark web, a collection of websites underneath a veil of anonymity (Greenberg, 2014), dark platforms are publicly accessible on the internet (Zeng & Schäfer, 2021). The dark platform ecosystem contains dark social media (Al-Rawi, 2019), which is often conceptualized through harmful content, anonymity, and inaccessibility (Al-Rawi, 2021). Our study illustrates that Telegram and BitChute are rife with harmful content, exposing users to misinformation in areas related to the Great Awakening, Islamophobia, COVID-19, and the Deep State (Al-Rawi et al., 2022). The anonymity of dark social media fosters legitimacy, avoidance of state surveillance, and online privacy (Gehl, 2016). Most alternative social media sites offer anonymity to users through lower platform governance, and, as a result of its smaller scale, is under less surveillance from the state. Dark social media content is often inaccessible to researchers (Al-Rawi, 2021). Platforms exist in shades of darkness, which is an important construct within dark social media because it marks a shift away from dichotomizing mainstream and alternative platforms (Zeng & Schäfer, 2021). Geography also plays a role in determining whether platforms are perceived as dark. For example, Twitter, now X, and YouTube are considered mainstream platforms in most countries but are banned in other nations like China (Zeng & Schäfer, 2021).

Mainstream social media sites like YouTube, Twitter, and Facebook have responded to growing hate speech and conspiracy theories by deplatforming vocal patriots (Buckley & Schafer, 2022). This type of infrastructure ostracization often results in exile congregation – the migration of extremists to alternative social media platforms (Zeng & Schäfer, 2021). Infrastructure ostracization on mainstream social media correlates to higher levels of content moderation on mainstream platforms, propelling user migration to dark platforms (Al-Rawi, 2019) like Gab, Voat, Minds, 4chan, Parler, Gettr, Telegram, and BitChute, all of which operate in a low content moderation ecosystem (Buckley & Schafer, 2021; Trujillo et al., 2020). These alternative sites promote censorship-free, "free speech zones", that promise an anti-cancel culture (Buckley et al., 2021). Platforms like Telegram and BitChute have content moderation protocols, but typically adopt more flexible policies and use less stringent enforcement procedures. Content moderation provides a layer of governance and regulation over platforms, and often includes user-generated content.

Content moderation and infrastructure ostracization are two procedures platforms use to combat disinformation, hate speech, and conspiracy theories. For example, Google and Apple have refused service to alternative social media sites (Buckley et al., 2021), further underscoring the import of the profitability of platforms under capitalism (Srnicek, 2017) and the ability for dark platforms to remain productive online. Today, demonetized content creators on YouTube have migrated to "darker" counterparts like BitChute and Rumble, where viewers can send virtual tips to content producers without having to pay the platform (Zeng & Schäfer, 2021, p. 3; BitChute, 2021).

Below, we focus on BitChute and Telegram using our novel methodological codebook around conspiracy theories. We also examined similar emergent themes on 4chan, 8kun, Amazon, Dark Web, Discord, Facebook, Instagram, Gab, GETTR, Google, Parler, Rumble, Tumblr, Twitter, and YouTube (see the Appendix). Our exhaustive search illustrates that platforms with lower moderation have higher levels of conspiratorial content and an overemphasis on COVID-19-related concerns, and as our analysis of Facebook and Twitter illustrate, it is easier for text-based platforms to moderate content, in comparison to sites like Instagram. Additionally, platforms like Gab, GETTR, Telegram, and BitChute operate as hotbeds of hate, with a high volume of conspiratorial content and RWE groups/actors.

3.2 Platforms and means

Based on evidence from RWE in Canadian history, we find it important not to limit our analysis of current RWE actors in terms of conspiracies, the extremist ideology, but also to look at the platforms and means, or the infrastructure where these ideas spread and how they come together and, at times, profit economically. Conspiracy theories mixed with RWE have not only moved into the mainstream with right-wing populism catering to both in their political responses, but have also seen conspiracies intermingle with RWE in events such as January 6, 2021, the freedom convoys, anti-immigration sentiments and proposed policies, moral panics such as the "groomer" anti-LGBTQ2SA and anti-sexual orientation and gender identity (SOGI) in schools, the anti-Critical Race Theory movements, and the banning of books and curricula. *Gender identity* is defined as an internal concept of the self as male, female, a mixture of both, or neither (Belew & Gutiérrez, 2021). Importantly, what may begin in America soon advances to Canada, and we are seeing the impact of violent acts, such as the first individual charged with terrorism in Canada, Nathanial Veltman. Veltman intentionally ran over a Muslim family in London, Ontario, and in his confession cited active consumption of both conspiracy theories and extremism. This is identical to the case of Alexandre Bissonnette, the terrorist whose media consumption is described above. In Veltman's manifesto, he claimed to be a white nationalist, anti-Islam, and anti-immigration. Copies of the manifestos from the Christchurch shooter and the Norway mass shooter were found on his thumb drives. Veltman also wrote about "white genocide" and "white replacement" terms also found in the other manifestos. He did not belong to a specific RWE group, but did engage in RWE-related hate and conspiratorial material online. The real-world implications of conspiracy and extremism online and offline are being felt internationally as attacks on politicians, individuals, marginalized communities, and democracy are occurring internationally. The politically charged nature of society is encompassing calls for equality and rights rising, with movements such as Black Lives Matter (BLM), Indigenous Lives Matter, and sexual gender minorities (SGM) rights.

While the internet was once viewed as a medium to strengthen democracy, it is now often considered a popular medium for the spread of misinformation. Traditional websites such as *The Daily Stormer* and *Iron March* were integral to the proliferation of RWE groups worldwide. Over time, RWE groups migrated from discussion-board websites to social media platforms. Importantly, we can distinguish Web 2.0 from its predecessor because it implements collaboration, dialogue, and participation (Caballero, 2020). For example, TikTok's popular Conspiracy Tok, tagged with the hashtag #ConspiracyTok, is a dedicated channel that brings together a large and decentralized community of people who like to discuss conspiracies (Grandinetti & Bruinsma, 2023).

Kim and Chen (2022, p. 5) describe social media as a "playground of contestation in which conspiracies and debunking messages co-exist and compete". Dentith (2021, p. 9897) argues we should avoid using the term "debunk" (and other similarly loaded terms) and, similar to the focus of our work in Chapter 3, "focus on *investigating* conspiracy theories". Social media platforms have made it easy for RWE actors to propagate conspiracies. A central feature of social media platforms is that they offer a low barrier of entry for sharing information, including conspiracy theories and mis/disinformation (Kim & Chen, 2022; Tingley & Wagner, 2017). While it may *feel* like conspiracies are more rampant today than ever, conspiracies are actually no more widespread today than they were in the past, but there is a greater appreciation for how ingrained and mainstream they are (Uscinski, 2018), as well as the consequences they can have on democracy. Dentith (2023, p. 410) argues that if "we think conspiracy theories seem more common despite the survey work suggesting they are not, then that suggests (strongly I would argue) that what we are seeing is people being more inclined to express (or indulge in) their conspiracy theories than previously seen". Social media platforms have made it easy for conspiracies to move from the fringe into the mainstream (Dentith, 2023).

Conspiracy theories can gain traction and spark an emotional contagion effect among RWE groups. Many conspiracy theories use emotional appeals on social media (Kim & Chen, 2022). In these platform ecologies, conspiracy theorists overwhelmingly try to persuade audiences by using negative emotions that will incite anger (Fong et al., 2021). Tweets with misleading information on COVID-19, for instance, contained more instances of negative sentiments compared to tweets with no misleading information (Gerts et al., 2021). Similar to how hate influencers use emotional contagion as a way to create cohesive group bonds (Stewart et al., 2023), "conspiracy theories are infamous for utilizing emotional appeals to arouse distrust and fear among audiences" (Kim & Chen, 2022, p. 4). RWE groups connect through codes or symbols to "mark their territory and communicate with one another" (Mattheis & Kingdon, 2023, p. 485).

The complexities of conspiracy theories in online environments have unleashed an era of *platformed conspiracism* (Mahl et al., 2023; Packer & Stoneman, 2021). Drawing from platformization studies (Helmond, 2015; Nieborg & Poell, 2018), platform conspiracism illustrates how conspiracy theories are reconfigured around the technical, economic, and regulatory specificities of platforms (Mahl et al., 2023). Platform specificities include technological features, platform business models, and governance strategies (Mahl et al., 2023). According to Mahl et al. (2023, p. 3), "platformed conspiracism can vary spatially and temporally depending on platform and user cultures". Similar to the concept of platformed racism (Matamoros-Fernández, 2017), platform conspiracism accounts for the "appropriation of platform specificities by social groups to promote harmful discourses, and by implication, the accountability of technology companies for facilitating such practices" (Mahl et al., 2023, p. 3). Importantly, platform specificities can result in user practices such as the communication, monetization, or insulation of conspiracism (Mahl et al., 2023).

A central "technical specificity" is the way social media platforms use algorithms to disseminate conspiratorial content. A study on the affective algorithms of #conspiracy on TikTok illustrates how platforms spread mis/disinformation for the purpose of data collection and commodification (Grandinetti & Bruinsma, 2023). This monetization illustrates the importance of capturing "user desire" that can manifest into a "mix of love, loyalty, and habituation for the platform" (Grandinetti & Bruinsma, 2023, p. 283). As social media algorithms encourage personalized environments, it's perhaps not surprising that, at least on TikTok, the "For You" algorithm heavily recommends conspiratorial content to users because of its "affective gravity" (Grandinetti & Bruinsma, 2023). On YouTube, both videos intending to propagate or quote-unquote "debunk" COVID-19 conspiracies often used emotions like trust and fear – rather than aspects of affect, such as joy or disgust – to frame conspiracies (Kim & Chen, 2022). These emotional frames often focus on "who to blame" for the conspiracy and "who to protect" (Kim & Chen, 2022, p. 5). Using social network analysis to follow conspiracies online, Estrella Gualda Caballero (2020, p. 143) was able to demonstrate the "strong emotional component" in the polarization of online communities.

Platform affordances similarly encourage users to become "prosumers" – both producers and consumers of conspiratorial content. In relation to platformed conspiracism, QAnon encouraged conspiracy followers to read and write in an esoteric manner, largely in relation to President Donald Trump, forming a type of amateur "produsage" transpiring from a "serpentine pipeline of digital-cultural interactivity and networked internet platforms" (Packer & Stoneman, 2021, p. 255). The ability of conspiracy influencers to encourage followers to engage in amateur "produsage" has resulted in YouTube channels, Reddit threads, memes, and a number of QAnon members "devoted to the task of actively decoding hidden messages intended for the faithful while cryptically encoding and distributing some of their own" (Packer & Stoneman, 2021, p. 255). This type of *conspiratorial prosumption* is visible across many mainstream and alternative social media platforms.

Platform business models can vary dramatically, but all social media platforms "commodify user activities, social relations, and various forms of transactions" (Mahl et al., 2023, p. 5). "Mainstream" platforms often rely more heavily on targeted advertising, whereas the revenue models for "alternative" platforms often consist of memberships, subscriptions, or donations (Mahl et al., 2023). Business models are essential to understanding platform conspiracism as platform choices are often driven and "justified by strategic decisions and marketed in politicized ways" (Mahl et al., 2023, p. 5).

Governance often refers to the ways platforms regulate and intervene to moderate both users and content (Mahl et al., 2023). Buckley and Schafer describe three aspects of governance. First, platforms code prohibited content, often through regulation documents like terms of use, terms of service, or community guidelines. Second, social media platforms use content moderation – human moderators, algorithms, users, or all three – as a defense mechanism against content that violates the platform's policies (Mahl et al., 2023). Moderation practices can vary drastically across social media platforms and chat apps. Chat apps like WhatsApp, Signal, and Telegram enable the use of encrypted private messaging to what is expected regarding appropriate scrutiny. For instance, there is often public scrutiny on Telegram channels compared to the back-end messaging features where content and information largely sit in the dark. Digital platforms enable the assemblage of online communities, constructed of online profiles, rating systems, and content moderation (Rafail & Freitas, 2019). In platform ecologies, social hierarchies "involve formal positions such as moderators who can censor posts and ban users for offensive material or informal positions such as a status as a long-standing community member" (Rafail & Freitas, 2019, p. 3). Third, platforms enforce these "policies" and "rules" by applying warnings to the content, demonetizing content, or removing users through temporary or permanent bans (Mahl et al., 2023).

The majority of mainstream platforms have deplatformed terrorist groups, RWE groups, and notable RWE actors and influencers. Platforms like YouTube, Twitter, and Facebook have responded in varying ways to growing hate speech and conspiracy theories, including shadow banning or deplatforming vocal "patriots" (Buckley et al., 2021; Cole, 2018). In 2022, when Elon Musk purchased Twitter, significant changes to the moderation and replatforming of those who were banned occurred, Twitter, now X, has been plagued with issues regarding hate speech, conspiracy theories, and disinformation, including posts by Musk himself. After initiating monetization for influencers on the platform, conspiracists, those peddling in disinformation, and extremism have benefitted from the dissemination of their posts. *Shadowbanning* is a moderation technique that bans users from online forums without disclosing the ban to the user, which means users are able to post but these posts are invisible to the online community (Cole, 2018) and proscribes the possibility that posts will extend in reach to non-followers (Cotter, 2021). A more common platform practice to deal with far-right extremists and conspiracists is deplatformization, whereby technology companies prohibit services to the users (Zeng & Schäfer, 2021; Rogers, 2020). *Deplatforming* is a countermeasure that social media platforms undertake to control disinformation and entails the removal of social media accounts that have "engaged in problematic behavior, in terms of authoring or amplifying malign or harmful content" (Innes & Innes, 2023, p. 1265). Extremist radicalization, sexual abuse, hate crimes, or risks and threats are all actions that can trigger the deplatformization of a user (Innes & Innes, 2023).

When far-right influencers Laura Loomer and Paul Joseph Watson were deplatformed from Facebook in 2019, the platform was criticized for announcing the ban beforehand, allowing the influencers to help redirect their audience (Innes & Innes, 2023). Even prominent figures like former President Donald Trump were previously deplatformed from Twitter, Snapchat, Facebook, Twitch, Shopify, and PayPal (Crichton, 2021).

Platformed conspiracism forms around network structures. Scholars have detailed how social media platforms are a productive medium to examine networks that encourage similarity among relational nodes (Figeac & Favre, 2023). With chat apps, like Telegram, followership can assume both symmetrical and asymmetrical relationships. YouTube (like BitChute) is not often a platform that people rely on for establishing social connections.

Innes and Innes (2023, p. 1266) argue deplatforming is a "mode of social control" exerted by platforms and intended to be used as a form of deterrence. These control mechanisms alongside the emergence of alternative, hybrid media platforms mean RWE groups are increasing at the mercy of platform policies and inclined to migrate to "darker" platforms. Al-Rawi (2019) argues that following the deplatforming on mainstream platforms, users can be propelled to alternative platforms such as Gab, BitChute, Parler, and 4chan, all of which provide comparatively limited content moderation. With the lack of oversight on these platforms, far-right actors can organize, spread misinformation and conspiracy theories, or help inspire attacks on marginalized groups (Perry & Scrivens, 2016; Jasser et al., 2021), enabling them to fund their work. It is in this more recent context we can see not only the import of RWE communication but also the other channels used that enable such reach.

Where deplatformization is not an issue, right-wing content creators often develop a social media presence across platforms. Content creators like Kevin J. Johnson cross-post identical content across platforms, but routinely remind viewers that if they are deplatformed from YouTube, they are also available elsewhere. Deplatforming users has historically been viewed as a pro-social solution, but, more recently, scholars argue it is limiting our understanding of how online cultures form and propagate on fringe platforms (Trujillo et al., 2020). Additionally, it is an unproductive way to reduce or remove conspiratorial thought from social media sites as actors and information simply permutate or migrate to other platforms.

In the following analysis, the operationalization of RWE communication, and respective conspiracy theories, involved four categories: topics, concerns, targets, and actors (see Chapter 1). As mentioned above, the development of our conceptualization of conspiracies in Chapter 1 emerged through our extensive empirical studies on BitChute and Telegram in this chapter. We focused on these two platforms only, and we believe that they are sufficient to show the applicability of our conceptual framework and its operationalization of conspiracy theories.

3.3 Telegram

Below, we empirically examine Canadian far-right conspiracies on the messaging application, Telegram.[1] Using mixed-methods that involved traditional content analysis of a sampled data and a digital investigation of the overall dataset, our findings illustrate a tendency to delegitimize the legitimate, with a prominent focus on conspiracies related to COVID-19, followed by technology (5G Network, QR Codes, etc.), and the Great Awakening. We discuss the implications of our study in the conclusion by focusing on the dark type of content that Telegram allows its users to circulate.

As mentioned previously, the social media ecosystem is dominated by a few major players, but there are several lesser-known platforms, like Telegram, that have high user bases (Baumgartner et al., 2020). Right-wing extremists are often hostile toward the mainstream press and social media, routinely using "new media for mobilization, coordination and information dissemination" (Urman & Katz, 2020, p. 1). Far-right actors commonly argue that mainstream media are biased, misrepresent their ideas, or disregard them entirely (Urman & Katz, 2020). The closure of the 8chan image-board alongside deplatformization on mainstream social media resulted in a growing, far-right user base on Telegram (Urman & Katz, 2020). Telegram has become a "popular online gathering place for the international white supremacist community and other extremist groups who have been displaced or banned from more popular sites". Similar to mainstream social media, far-right networks on Telegram form along ideological and national lines (Urman & Katz, 2020). RWE and groups disseminate hateful discourse on all social media platforms as a way to "bypass traditional media and political institutions" (Al-Rawi, 2021, p. 823). Dark platforms like Telegram make it even easier to circumvent traditional gatekeepers of discourse (Urman & Katz, 2020).

In 2018, Telegram increased in popularity after the mainstream social media platforms like YouTube, Twitter, and Facebook tightened moderation protocols. Telegram's main competitor, WhatsApp, made an update to its privacy policy in January 2021, which prompted 25 million users to migrate to Telegram within 72 hours (Statista, 2021). Telegram's founder, Pavel Durov, called it "the largest digital migration in human history" (Cuthbertson, 2021).

Telegram (2022) also features a secret chat where messages can be unsent or set to self-destruct, which is appealing to far-right users who seek digital refuge on platforms with low content moderation. Not surprisingly, Telegram experienced a spike in users in January 2021 (see Figure 3.1), corresponding with the attack on Capitol Hill (Molla, 2021), the closure of Parler, Donald Trump's deplatformization from mainstream social media, and the aftermath of WhatsApp's revised terms (Audrey et al., 2021), making it a prime platform to examine the kind of conspiratorial topics Canadian RWE circulate on Telegram. The platform's security features are the main selling point to its growing user base. Telegram users can join public (searchable) or private (invite-only) channels where the creator/administrators broadcast messages to an unlimited number of subscribers (Urman & Katz, 2020). This allows RWE to gain publicity while preserving security (Guhl & Davey, 2020). Group chats are similar to other platforms, where users can join, either by searching or sending an invitation to chat with other members. Private groups provide more secretive communication, while public groups are helpful for coordination and mobilization of up to 200,000 users (Urman & Katz, 2020).

All messages are encrypted on Telegram's servers with encryption keys stored in multiple locations so technical personnel cannot access messages. Users can also utilize the secret chat feature for enhanced security, where messages are stored on the user's devices rather than the Telegram's servers. These messages self-destruct after a specified period, making them impossible to recover. Additionally, users can also un-send messages and permanently delete them (Telegram, 2022). According to ADL, these enhanced security features have inadvertently attracted the interest of RWE and terrorist organizations.

To apply our conceptual model, we deployed traditional content analysis alongside a digital method to analyze the whole dataset in our analysis of Telegram.

In terms of analytical method, we used a mixed approach to combine the traditional content analysis approach on a representative sample data alongside a digital method to analyze the whole dataset. We retrieved the data using a Python script to collect all the available Telegram messages posted on Canadian far-right group channels (Al-Rawi, 2021). To find these relevant channels, we consulted previous literature, thoroughly searched the messaging app using our mobile phones and the web, and used the Telegram Analytics site (https://tgstat.com/). We cannot claim that we covered all the available Canadian RWE channels on this site because it is not possible to know them all, but we believe that we have included the major ones. All the 270,806 posts were retrieved from 21 Telegram channels selected based on their affiliation and/or association with Canadian RWE. These Telegram messages were posted between April 14, 2019 and September 4, 2021, when the data was collected (Figure 3.1 and Table 3.1).

To operationalize conspiracy theories, we inductively and deductively designed a codebook. In this respect, a group of four researchers used emergent coding in content analysis to inductively identify the major topics (Wimmer & Dominick, 2013). After reviewing the dataset, the researchers outlined four key areas including (1) topics; (2) actor; (3) target; and (4) fear element (which was later changed to "concern"). The first draft of the codebook contained topics like "Blue Beam", "White Replacement", and "Survivalist" but the instances of these conspiracies were not as prevalent as we originally thought, so we added an "Other" category. While the researchers initially identified specific "targets" such as "Liberals" and "United Nations", this ultimately produced too many codes and made it difficult to fit content into the defined box we created. To solve this problem, the researchers designed broader codes such as "Liberal government, figures & supporters" and "International organizations (e.g., WEF, UN, WHO)". This reveals some important findings about developing a codebook to study conspiracy, including the need for an overarching framework and using broad terms that cover a larger range of topics/targets.

The researchers identified the following ten topics that were both exhaustive and mutually exclusive: (1) The Great Reset (World economic forum-Klaus Schwab), (2) Great Awakening, (3) UN (Agenda 2030-/C-15/UNDRIP), (4) Technology-software-microchip Q/5G Network/R Codes/4th Industrial Revolution, (5) China displacement/infiltrations/military (Chinese takeover of the government and military via CCP influence), (6) Deep State, (7) COVID-19 related, (8) Islamophobic,

(9) NWO (conspiracy of a secretly emerging totalitarian "one-world" government), and (10) other (minor topics like Social Credit System, White Replacement, Blue Beam Project, Survivalist movement, Climate change, Anti-Semitic, etc.). Though these categories are exhaustive and mutually exclusive, each Telegram post is coded with the potential of having more than one topic that can assist the researchers in identifying the salience of conspiracies.

To quantify dark participation on Telegram, the conspiracies were divided into four overarching categories, as stated in Chapter 1. It is important to note here that some of the topics, targets, actors, and concerns might vary when conducting other studies, depending on the examined platform, timeframe, and sample analyzed.

The category for topics included the following items:

1. The Great Reset (World economic forum-Klaus Schwab);
2. Social Credit System;
3. Great Awakening;
4. UN (Agenda 2030-/C-15/UNDRIP);
5. Technology-software-microchip Q/5G Network/R Codes/4th Industrial Revolution;
6. China displacement/infiltrations/military (Chinese takeover of the government and military via CCP influence);
7. Deep State;
8. COVID-19 related;
9. Islamophobic;
10. NWO (conspiracy of a secretly emerging totalitarian "one-world" government);
11. Anti-Semitic;
12. Climate change;
13. White replacement; and
14. Other (less frequent or minor issues like Blue Beam, Survivalist movement, etc.).

For Actors, this included:

1. RWE provocateur/content creator;
2. Fake/fringe expert;
3. Politician(s);
4. Citizen(s); and
5. Other (journalists, etc.).

For Targets:

1 Liberal government, figures, and supporters (e.g., Bill Gates, George Soros, Trudeau, Obama, Biden);
2 China/Communism;
3 International organizations (e.g., WEF, UN, WHO);
4 Indigenous;
5 Telecommunication and technology companies;
6 Jews;
7 Muslims; and
8 Other.

Finally, for Concerns, this included:

1 State control, censorship, and surveillance: Loss of rights and freedoms (slavery, encampment, concentration camps) and mass control;
2 Social chaos: Destruction or loss of traditional Christian values, loss of internet, access to banking etc., social chaos with individuals being controlled/tackled by police;
3 Nationalism: Foreign infiltration, espionage, military invasion, fifth column, migrants are flooding Western countries, etc.;
4 Harm to children: Pedophiles (e.g., Pizzagate conspiracy theory);
5 Harm to women: Kidnapping/marrying/raping/enslaving women;
6 Public health policies are harming people, or they don't work; and
7 Other.

Two coders examined over 10% of the total sample or 200 Telegram posts, and the intercoder agreement was acceptable in the second attempt $\alpha \geq 0.760$, using Krippendorff's Alpha (Krippendorff, 2010).

Next, we manually content analyzed the top 1,000 most viewed Telegram posts from all the channels after removing irrelevant, vague, or replicated posts. Google Translate was used to decode ten posts in other languages, which typically included German or Spanish. These top Telegram posts received a total of 351,001,320 views. Specifically, we found 1,153 Telegram posts that fell into the other category and were removed from our dataset. When calculating the percentages, we removed this category from the analysis to focus on the major topics. We used the views metrics because it was the only one that we were able to extract, and we needed to follow a systematic procedure to filter our data for the manual analysis. Because the dataset is large and we wanted to fully understand the dataset, we decided to use a digital method to identify the most frequent words, phrases, hashtags, and emojis (Al-Rawi, 2021).

Below we highlight seven main findings linked to primary conspiracies or conspiratorial trends, including COVID-19, the interwoven nature of conspiracies, technology, #TheGreatAwakening, the Deep State and political polarization, #Savethechildren, and conspiracies related to race and/or religion.

As we found in Table 3.2, pandemic-related messages on Telegram represent the highest percentage of posts (42.2%) as well as views (38.9%). This was expected due to the magnitude of the COVID-19 pandemic and its impact on the whole world. This finding is corroborated with our digital analysis. For example, we observe from the top 50 most recurrent hashtags in Table 3.3 that 18 out of 50 (36%) hashtags directly relate to the pandemic, indicating that this is the most widely discussed topic among Canadian RWE. In this respect, the word "Covid" is the seventh most frequent term found in the whole dataset (n = 5,180). We can also see that among the top 20 most used emojis are 💉 (n = 1,079), while other related ones include 💊 (n = 231) and 😷 (n = 84) which all refer to the pandemic. The discourses around COVID-19 are centered around freedom of choice and resisting anti-authority measures in an attempt to delegitimize the public health directives and guidelines.

These information pathologies gain traction because posters include fake experts to foster credibility and delegitimize the legitimate. For example, one post features an alleged list of 49 doctors who "clearly explain why vaccines aren't safe or effective", while another post says, "Army Doctor Reveals More Soldiers have died from the Vaccine than died from COVID". Another trend to delegitimize COVID-19 vaccinations is to claim that elites are not being vaccinated. For example, one post says, "Nurse exposes how Justin Trudeau and his wife didn't actually take the Covid Vaccine". The most recurrent hashtag is #Justsayno, suggesting that "resisting" public health measures is the appropriate path for RWE because the liberal government has an agenda in implementing public health measures. The #Justsayno hashtag often connects to Toronto's anti-lockdown leader and self-proclaimed anti-vaxxer "Chris Sky" (n = 304) (also known as Christopher Saccoccia), who authored a book *Just Say No* to encourage public opposition to COVID-19 vaccinations and restrictions.

Telegram users share right-wing media clips from outlets like The Stew Peters Show and personal social media posts with captions like, "Chris Sky lays out the COVID-19 hoax and medical tyranny in 2 minutes" and "Chris Sky on the Quackccine Passport: 'Do Not Comply'". The majority of "Chris Sky" posts reference information pathologies around COVID-19, but a few also connect him to the Great Awakening. One post says, "Canada Huge Demonstrations Against Tyranny, Chris Sky leading the way in Montreal, The Great Awakening CA WWG1WGA".

Similar hashtags are used to communicate the idea of collectivizing to counter governmental policies like #Weareallessential (n = 29), #Riseup (n = 24), #Joinus (n 22), #Hugsovermasks (n = 20), #StayOpen (n = 16), #MakeCanadaFreeAgain (n = 15), #Unitednoncompliance (n = 14), and #Nomorelockdowns (n = 14). There are clearly attempts to form a dark social movement whose objective is to establish some kind of collective anti-pandemic behavior by appropriating the language of resistance and civil disobedience. These dark social movements collectivize to form networks, and subsequently group identities around political, financial, and ideological interests as a way to amplify resistance. For instance, we find among the most frequent words and phrases terms like "freedom" (n = 1,807) and "Keep Canada Free" (n = 48). One trend within the dataset was for RWE to denounce COVID-19 entirely, considering it a hoax, which is one aspect of these information pathologies. For example, one post claimed that COVID-19 was a "lie" and "was developed by the pharmaceutical company that produces biological weapons". Another post said, "None of this was about Covid. That's just a flu. Operation Warp Speed is a global military operation".

Some of these discourses are meant to spread conspiracies about the government and health authorities, which is evident in the use of some conspiratorial terms like #Wwg1wga (n = 92), which is mostly used by the QAnon group, #clotshot (n = 19) or #Covidvaccinevictims (n = 14), which both serve to disseminate fear about the efficacy and safety of the vaccine, and other conspiracies like #Thegreatawakening and #Agenda2030. Generally speaking, QAnon is an umbrella conspiracy, which includes several COVID-19 and political-based conspiracies. The Great Awakening is a conspiracy where people believe the masses will "wake up" and see the conspiracies of the world and rise up against the governments and cabals to save the world. As one post indicates, people who are red-pilled are "awakened to truth that has been hidden by the media", blue-pilled individuals are in "a state of bliss believing the media", and black-pilled people were "awakened at one point" but have gone "back to sleep". Posts often include references to "powerful white hats", corrupt bankers, governments, politicians, and elites, the Deep State, and the integration of pedophilia in military and governments.

3.3.1 Connecting conspiracies with other conspiracies

Conspiracies are often interwoven with other conspiracies. For example, the COVID-19 vaccine is also associated with other conspiracies around the alleged attempt by the Canadian government to create genocide for the sake of depopulating the masses. This is evident in the use of some sinister-sounding hashtags like #Depopulation (n = 24), Death (n = 22), #Crimesagaisthumanity (n = 17), and #Genocide (n = 17). In fact, the word "vaccine" (in singular and plural forms) is the second top word in the whole dataset (n = 8,773), while other related words like "vaccinated" (n = 2,045) are among the top 50 ones. In terms of recurrent phrases, we can find that the top phrase is actually "Vaccine passports" (in two formats) (n = 782) followed by other related ones such as "covid vaccine" (n = 684), "vaccinated people" (n = 303), and "covid vaccines" (n = 300). It is important to mention here that there are many conspiracies surrounding the vaccine passport, producing a high volume of posts related to protests and opposition to government-regulated passports. One post encouraged people to "flood" the Human Rights Commission's phone numbers across Canada with "complaints and concerns about health passports".

A large volume of posts were related to concerns, protests, or state-wide bans of vaccinations in other countries, including France, the United States, and China. The concern over vaccination passports is also evident from the use of the following emoji sequence 🔬☠️ (n = 25), which refers to the alleged lethal impact of the vaccine. For example, one Telegram post mentioned the following: "Choice to be Silent, is NO LONGER YOURS. this is Genocide!! 🔬☠️🔬", while another example offers clear disinformation on the vaccine: "HIV IN THE VACCINES! 🔬☠️🏷️". This fear and conspiracies about the vaccine stem from the Tuskegee experiments in the 1930s, where African American men were tested for the long-term effects of suffering from syphilis but the men were never told the purpose of the experiment. The subjects were told they were being treated for bad blood but were not receiving any treatment whatsoever. In 1972, a whistleblower revealed the truth and ended the experiment (McVean, 2019).

There is a great deal of disinformation about the nature of the vaccines and their ingredients. For example, one Telegram post mentions the following: "MY POST LISTING ALL THE INGREDIENTS PRESENT IN THE INOCUPUNCTION 🔬🧪, SUCH AS POTASSIUM CHLORIDE ALSO USED IN DEATH-JABS, ETC, SAYING THAT "THIS CANNOT BE SO AND IS THEREFORE A PSYOP, SINCE WE NOW KNOW THAT THE VILES CONTAIN 99% GRAPHENE". 😵🤢 WHAT AN IDIOT, EH!! 😂😀😆) SO HERE YOU GO. 🔺🔪💅" The high volume of posts with cross-over conspiratorial topics suggests dark social movements attach to pandemic issues as a way to co-opt and subvert others to existing causes. As stated below, there is a clear attack against liberal figures who are often associated with Jews and/or Muslims. For instance, the star of David emoji ✡ (n = 6), often used in pejorative ways as one Telegram post, mentions the following conspiracy: "Johnson & Johnson ✡ sold baby powder containing cancer-causing asbestos. IMAGINE TRUSTING THESE COMPANIES TO INJECT YOU WITH A RUSHED EXPERIMENTAL GENE THERAPY DRUG? 🤣🤣🤣🤣🤣 🤣🤣". As part of the conspiracies, it seems here that the poster believes that Johnson & Johnson is run by Jews and its intention is to harm people. Other vaccine-related conspiracies can be seen in the frequent use of phrases like "Chinese communist party" (n = 83) and "social credit system" (n = 41), with one post stating, "Vaccine Passports" are a coercive tool to force social compliance and a China-like social credit score upon the public". Within the posts, COVID-19 is often referred to as "the China Virus". In fact, the #China (n = 26) hashtag is among the top 50 most used ones in the dataset. A number of posts are also about alleged Communist infiltration, boycotting Chinese products, cyber attacks originating from China, and artificial intelligence technologies developed in China that surveil global citizens so "nobody can hide".

3.3.2 Technology conspiracies: 5G, cryptocurrency, and platform surveillance

Based on our manual analysis of the data, conspiracies around technology make up the second highest percentage of topics (25.9%) as well as Telegram views (27.5%). In relation to the digital analysis, we found several references to the site (www.drcharlieward.com) (n = 48), which provides fake medical advice on the alleged harmful effects of the 5G networks with links to My Patriots Network

RWE site (https://mypatriotsnetwork.com/?ref=5). Discourse was also centered around untraceable technologies and cryptocurrencies, platform surveillance, censorship, and governance, as well as dark platforms. The linking of 5G technology through conspiracy theory is the belief that the new technology is the cause of the spread of the COVID-19 virus and the waves spread by 5G are a tool used by the evil cabal to control and eventually enslave humanity. This is a global conspiracy theory that is not uniquely connected to Canada, yet it is popular among some Canadians. Unfortunately, the resistance against such potentialities has led some individuals to destroy 5G towers through arson (Jolley & Paterson, 2020, p. 628) including a few incidents that occurred in Quebec. Here we see a conspiratorial convergence occurring with technological fears of 5G and the fear of the digital age articulated through the social credit system established in China. Vaccine passports are equated to the idea of identification such as banking information, government identification, and health information being digitized and under the control of the federal government. This leads some to believe that the government through surveillance can block access to your finances for social infractions, such as jaywalking or travelling too far from home. Technology advancements can lead to fears of control or depopulation, but when connected to COVID-19 mandates and resulting concerns convergence can link technology to conspiracies about government overreach, 15-minute cities, depopulation, social credit controls, and the Great Reset, to create a narrative of distrust of all of the institutions of society working in collaboration to control the population under the guise of pandemic measures.

3.3.3 *#TheGreatAwakening*

The third most frequent topic is the Great Awakening (12.4%), which scored (11.7%) in terms of the percentage of views. This finding also aligns with our digital analysis, for the term #TheGreatAwakening (n = 17) is found among the top 50 most frequent hashtags. In this respect, we find a summary of different conspiracies including the Great Awakening articulated with the use of emojis in the following message posted on @Keepcanadafree Telegram channel:

102 *The Canadian Far-Right and Conspiracy Theories*

|| ⚡#Divine #Wisdom ||
|| 🗡New World Order 🔒||
||US #Election #News
||GB#BREXIT
|| 💊#Covid #Plandemic #Agenda
|| 🗡The #Matrix
|| ❄ #Quantum
|| ♡ #GoOD Vs #Evil ☠
#DominionVotingSystems #Dominion #ElectionDay2020 #TheMoreYouKnow #HoldTheLine #FuckTheTraitors #wwg1wga #news #nwo #agenda21 #areyouawake #Trumpwon #releasethekraken #nothingcanstopwhatiscoming

#Q̧ #QSent Me #WWG1WGA

🛡 WWG1WGA 🛡 🗡
👥🛡TELEGRAM GROUP CHAT
https://t.me/areyouawakeyet
👥📢TELEGRAM CHANNEL
https://t.me/areyouawake1
👥📢WHATSAPP CHAT
https://chat.whatsapp.com/Cmd0jh8kEY2IFhMGl0gPCp

3.3.4 Deep State, NWO, and political polarization

The fourth major topic that is identified in our manual analysis is related to the Deep State conspiracy (9%) with (10.7%) views. Our digital analysis shows similar results, for some of the most frequent phrases include "Deep State" (n = 321) and other related ones like the [New] "World Order" (n = 241). The Deep State is understood as a secretive network of compromised politicians, military officials, and others who have infiltrated the institutions operating worldwide, and are able to control the policies of nations. The Deep State is a term derived from the QAnon conspiracy theory that believes that there is a satanic cabal of pedophiles and cannibals controlling media, education, science, politics, and similar institutions. The members of this cabal include liberal politicians, wealthy leaders such as Bill Gates and George Soros, and the entirety of the Democratic Party.

There is also clear political polarization in the Telegram discussion mostly represented in the affiliation with American politics, especially to express support for the former US president, Donald Trump. For example, the word "Trump" is the 15th most recurrent term (n = 3,446), while "Trudeau" (n = 2,199) and Biden (n = 1,872) are in the top 50 words. As for the top phrases, they include "Justin Trudeau" (n = 558), "President Trump" (n = 527), "Bill Gates" (n = 488), "Joe Biden" (n = 361), and "Donald Trump" (n = 246). For example, one Telegram post mentions the following: "🔔🔔🔔BILL GATES IS AN EVIL 👑 🐍 SCUMBAG🔔". In line with this polarization, we find attacks against "mainstream media" (n = 360), often accusing it of being "fake news" (n = 265). In fact, the analysis of the most frequent emojis shows the use of far-right symbols such as Pepe the frog 🐸 (n = 1,072), the OK sign 👌 (n = 128), and the snake 🐍 (n = 10). Others who are not white are often described as aliens 👽 (n 52), such as in the following post: "Canada does NOT need a lil terrorist commie mini Jagmeet. 😒 🤮 👽".

3.3.5 #Savethechildren

The other theme is related to children, which is evident in the use of hashtags like #Savethechildren (n = 39), (n = 37), and #Children (n = 14). In fact, this is related to an aspect of the QAnon conspiracy theory, which focuses on the alleged human trafficking attempts by liberal figures to sexually exploit children, and the roots of these claims can be traced back to the Pizzagate conspiracy theory – "a false rumor that Hillary Clinton and her top aids were involved in various crimes", including "running a child-trafficking ring out of a Washington pizza parlor" (Aisch et al., 2016). A similar disturbing and related hashtag is #Adrenochrome (n = 16), which is a reference to a century-old anti-Semitic myth that global elites are harvesting children's blood to extract adrenochrome, a chemical that is injected into the elites to keep them young and healthy (Friedberg, 2020). One post combines the adrenochrome conspiracy with other conspiracy theories noting, "Wuhan is the epicentre of nucleaire reactors, Bitcoin corruption, adrenochrome production, human slavery, biochem laboratories. This is why the three gorges dams need to go down and wipe out evil from the earth". The posts about adrenochrome often reference "elites" and the "3 Gorges dam". Upon examining phrases that are made up of two to three words, we can find that terms such as "human trafficking" (n = 256) and "Child sex trafficking" (n = 90) are among the most frequent ones, too.

3.3.6 *Race and religion*

Finally, there are minor conspiracies that discuss other issues like "critical race theory" (n = 83), "Black Lives Matter" (n = 49), and "dominion voting system" (n = 40). For instance, one post states the following false claim about BLM: "💣 CIVIL UNREST – Leaked audio has surfaced of (allegedly) John Sullivan admitting Antifa and BLM involvement in US Capitol Siege". Similarly, some of the most frequent phrases include the Blue Beam project, a Canadian-based conspiracy where the Devil/Satan takes over as the world leader and a blue beam will form a holograph that will confuse, and then lead the public astray. At that point, the gods will emerge as holograms and explain all religions are wrong, before Satan takes the throne and the world is enslaved. For instance, the following Telegram post states: "Check out this link, it is a document detailing '3D holographic display using strontium barium niobate'. AKA Project Blue Beam; how they can stage a fake alien 👽 invasion or a solar deity in the skies. 📄https://apps.dtic.mil/sti/citations/ADA338490".

In brief, we empirically examined in this section dark social movements across 21 Telegram channels. Our work fills a substantial gap in the literature by offering a first look at salient conspiratorial topics in Canada. The combination of lax moderation protocols and mass communication to users provides a safe haven for far-right actors to mobilize their followers to spread hate and misinformation without fear of any legal repercussions. The technological affordances of Telegram encourage dark social movements by the Canadian far-right. As a result, our findings illustrate how Telegram is rife with conspiracy theories.

Within the overall dataset, the highest percentage of posts (42.2%) and views (38.9%) were related to the pandemic. The use of hashtags such as #Weareallessential (n 29), #Riseup (n = 24), and #Joinus (n = 22) helps to amplify the calls to resistance against the perceived tyrannical measures made by the government. Additionally, popular leaders such as "Chris Sky" (n 304) can use Telegram to mobilize their followers and encourage a larger anti-lockdown, anti-vaccine movement. The organized and coordinated information networks on Telegram demonstrate how the use of hashtags, such as #Depopulation (n = 24), Death (n = 22), #Crimesagaisthumanity (n 17), and #Genocide (n = 17) can help spread global conspiracies related to the pandemic such as 5G technology (25.9% of posts) the Great Awakening (12.3% of posts) and the Deep State (9% of posts). In the following section, we discuss BitChute, the other alternative SNS site.

Table 3.1 The frequency of Telegram messages posted by 21 channels

No	Channel Name	Username	Bot	Frequency
1	Canadian Fact Checked News	@canadian_fact_checked_news	No	2,052
2	The Canadian Stormer	@TheCanadianNationalist	No	127
3	Clown World	@clownworld1984	No	2,495
4	WLM_Canada_Toronto	@WLMTorontoChat	No	2,492
5	White Ontario Active Club	@WhiteOntarioActiveClub	Yes	706
6	Canadian Patriots	@canadiansoldiersoftruth	No	30,671
7	Keep Canada Free	@keepcanadafree	Yes	83,635
8	Pepe Lives Matter	@PepeMatter	No	3,651
9	SOS Canada Patriots	@soscanada	Yes	97,145
10	Saskatchewan Patriots	@SaskatchewanPatriots	No	44,741
11	Beyond the Narrative	@BeyondtheNarrative	No	448
12	Canadian Nationalist Party[2]	@canadian_nationalist_party	No	304
13	WLM- Alberta	@WLM_CANADA_ALBERTA	No	21
14	WLM-Alberta-chat	@WLM_ALBERTA_CHAT	Yes	97
15	WLM-SWO	@WLM_CANADA_SWO	Yes	125
16	WLM-SWO-chat	@WLMSouthwestOntarioChat	Yes	576
17	WLM-Toronto	@WLM_CANADA_TORONTO	No	172
18	WLM-Niagara	@WLM_CANADA_NIAGARA	No	3
19	WLM-Niagara-chat	@WLM_NIAGARA_CHAT	Yes	24
20	Faith Goldy	@faith_goldy	No	42
21	Maxime Bernier	@MaximeBernier	No	1,279
	Total			270,806

Source: Created by the authors.

RWE sites 105

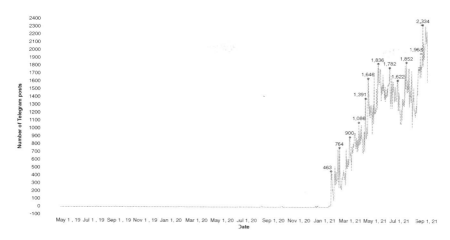

Figure 3.1 The frequency of Telegram posts highlighting some important landmark dates.
Source: Created by the authors.

Table 3.2 The frequency and percentage of Telegram topics and their views

No	Topic	Freq. and Perc.	Views
1.	Great Reset	19 (1.6%)	6,860,951 (1.6%)
2.	Great Awakening	142 (12.4%)	48,512,003 (11.7%)
3.	UN	9 (0.7%)	3,436,262 (0.8%)
4.	Technology	296 (25.9%)	113,857,951 (27.5%)
5.	China	57 (5%)	22,715,623 (5.4%)
6.	Deep State	103 (9%)	44,596,661 (10.7%)
7.	COVID-19	482 (42.2%)	160,795,920 (38.9%)
8.	Islamophobic	22 (1.9%)	7,761,298 (1.8%)
9.	NWO	10 (0.8%)	4,500,791 (1%)

Source: Created by the authors.

3.4 BitChute

The second platform we examined is BitChute, which is a UK-based platform established in 2017 by Ray Vahey. BitChute is a peer-to-peer UK-based video-hosting platform founded by Ray Vahey, launched as an alternative to YouTube in 2017 (Trujillo et al., 2020; BitChute, 2021). BitChute has similar architecture and technological affordances as YouTube, which fosters the facilitation of knowledge sharing. The technological affordances of BitChute include the ability for users to post, watch, and interact with user-generated video content through the comments feature. BitChute's digital infrastructure operates through mobile applications for iOS and Android devices, as well as through a website that can be located using a search browser on any device with internet access. BitChute (2021) supplements

Table 3.3 The top 50 most frequent hashtags used in the dataset

No	Hashtags	Frequency	No	Hashtags	Frequency
1	#Justsayno	255	26	#Godwins	21
2	#Covid19	136	27	#Hugsovermasks	20
3	#Cdnpoli	119	28	#Bitcoin	19
4	#Breaking	95	29	#Click	19
5	#Wwg1wga	92	30	#Vaccine	19
6	#Covid	43	31	#Clotshot	19
7	#Savethechildren	39	32	#Crimesagaisthumanity	17
8	#Lockdown	39	33	#Thegreatawakening	17
9	#SaveOurChildren	37	34	#Winning	17
10	#Newsletter	37	35	#Genocide	17
11	#Echobox	30	36	#Adrenochrome	16
12	#Canada	30	37	#StayOpen	16
13	#Weareallessential	29	38	#MakeCanadaFreeAgain	15
14	#China	26	39	#Lockdowns	15
15	#Vaccines	25	40	#NSA	14
16	#ExposeCNN	24	41	#SP	14
17	#Depopulation	24	42	#Australia	14
18	#Riseup	24	43	#Berlin	14
19	#Thankyou	24	44	#Children	14
20	#Ebs	23	45	#Name	14
21	#Astrazeneca	22	46	#Covidvaccinevictims	14
22	#Joinus	22	47	#Unitednoncompliance	14
23	#Death	22	48	#Nomorelockdowns	14
24	#Agenda2030	21	49	#Kabul	13
25	#Pfizer	21	50	#Moderna	13

Source: Created by the authors.

technological affordances with policies that encourage equal treatment regardless of sex, race, age, religion, or political beliefs, and prohibits harmful content like violence, animal cruelty, and child abuse.

BitChute produces low user engagement but has a high volume of channels that contain hate speech and conspiracy theories (Trujillo et al., 2020). In particular, a recent study found that 75% of comments on BitChute include at least one hate speech term, including ethnically-based hate (45%), gender-based hate (23%), and class-based hate (13%) (Trujillo et al., 2020). The majority of content on BitChute is "loosely-related to news and politics" with a significant number of keywords related to conspiracy theories (Trujillo et al., 2020, p. 4). This finding is consistent with the tendency for far-right extremists to use dark platforms to insert racism, anti-Semitic, Islamophobic, heterosexist, and ableist discourse into mainstream political avenues. Despite the fact that BitChute has community guidelines, the platform is not doing enough to remove hateful content. While right-wing extremism has flourished on mainstream and alternative platforms, dark platforms like BitChute are often excluded from social media research (Zeng & Schäfer, 2021).

BitChute is an alternative social media platform where content is not as moderated. Joining the ranks of Gab, Voat, GETTR, and 4chan, BitChute differentiates itself as being the first of these platforms to focus on video content. Like YouTube content, providers can choose to monetize their channels and content. Vahey created BitChute in response to what he perceived as being "censorship" by mainstream social media sites through the use of deplatforming, demonetization, and the use of algorithms to "obscurity" (David, 2021). According to the Anti-Defamation League, BitChute's domain registrar and hosting provider is Epik, a company that in the past has provided services to other extremists' websites, and Twitter alternative Gab. BitChute, as one of the first alternative platforms to YouTube, is designed in a very similar fashion and layout. Both platforms provide a format for users to interact with the user-posted content through comments beneath the videos.

In the months leading up to the 2020 U.S. presidential election, mainstream social media began closer and more stringent moderation. In response, some conservative pundits and social media users alleged that they were being censored by "big tech". This led to a migration of many conservatives to alternative social media platforms like BitChute to avoid strict moderation. These alternative platforms capitalized on this migration and perceived censorship to define themselves as hubs for "free speech". These unmoderated platforms soon became a hotbed for disinformation, hate speech, and conspiracy theories. Trujillo et al. (2020) in their research found that the content provided on BitChute was predominately composed of videos promoting conspiracy theories and hate speech. The videos collected and their corresponding between June and December 2019, by Trujillo et al. (2020), found that they were mostly related to conservative politics and conspiracy theories. Consistent words and phrases found in the comments included misogyny, references to the male supremacist group Men Going Their Own Way (MGTOW), and the term "red pill".

Indeed, the migration of "digital refugees" to darker corners of the internet is known as exile congregation (Zeng & Schäfer, 2021, p. 1323). After Trump was banned from YouTube, the president and his supporters migrated to BitChute which is a video-sharing platform. The popularity of BitChute climbed to its highest levels shortly before the 2020 US election and the Capitol Hill attack. BitChute now houses several far-right conspiracists who were embargoed from YouTube, including Alex Jones, the radio host of Infowars. Another example is Kevin J. Johnson, who ran as a fringe candidate in Calgary's 2021 mayoral election. On social media, Johnson describes himself as "Canada's most censored man" (Gettr, 2021; Gab, 2021). Johnson runs a network of websites called Freedom Report and is a far-right extremist that "pushes misinformation and promotes hate towards Muslims, women, and the LGBTQ+ community" (Lamoureux, 2019). Johnson built his following on YouTube by spreading hate but was deplatformed as a result of a targeted campaign towards Toronto restaurateur, Mohamad Fakih (Lamoureux, 2019). Johnson called Fakih an "economic terrorist" and suggested only guests who were jihadists and rapists would be permitted entrance into the restaurant (Lamoureux, 2019). The hate speech resulted in bans on Facebook and YouTube, as well as the largest Canadian defamation suit related to online activity (Lamoureux, 2019). This was the second time Johnson was banned from YouTube, despite the fact that terminated accounts are supposedly prohibited from returning to the site (Lamoureux, 2019). Johnston circumvents deplatforming procedures by creating new pages or channels (Lamoureux, 2019), as well as posting video content related to the dangers of Islam, promotion of Maxime Bernier, and his personal political ambitions as mayor of Calgary on BitChute. In 2018, the videos Johnston posted to BitChute (2021), which were presumably cross-posted to YouTube, finished with "IN CASE YOUTUBE KILLS US, FOLLOW ON BitChute: https://www.BitChute.com/channel/kevinjjohnston". Many content creators on YouTube mirror video content on BitChute in case YouTube bans them at some point (Anti-Defamation League, 2020). Johnson's platform history illustrates a key problem with infrastructure ostracization and highlights the ability for exile congregation to exist within a single platform. "So far the only site that seems to have been able to de-platform Johnston for good is Twitter" (Lamoureux, 2019). This underscores the problem of infrastructure ostracization and the need to examine the shades of darkness within platforms.

Indeed, BitChute and Telegram are considered dark social media channels laden with dark participation because users' activities mostly contain conspiracy theories. The concept of dark participation originates from journalism studies, and in Chapter 3, we use it as a framework to investigate some of the platforms used by RWE. For example, to understand the most viewed and commented BitChute videos. The concept of dark participation is defined as "negative, selfish or even deeply sinister contributions such as a "trolling", strategic "piggy-backing" on journalistic reputation, and large-scale disinformation in uncontrolled news environments" (Quandt, 2018, p. 41). Dark participation includes "misinformation and hate campaigns, individual trolling, and cyberbullying" (Quandt, 2018, p. 41). Dark users are often referred to as comment trolls and "paint the picture of angry, malevolent participants who project their personal issues and a general hatred of fellow human beings or "the system" onto others with a grim will to stir up forum debates" (Quandt, 2018. p. 41). Dark participation is also defined as deviant engagement by individuals, groups, or states who do so for "sinister strategical, tactical, or 'pure evil'" to attack targets directly or indirectly for the purpose of manipulation (Frischlich et al., 2019, pp. 2015–2016). Dark participation includes emotionally-charged comments and posts loaded with rage, often incorporating fake news, disinformation, and conspiracy theories by troll armies and social bots (Frischlich et al., 2019, p. 2016). Dark social media offers an avenue for harmful content to thrive within a largely anonymized ecosystem (Al-Rawi, 2024), fostering an environment of dark participation that encourages venting, attacks, and trolls commenting on videos with opposing ideological viewpoints. We argue this type of dark participation is not only confined to negative news site commentary and/or attacks against journalists, but expands to other unconventional platforms like BitChute and Telegram, as illustrated in this chapter.

Similar to Telegram, this study analyzes the main conceptual components observed in conspiracy theories within the theoretical framework of dark participation within the dark platform ecosystem. Dark platforms such as BitChute are characterized by their perceived harmful content, anonymity, and inaccessibility, enabling users to spread hate and conspiracy theories through content liberation (Al-Rawi, 2021).

To conduct this study, we programmatically downloaded all available BitChute videos for 38 search terms representing different Canadian issues, figures, and places: "Harjit Sajjan", "Maryam Monsef", "Catherine McKenna", "Patty Hajdu", "Ahmed Hussen", "Anita Anand", " Omar Alghabra", "Iqra Khalid", "Erin O'Toole", "Jagmeet Singh", topoli, quebec, qcpoli, Halifax, Edmonton, Calgary, Alberta, Ontario, Winnipeg, Manitoba, Saskatchewan, "British columbia", "Chrystia Freeland", "Stephen Harper", "Thomas Mulcair", "Maxime Bernier", "Toronto", "Montreal", "Vancouver", "Ottawa", "onpoli", "polqc", "cdnpoli", "Andrew Scheer", "Canadian", "Trudeau", "Canada", "Canadian". The search retrieved all the available videos from January 1, 2017 to September 30, 2021, when the data was collected (Figure 3.2). After removing duplicates, we found 35,153 videos in total to include in the study. These videos generated 24,727,471 views, 590,076 likes, and 5,340 comments. Since the collected video data is very large, we focused our attention on the top 500 most viewed videos that received 9,271,211 views (37.4% of the overall views), 172,890 likes (29.2% of the overall likes), and 4,217 comments (78.9% of the overall comments). This approach is connected to the theoretical concept of dark participation because we wanted to see what the BitChute users mostly viewed. The total number of hours of these 500 videos is 197.8. This procedure is followed by several previous social media studies because there is so much "noise" in the data, and it is better to focus on what the users of the platform mostly viewed. Another procedure is to focus on the most active users on the platform (see Table 3.4); however, this method can produce bias in the findings and focus our attention on only a few selected users, some of whom may be spamming others.

To proceed with the study, four researchers selected a sample from an earlier BitChute download and examined the main conceptual components that can be observed in conspiracy theories. Using manual content analysis, the researchers relied on emergent coding to identify these conceptual components (Wimmer & Dominick, 2013). To be comprehensive, the coders divided conspiracies into four overarching categories after several deliberations: (a) topics; (b) actors; (c) targets; and (d) concerns. Each major category contained several items. In the third attempt, the researchers were able to refine the designed codebook to include the following items for topics: (1) The Great Reset (World Economic Forum – Klaus Schwab), (2) Social Credit System, (3) Great Awakening, (4) UN (Agenda 2030-/C-15/UNDRIP, (5) Technology-software-microchip Q/5G Network/R Codes/4th Industrial Revolution, (6) China displacement/infiltrations/military (Chinese takeover of the government and military via CCP influence), (7) Deep State, (8) COVID-19 related, (9) Islamophobic, (10) NWO (conspiracy of a secretly emerging totalitarian "one-world" government), (11) Anti-Semitic, (12) Climate change, (13) White replacement, and (14) Other (less frequent or minor issues like Blue Beam, Survivalist movement, etc.). As for actors, the following categories are listed: (1) RWE provocateur/content creator, (2) Fake/fringe expert, (3) Politician(s), (4) Citizen(s), and (5) Other (like journalists, etc.). For targets, the categories: (1) Liberal government, figures, and supporters (Bill Gates, George Soros, Trudeau, Obama, Biden), (2) China/Communism, (3) International organizations e.g., WEF, UN, WHO,

(4) Indigenous, (5) Telecommunication & technology companies, (6) Jews, (7) Muslims, and (8) Other. For concerns, the categories were: (1) State control, censorship, & surveillance: Loss of rights and freedoms (slavery, encampment, concentration camps) and mass control, (2) Social chaos: Destruction or loss of traditional Christian values, loss of internet, access to banking, etc., social chaos with individuals being controlled/tackled by police, (3) Nationalism: Foreign infiltration, espionage, military invasion, fifth column, migrants are flooding Western countries, etc., (4) Harm to children: Pedophiles e.g. Pizzagate conspiracy theory - children, (5) Harm to women: Kidnapping/marrying/raping/enslaving women, (6) Public health policies are harming people or they don't work and (7) Other, e.g., White people are systematically displaced, etc. (see Chart 1).

To test the codebook, three coders completed an analysis of 50 sample videos. The initial results showed significant differences between them, who later met to discuss their selections. After much deliberation, the coders agreed on using more unified definitions to determine their articulation within the BitChute videos.

After discussing and agreeing on the categories' definitions, two coders both re-coded their choices, and with this clarity, they reached a higher intercoder agreement in the third attempt. Using Krippendorff's alpha, the agreements were all acceptable (Krippendorff, 2010): (A) topics $\alpha \geq 0.833$, (B) concerns $\alpha \geq 0.825$, (C) actors $\alpha \geq 0.833$, and (D) targets $\alpha \geq 0.894$. To add more insight to our findings, we further filtered the data based on the number of comments along these major categories because commenting on the videos shows a more engaged level in dark participation, requiring more time and effort than liking or viewing a video alone. In terms of comments, we found it is important to skip the "other" category as there is a single unrelated video on a personal encounter at a Canadian bank which got 1,058 comments. We followed the same rule on this video with regard to all the major categories of the study (topics, actors, targets, and concerns).

Finally, we used a Python script (Al-Rawi & Shukla, 2020) to extract the most frequent words, phrases, and hashtags that are made up of two words taken from the subject and description of BitChute videos. We followed this digital procedure to make sure we cover the full range of possible other issues covered in the entire dataset.

The results of our study show that the most frequent topic 47% (n = 409) is related to COVID-19 as this issue seems to attract the attention of Canadian far-right users due to its association with government policies like vaccinations, lockdowns, mask policies, and physical distancing mandates (see Table 3.5). The COVID-19 topic received the highest percentage of comments, situated at 53.4% (n = 2,925). In the digital analysis, the word "vaccine" is among the top 100 words used in the entire dataset (n = 2,669). Other frequent words used include the "flu" (n = 1,373) which is often used to discredit the existence of COVID-19, "anti-lockdown" (n = 1,368), and "virus" (n = 1,309). Also, the top 100 most used hashtags include several pandemic-related terms including controversial ones like #Endthelockdowns (n = 45) and #covid1984 (n = 30). Some of these conspiratorial views are associated with the QAnon group, for we also found relevant hashtags like #wwg1wga (n = 51) and #Greatawakening (n = 39). For example, the most popular video in our sample, titled: "Yuge!!! Canadian Court Victory Proves Covid-19 is a Hoax & All Restrictions have Now Been Dropped" garnered 896,018 views and 682 comments and was shared across 20 different channels. It is important to note that many topics are discussed interchangeably; for example, COVID-19 is often associated with the UN as well as the NWO conspiracy. This is similar to a blame game and a psychological projection tactic since blaming external parties makes far-right members feel that major world problems are caused by other parties who are ideologically different from them. Conspiracy theories can provide not only a rationale for what is occurring but also provide an instigator, who meets the narrative of many of the dark participants' worldviews. Dark participants seek news sources that appeal to their political fears or concerns, which is fundamentally how they create their sinister narrative of the world around them. Through conspiracy theory their relevant fears and concerns are met. In another video titled: "Canadian Speaks out with a Warning to All", with 80,862 views, a nurse alleges that there are UN troops marching across Canadian cities and acting as "COVID marshalls", ensuring compliance with COVID-19 measures.

The second most frequent category is the Great Awakening 8.1% (n = 71). This refers to the QAnon conspiracy theory, where people will allegedly awaken and rise up against tyrannical governments/the cabal and save the world. In one video titled: "Trudeau Faces Rape and Murder Charges- Trump Prepares Dagger Plunge to Heart Of Democrats", with 66,843 views, Nicholas Veniamin and former CIA agent Robert David Steele, prominent far-right actors on BitChute, call for people to rise up to Trudeau's alleged crimes against humanity, illuminating how dark participation emphasizes harmful content. According to the conspiracy, former President Donald Trump holds compromising intel on prominent liberal figures, including videos of Trudeau raping and killing children. Those who believe in this conspiracy view Donald Trump as a revolutionary, leading the charge against the perceived cabal and evil-doers to save humanity.

As for the third most frequent topic, it deals with the NWO at 7.7% (n = 67). Similar to the discussion above on the Great Awakening, far-right group members believe there is a silent push by the liberal elites for a tyrannical one-world government. For example, a video titled: "Deepest dark documentary 2021 warning!! Very graphic and disturbing" aimed to expose this conspiracy and garnered 60,463 views. In detail, it discusses how the world is allegedly controlled and manipulated by members of the liberal elite, who are also part of secret satanic pedophiles. This topic is often discussed interchangeably with the Great Awakening as the conspiracy of a global ring of child sex trafficking is part of the transition toward establishing a NWO. Conspiracy theories such as these have provided a conduit for the expression and symbolic representation of the extreme-rights' fears, the same fears that acted as the catalyst to dark participants lashing out on social media and in news media forums. In defining the extreme-right and the use of fear and conspiracy for mobilization, important commonalities need to be acknowledged, for there is a trope of making their nation more ethnically homogenous and demanding a return to more traditional values. Descriptions of those in power and national institutions are seen as being under the control of elites who place internationalism before the nation. Elites, or powerful individuals, are described by the extreme-right as putting their own self-interests ahead of those they represent. This notion of fear and dread is an important component of the power of conspiracy theories, in that they can provide an "answer' or rationale as to why these fears manifest. Linked to politics, religion, and racism conspiracy theories have served as justification for political mobilization, activism, and in some cases, violence. Politically, populism, dark participation, and conspiracy are usually connected.

We also found that the topic of technology received the second-highest percentage of comments at 7.9% (n = 435). This is often linked to COVID-19 as it refers to the merging of the biological and digital worlds through measures such as the implementation of software-microchips in vaccines, QR codes, and 5G networks. In a video titled: "David Icke in Powerful Exposure of 'covid' Hoax in Awakening World Interview on Toronto Caribbean" with 31,361 views, the renowned conspiracy theorist David Icke argues that COVID-19 is a computer-generated fiction and part of a larger plan to replace the human perception with artificial intelligence. David Icke is a good example of how infrastructure ostracization from YouTube resulted in the exile congregation to BitChute and this subsequent conspiratorial content liberation. This is followed by the Great Awakening at 7.1% (n = 392) and the Great Reset at 4.3% (n = 239). Hence, we can see that the comments metrics provide a slightly different insight on dark participation from the ranking of topics.

As for the featured actors, the most frequent category is related to RWE provocateurs and content creators at 66.3% (n = 375). This was expected because the majority of videos were posted by the same community members who are often featured or discussed in these videos. Similarly, this category received the highest percentage of comments at 42.4% (n = 1,997). The second most frequent actors are related to fake experts at 17.1% (n = 97) who also received the second-highest percentage of comments at 28.5% (n = 1,341). When discussing topics such as COVID-19, far-right actors often bring on fringe medical doctors in an attempt to strengthen the credibility of their arguments. One video with 273,856 views titled: "Canadian Doctors Speak Out", had doctors such as Stephen Malthouse downplay the pandemic while also promoting alternatives to the vaccine such as using hydroxychloroquine. Malthouse appeared repeatedly on both Telegram and BitChute as an "authority" or "expert" figure on COVID-19 vaccines. In some videos, Malthouse argued that COVID-19 is not more dangerous than the flu, and that vaccinations are far more dangerous than COVID-19. He also promoted his website where he was allegedly signing fake vaccine exemptions (see also CBC News, 2022). In 2022, the College of Physicians and Surgeons of British Columbia suspended Dr. Stephen Malthouse's license for spreading COVID-19 misinformation (CBC News, 2022). The third most frequent actors found are related to citizens at 6.7% (n = 38). Many of BitChute's most popular videos involve people protesting against pandemic restrictions set by the government. In a video with 53,717 views titled: "Pastor Arrested – Canada the Great Awakening", a pastor can be seen getting arrested on the highway after defying COVID-19 orders by hosting maskless church services and denying health inspectors into his church. However, the category that received the third highest percentage of comments is related to RWE-related whistleblowers at 6.5% (n = 309).

Regarding the targets, we find that the most frequent one is related to targeting the liberal government, figures, and supporters at 59.4% (n = 469). The targets varied but focused on attacking prominent liberal political leaders, especially Justin Trudeau. It is important to note our dataset did not contain one positive video about Trudeau which can be attributed to the ideological differences between the two and the outcry surrounding the provincial and nationwide pandemic measures. In fact, the digital analysis shows that Trudeau is the most mentioned person (n = 9,083) and ranks as the eighth most referenced word. "Justin Trudeau" is the third most used phrase (n = 3,582) in the entire dataset and the third most used hashtag #Justintrudeau (n = 554) or #Trudeau (n = 310) which is ranked 9th. This category also received the highest percentage of comments 51.5% (n = 3,042), indicating that liberals are enemy number one for far-right members. In a video with 319,111 views titled: "Dr. David E. Martin Drops Shocking Covid Info on Canadians", fringe medical expert Dr. David E Martin accused Justin Trudeau of being compromised by the vaccine manufacturers to take part in a global respiratory virus experiment.

The second most frequent category is related to telecommunication and technology companies 15.8% (n = 125) because of their perceived role in supporting the Deep State and maintaining a global system in which liberal elites have more power over far-right groups. Again, this category received the second highest percentage of comments 23.1% (n = 1,363). In one video with 51,200 views titled: "B E T R A Y A L: At Every Turn", a user discussed an alleged secret plan to track information from those who have been vaccinated through an imaginary pharmacovigilance surveillance system.

The third targeted group is related to attacking China and/or communism 10.6% (n = 84). In this respect, the digital analysis shows that China (n = 1,128) is the only country mentioned in the top 250 words, mostly in relation to the pandemic and the alleged ongoing military training of the Chinese Army in Canada. Members of the far-right, including Ezra Levant, allege that Trudeau is controlled by and allows infiltration of Canadian institutions by the Chinese Communist Party (Levant, 2020). Despite a focus on the liberal government, the far-right also blames China for the pandemic, accusing government of weaponizing COVID-19 while continuing to influence nations as part of its alleged communist takeover of the Western world. In a video with 22,844 views titled: "Legislation Allows Chinese Troops in Canada, Death Squads, Preserving Your Rights W/ Kevin Annett", the video posters alleged that the Chinese state has infiltrated the government in British Columbia. In fact, the hashtag #China was also prominent in the data (n = 88), while pejorative expressions against the perceived enemies include hashtags like #thewolvesarecoming (n = 60). However, the category that received the third highest percentage of comments is related to conspiracies around the UN 3.5% (n = 210). Conspiracy theories can delineate the attributes of a patriot or social hero who can save the nation from the "enemy" whether domestic or foreign. They also serve to formulate the components of the identity of the enemy, for example, via religion, race, culture, and/or political leaning. In this respect, the perceived enemy can be the UN, China, and/or the liberals.

As for the most frequent concerns expressed by far-right groups, they are first related to public health measures 31% (n = 352) particularly related to COVID-19 that also received the highest percentage of comments 30.1% (n = 2,924). This category aligns well with the findings above on the most frequent topics. The far-right politicized the pandemic and utilized it as a recruitment tool, targeting citizens frustrated with public health measures. In a video with 125,771 views titled: "Dr. Buttar Leaked Email from Liberal Party Lays out the Plan", fringe medical experts claimed to have received a leaked message from a whistleblower within the liberal party stating that the pandemic is merely part of the globalists' agenda for a technocratic future in exchange for people's rights. This is related to the Great Reset conspiracy cited above, where all debt will be erased, but people will be enslaved and the rich will own everything.

The second category is related to social chaos such as the destruction and/or loss of traditional Christian values, loss of internet, or access to banking 27.9% (n = 317) which also received the second highest percentage of comments 28.8% (n = 2,795). As a matter of fact, the far-right utilizes the social chaos they create in order to further destabilize the democratic institutions they despise. In a video with 78,530 views titled: "Canadian Court Ends Covid Emergency | Mask Mandates, Lockdowns, & Emergency Use Jab are Now Unlawful", a user reports that the state of emergency orders in Ontario are criminal and a constitutional lawyer called Rocco Galati will be holding them accountable. The user also tells his viewers that now is the time to fight back harder than ever before through unified non-compliance.

This is followed by concerns around the issue of perceived state control, human rights infringement, censorship, and surveillance 27.6% (n = 314) that got the third highest percentage of comments 28.3% (n = 2,751). For example, some of the most frequent words in the dataset include "freedom" (n = 3,015) and "patriots" (n = 2,680) in reference to far-right group members who resist the Canadian government. The most frequent hashtags show a similar pattern, for we can see relevant terms like #freespeech (n = 61), #censorship (n = 47), #freedom (n = 42), #fightforfreedom (n = 37), #endthetyranny (n = 37), and #worldwidefreedomprotest (n = 36). In one video with 92,441 views titled: "Supreme Court of Canada Will Hear Crimes Against Humanity – Indictments Served to Trudeau and More", one small business owner accused the Ontario Provincial Police of committing crimes against the people of Ontario by restricting their freedoms and forcibly injecting poison into peoples' arms. Again, this kind of dark participation shows that BitChute offers its users a suitable venue for the dissemination of threats and conspiracy theories.

Finally, the digital analysis of words, phrases, and hashtags shows clear affiliation with Ezra Levant and his *Rebel News* media organization. For example, the word "Rebel" was used 17,828 times and is ranked 4th immediately after "News" (n = 18,846), while the phrase "Rebel News" is the most frequent one (12,533) similar to the hashtag #rebelnews which is the most used one (n = 1,618). Following the reference to Trudeau, there are some conservative figures that are commonly mentioned like "Trump" (n = 1,725) and "Ezra" (n = 1,615). In terms of phrases, other figures include "Sheila Gunn" (n = 916) and David Menzies (n = 854) from Rebel News, the conspiracy theorist, "Alex Jones" (n = 716) as well as "Maxim Bernier" (n = 610), the political leader of the People Party of Canada (PPC). In one video with 5,849 views titled: "Firetam.Com: Canada's Chief Public Health Officer Must Resign or Be Fired", Ezra Levant, founder of *Rebel News*, personally targeted Canada's Chief Public Health Officer, Theresa Tam, for listening to the allegedly Chinese Communist Party controlled World Health Organization (WHO).

One of the other insightful findings from the digital analysis shows that far-right group members are using BitChute and similar alternative platforms to solicit financial donations mostly to support *Rebel News*, for words like "Paypal" (n = 3,493), "donate" (n = 3,103), "donations" (n = 1,336), "cryptocurrency" (n = 1,107), "deposit" (n = 1,089), and "e=transfer" (n = 970) are among the most frequent words. *Rebel News* is often described as a "fearless source" (n = 822) and is mentioned in relation to donations, such as the use of phrases like "support independent journalism" (n = 2,073). Further, far-right actors on BitChute often end their videos with a call to action, citing the need for donations in order to continue supporting their channel. For example, in the video titled: "Yuge!!! Canadian Court Victory Proves Covid-19 is a Hoax & All Restrictions have Now Been Dropped", one user asks his supporters to donate and "be a banner for truth". In addition to donating directly, far-right actors and larger BitChute channels sell products and supplements as an alternative form of funding. For example, Dr. Charlie Ward, a channel with 134,969 subscribers promotes products aimed at allegedly protecting people from the dangers of 5G networks. Indeed, these examples underscore how content liberation often evades content moderation in the dark platform ecosystem.

In conclusion, we explored in this section how BitChute, as one form of dark social media platform, offers users an avenue to widely disseminate negative content and conspiracy theories. These information activities are considered a type of dark participation because the main intention is to express hate, attack, and spread disinformation. BitChute is a rich platform for dark participation because there is less content moderated than mainstream social media channels. Interestingly, the far-right group members often discuss being censored or deplatformed on other social media sites such as Twitter, Facebook, and Instagram, in addition to discussing alternative venues like podcasts and GAB that are used as their preferred dissemination tools. In other words, BitChute offers a space where far-right actors seek exile congregation in response to infrastructure ostracization on other social media platforms. Dark platforms like BitChute allow the far-right to continue spreading their disinformation and hate without fear of censorship.

We also found that *Rebel News* played a large role in discrediting and misrepresenting information related to the COVID-19 pandemic, targeting Justin Trudeau and Doug Ford in particular for their strict lockdown measures. Several of *Rebel News*' more popular videos (32,285 views combined), covered the quarantine hotels in Toronto, Ontario, likening them to prisoner isolation camps. *Rebel News*, however, freely posts its negative content on traditional social media outlets like YouTube; hence, BitChute serves in amplifying content liberation and dark participation across platforms, even though sites like YouTube are still complicit in conspiratorial dissemination. Moreover, the funding solicitations on BitChute intertwine with concepts like platform capitalism (Srnicek, 2017) because fringe outlets provide a lifeline and alternative routes to economic survival.

We also found that the final dimension of dark participation, which is content liberation, is evident in many BitChute videos, especially in relation to COVID-19-related conspiracies that encourage vaccination hesitancy. Pages like Vaccine Choice Canada (VCC) post videos on BitChute intended to provide citizens – and "especially Canadians" – with "shocking news" around the "potentially treasonous acts" related to COVID-19 regulations, mandates, and vaccination protocols. The video features the VCC President Ted Cruz and Dr. David E. Martin (VCC, 2021), a speaker from *Plandemic*, the documentary that claimed the coronavirus was a human-made disease. The 2021 VCC video titled, "DR. DAVID E. MARTIN DROPS SHOCKING COVID INFO ON CANADIANS", is rife with misinformation and conspiracies about COVID-19 and has generated over 370,900 video views and 1900 likes. The architecture on BitChute (2021) allows playlists to be public or private and users can hide or delete a video after it is posted. Embedded within the norms and values inscribed by the architectural system (van Dijck et al., 2018), BitChute (2021) encourages content liberation through its slogan, "defend free speech".

Finally, there are some limitations that must be mentioned. For example, we only coded the top 500 most viewed videos because of the large dataset that we collected. Future studies can examine other metrics like the most liked videos instead of relying on the number of views. Second, we only focused on BitChute, so it is necessary to include other alternative social media sites that are known to encourage dark participation, including Telegram, Discord, Parler, GAB, Gettr, and Reddit. Further, our focus is on Canadian far-right groups, so it is necessary to compare them with other under-researched groups like those active in Australia and New Zealand in order to better understand the salience of topics, concerns, targets, and actors in conspiracy theories. We believe that the increasing deplatformatization of

Table 3.4 The top ten most active BitChutters discussing Canadian issues

No	Users	Freq.
1	canuck tv canada	2,899
2	Rebel News	2,083
3	Disclosure Quebec	1,386
4	ManFoWars.com	1,291
5	WDL_Northern_Ontario	1,251
6	Kevin J. Johnston	525
7	Digital Truth Calgary	452
8	News Now Canada Independent Media	418
9	OurCanadianTownhall.ca	380
10	CanadaPoli	369

Source: Created by the authors.

RWE sites 117

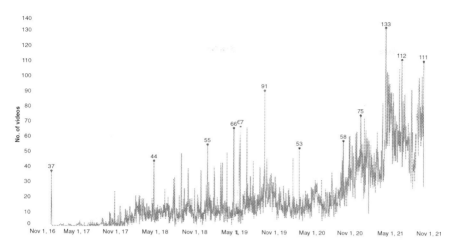

Figure 3.2 The frequency of videos referencing Canadian issues on BitChute.
Source: Created by the authors.

Table 3.5 The frequency of topics, concerns, actors, and targets and their respective comments

No	Topic	Freq. and Perc.	Comments
1	Great Reset	48 (5.5%)	239 (4.3%)
2	Social Credit	19 (2.1%)	41 (0.7%)
3	Great Awakening	71 (8.1%)	0
4	UN	35 (4%)	392 (7.1%)
5	Technology	63 (7.2%)	435 (7.9%)
6	China	41 (4.7%)	0
7	Deep State	35 (4%)	231 (4.2%)
8	COVID-19	409 (47%)	2,925 (53.4%)
9	Islamophobic	9 (1%)	0
10	NWO	67 (7.7%)	0
11	anti-Semitic	16 (1.8%)	147 (2.6%)
12	Climate change	3 (0.3%)	0
13	White Replacement	21 (2.4%)	0
14	Other	33 (3.7%)	1,058 (19.3%)

No	Concerns	Freq. and Perc.	Comments
1	State control	314 (27.6%)	2,751 (28.3%)
2	Social chaos	317 (27.9%)	2,795 (28.8%)
3	Nationalism	40 (3.5%)	0
4	Harm to children	77 (6.7%)	92 (0.9%)
5	Harm to women	9 (0.7%)	0
6	Public health	352 (31%)	2,924 (30.1%)
7	Other	25 (2.2%)	1,132 (11.6%)

(*Continued*)

Table 3.5 (Continued)

No	Actors	Freq. and Perc.	Comments
1	RWE member	375 (66.7%)	1,997 (42.4%)
2	Fake expert	97 (17.1%)	1,341 (28.5%)
3	Whistleblower	17 (3%)	309 (6.5%)
4	Politician(s)	26 (4.6%)	0
5	Citizen(s)	38 (6.7%)	0
6	Other	12 (2.1%)	1,058 (22.4%)

No	Targets	Freq. and Perc.	Comments
1	Liberal	469 (59.4%)	3,042 (51.5%)
2	China/Communism	84 (10.6%)	0
3	UN	72 (9.1%)	210 (3.5%)
4	Indigenous	2 (0.2%)	0
5	Technology companies	125 (15.8%)	1,363 (23.1%)
6	Jews	15 (1.9%)	147 (18.6%)
7	Muslims	6 (0.7%)	0
8	Other	16 (2%)	1,137 (19.2%)

Source: Created by the authors.

far-right members from mainstream social media outlets makes it difficult to fully map the growing trajectory of conspiracy theories because these actors simply migrate to new emerging platforms. In other words, the study of conspiracy theories will evolve to fit the affordances of new sites and their varied moderation policies.

3.5 Conclusion

Using a novel codebook entailing many major conspiratorial discourses, we highlight how the dissemination of these conspiracies cultivates dark social movements for members of the far-right to coordinate their activities, shares similar ideas, and troll their opponents, especially liberals, immigrants, and anyone who does not fit their white supremacist ideology. These findings demonstrate how dark users actively diminish credible authorities and the broader implications that occur when disinformation gains traction and becomes ever more mainstream. Delegitimization occurs across multimodal formats including texts, emojis, and hashtags.

The interwoven nature of conspiracies was particularly prevalent with COVID-19-related conspiracies. While conspiracies are timeless, there is also a degree of timeliness to them (Uscinski, 2018). As COVID-19-based issues anchored around anti-lockdown, anti-mask, anti-vaccination, and anti-vaccination-passport policies, dark social movements pre-dating the pandemic pivoted in such a way as to co-opt or subvert these causes as their own (Amarasingam et al., 2021). As our findings show, COVID-19 conspiracies dominated discourse attempting to discredit lockdown measures, mask-wearing mandates, and vaccinations using fake experts. Conspiracists argue that 5G technology spreads the COVID-19 virus and is a tool used by the evil cabal to enslave humanity. The third prominent conspiracy is the Great Awakening, which shows how conspiracies are rooted in politics and the tendency for conspiracies to overlap.

As "conspiracy theories are often difficult to parse" (Chess & Shaw, 2015), more attention to the salience of conspiracy topics in Canada is needed across platforms. Future studies should look at a range of discourses (text, memes, images, emojis, etc.) and explore these conspiratorial topics on alternative platforms, like Rumble, Gettr, BitChute, and GAB, which are frequented by the Canadian far-right. There is also a need to study conspiratorial topics by French-speaking RWE groups. Topics may need to be added or removed from the codebook as discourses evolve, for we found minor differences in the nature of these conspiracies when comparing Telegram and BitChute. Conspiracy as a mainstream phenomenon is a global concern, but given the lack of literature within this area, it is particularly important for further research to focus on conspiracies within the Canadian context.

As Mark Fenster (1999) argues, the exclusion of extremists is a form of de-legitimization of radicalism, creating an "other" from the "normal" of mass society. This separation can lead to conspiracy theories that can be used by political movements to disrupt existing political parties and create new coalitions. Conspiracy can also be a very valuable tool for populism to arise. The manual content analysis approach in combination with a digital method to analyze the whole dataset allowed us to develop our main findings, including identifying primary conspiracy theories and conspiratorial trends within Canada, all of which have an overarching tendency to delegitimize the legitimate. Some of these conspiracies include COVID-19, technology, the Great Awakening, the Deep State and political polarization, #Savethechildren, and critical race and/or religion. A conspiratorial trend that we uncovered was the tendency of conspiracists to weave conspiracies into other ones.

In brief, we operationalized conspiracy theories in this chapter to dissect the concept and understand its varied elements using Telegram and BitChute data. Using a mixed-method approach, we found that the framework we used can be adequate in understanding conspiracies, and we believe that other studies can borrow all or part of it to investigate other platforms and/or issues.

Notes

1 This section is borrowed from a previous peer reviewed study whose details are as follows: Al-Rawi, A., Stewart, N. K., Celestini, C., & Worku, N. (2022). Delegitimizing the legitimate: Dark social movements on Telegram. *Global Media Journal, 14*(1), 28–47.
2 In 2019, the Canadian Nationalist Party filed paperwork to participate in the federal election, which prompted The Canadian Anti-Hate Network to threaten to release the names of party members given leader Paul Fromm's connection to Blood & Honour (Lamoureux, 2019).

References

Aisch, G., Huang, J., & Kang, C. (2016, December 10). Dissecting the #PizzaGate conspiracy theories. *The New York Times*. Available online at https://www.nytimes.com/interactive/2016/12/10/business/media/pizzagate.html?searchResultPosition=1 (last accessed at: 010323)

Al-Rawi, A. (2019). Gatekeeping fake news discourses on mainstream media versus social media. *Social Science Computer Review*, *37*(6), 687–704.

Al-Rawi, A. (2021). Telegramming hate: Far right themes on the dark social media. *Canadian Journal of Communication*, *46*(4), 31–pp.

Al-Rawi, A., & Shukla, V. (2020). Bots as active news promoters: A digital analysis of COVID-19 tweets. *Information*, *11*(10), 461.

Al-Rawi, A. K. (2024). *Online hate on social media*. Springer Nature.

Al-Rawi, A., Celestini, C., Stewart, N., & Worku, N. (2022). How Google autocomplete algorithms about conspiracy theorists mislead the public. *M/C Journal*, *25*(1). https://doi.org/10.5204/mcj.2852

Amarasingam, A., Carvin, S., & Phillips, K. (2021). Anti-lockdown activity: Canada country profile. *ISD*. Available online at https://www.isdglobal.org/wp-content/uploads/2021/12/Anti-lockdown-canada-ISD.pdf (last accessed at: 010323)

Anti-Defamation League. (2020). BitChute: A hotbed of hate. Retrieved from https://www.adl.org/blog/bitchute-a-hotbed-of-hate

Audrey, S., Rand, A., Masoodi, M.J., & Tran, S. (2021). *Private messaging public harms: Disinformation and online harms on private messaging platforms in Canada*. Ryerson University. Available online at https://dais.ca/wp-content/uploads/2023/11/PrivateMessagingPublicHarms_2021.pdf (last accessed at: 010323)

Baumgartner, J., Zannettou, S., Squire, M., & Blackburn, J. (2020, May). The pushshift telegram dataset. In *Proceedings of the international AAAI conference on web and social media* (Vol. 14, pp. 840–847).

Belew, K., & Gutiérrez, R. A. (Eds.). (2021). *A field guide to white supremacy*. University of California Press.

BitChute. (2021, November). Prohibited entities list. Accessed from https://support.BitChute.com/policy/prohibited-entities-list

Buckley, N., & Schafer, J. S. (2021). "Censorship-free" platforms: Evaluating content moderation policies and practices of alternative social media. *SOC ARXIV*. https://doi.org/10.31235/osf.io/yf9qz

Buckley, N., & Schafer, J. S. (2022). 'Censorship-free' platforms: Evaluating content moderation policies and practices of alternative social media. For(e)Dialogue. https://foredialogue.pubpub.org/pub/bsh5uhll/release/1

Caballero, E. G. (2020). Social network analysis, social big data and conspiracy theories. In M. Butter & P. Knight (Eds.), *Routledge handbook of conspiracy theories*. Routledge.

CBC News. (2022, March 28). B.C. doctor accused of spreading COVID-19 misinformation suspended from practice. *CBC*. https://www.cbc.ca/news/canada/british-columbia/b-c-doctor-suspended-for-spreading-covid-19-misinformation-1.6400737

Chess, S., & Shaw, A. (2015). A conspiracy of fishes, or, how we learned to stop worrying about #GamerGate and embrace hegemonic masculinity. *Journal of Broadcasting & Electronic Media*, *59*(1), 208–220.

Cole, S. (2018, July 31). Where did the concept of "shadow banning" come from? *Vice*. https://www.vice.com/en/article/a3q744/where-did-shadow-banning-come-from-trump-republicans-shadowbanned

Cotter, K. (2021). "Shadowbanning is not a thing": black box gaslighting and the power to independently know and credibly critique algorithms. *Information, Communication & Society*, ahead-of-print(ahead-of-print), 1–18. https://doi.org/10.1080/1369118X.2021.1994624

Crichton. (2021, January 9). TechCrunch is part of the Yahoo family of brands. *Tech Crunch*. https://techcrunch.com/2021/01/09/the-deplatforming-of-a-president/

Cuthbertson, A. (2021). WhatsApp Exodus is 'largest digital migration in human history,' Telegram boss says as he welcomes world leaders. *Independent*. Available online at https://www.independent.co.uk/tech/whatsapp-privacy-telegram-world-leaders-b1787218.html (last accessed at: 010323)

David, G. (2021). *BitChute platforming hate and terror in the UK*. Hope Not Hate Charitable Trust.

Dentith, M. R. (2021). Debunking conspiracy theories. *Synthese*, *198*(10), 9897–9911.

Dentith, M. R. (2023). Some conspiracy theories. *Social Epistemology*, *37*(4), 522–534.

Fenster, M. (1999). *Conspiracy theories: Secrecy and power in American culture*. University of Minnesota Press.

Figeac, J., & Favre, G. (2023). How behavioral homophily on social media influences the perception of tie-strengthening within young adults' personal networks. *New Media & Society*, *25*(8), 1971–1990.

Fong, A., Roozenbeek, J., Goldwert, D., Rathje, S., & Van Der Linden, S. (2021). The language of conspiracy: A psychological analysis of speech used by conspiracy theorists and their followers on Twitter. *Group Processes & Intergroup Relations*, *24*(4), 606–623.

Friedberg, B. (July 31, 2020). The dark virality of a hollywood blood-harvesting conspiracy. *Wired*. Available online at https://www.wired.com/story/opinion-the-dark-virality-of-a-hollywood-blood-harvesting-conspiracy/ (last accessed at: 010323)

Frischlich, L., Boberg, S., & Quandt, T. (2019). Comment sections as targets of dark participation? Journalists' evaluation and moderation of deviant user comments. *Journalism Studies*, *20*(14), 2014–2033.

Gab. (2021). Gab social. https://gab.com/

Gabriel, Y. (2017). Narrative ecologies and the role of counter-narratives: The case of nostalgic stories and conspiracy theories. In S. Frandsen, T. Kuhn, & M. W. Lundholt (Eds.), *Counter-narratives and organization*. Routledge.

Gehl, R. W. (2016). Power/freedom on the dark web: A digital ethnography of the Dark Web Social Network. *New Media & Society*, *18*(7), 1219–1235.

Gerts, D., Shelley, C. D., Parikh, N., Pitts, T., Watson Ross, C., Fairchild, G., ... & Daughton, A. R. (2021). "Thought I'd share first" and other conspiracy theory tweets from the COVID-19 infodemic: Exploratory study. *JMIR Public Health and Surveillance*, *7*(4), e26527.

GETTR. (2021, September 25). Terms of use. https://gettr.com/terms

Grandinetti, J., & Bruinsma, J. (2023). The affective algorithms of conspiracy TikTok. *Journal of Broadcasting & Electronic Media*, *67*(3), 274–293. https://doi-org.libproxy.txstate.edu/10.1080/08838151.2022.2140806

Greenberg, A. (2014). Hacker lexicon: What is the dark web? *Wired*. https://www.wired.com/2014/11/hacker-lexicon-whats-dark-web [dostęp 6.02. 2017].

Guhl, J., & Davey, J. (2020). A safe space to hate: White supremacist mobilisation on Telegram. *ISD Global*. https://www.isdglobal.org/isd-publications/a-safe-space-to-hate-white-supremacist-mobilisation-on-telegram/

Helmond, A. (2015). The platformization of the web: Making web data platform ready. *Social Media+ Society*, *1*(2), 2056305115603080.

Innes, H., & Innes, M. (2023). De-platforming disinformation: Conspiracy theories and their control. *Information, Communication & Society*, *26*(6), 1262–1280.

Jasser, G., McSwiney, J., Pertwee, E., & Zannettou, S. (2021). 'Welcome to #GabFam': Far-right virtual community on Gab. *New Media & Society*. https://doi.org/10.1177/14614448211024546

Jolley, D., & Paterson, J. L. (2020). Pylons ablaze: Examining the role of 5G COVID-19 conspiracy beliefs and support for violence. *British Journal of Social Psychology*, *59*(3), 628–640.

Kim, S. J., & Chen, K. (2022). The use of emotions in conspiracy and debunking videos to engage publics on YouTube. *New Media & Society*, *26*(7), 3854–3875.

Krippendorff, 2010 Krippendorff, K. (2010). Krippendorff's alpha. In N. Salkind (Ed.), *Encyclopedia of research design* (Vol. 10). Thousand Oaks, CA: SAGE Publications, Inc. https://doi.org/10.4135/9781412961288

Lamoureux, M. (2019, July 23). Far-right group tries to run for office, discovers that means outing themselves. *Vice*. https:// www.vice.com/en/article/8xzzma/far-right-canadian-nationalist-party-led-by-travis-patron-faces-doxxing-threat

Levant, E. (2020). *China virus: How Justin Trudeau's pro-communist ideology is putting Canadians in danger*. Rebel News Network Limited.

Mahl, D., Zeng, J., & Schäfer, M. S. (2023). Conceptualizing platformed conspiracism: Analytical framework and empirical case study of BitChute and Gab. *New Media & Society*, *0*(0). https://doi.org/10.1177/14614448231160457

Matamoros-Fernández, A. (2017). Platformed racism: The mediation and circulation of an Australian race-based controversy on Twitter, Facebook and YouTube. *Information, Communication & Society*, *20*(6), 930–946.

Mattheis, A. A., & Kingdon, A. (2023). Moderating manipulation: Demystifying extremist tactics for gaming the (regulatory) system. *Policy & Internet*, *15*(4), 478–497.

Mcvean, A. (2019, January 25). 40 years of human experimentation in America: The Tuskegee study. *Office for Science and Society*. Available online at https://www.mcgill.ca/oss/article/history/40-years-human-experimentation-america-tuskegee-study (last accessed at: 010323)

Molla, R. (2021, January 20). Why right-wing extremists' favorite new platform is so dangerous. *Vox*. Available online at https://www.vox.com/recode/22238755/telegram-messaging-social-media-extremists (last accessed at: 010323)

Nieborg, D. B., & Poell, T. (2018). The platformization of cultural production: Theorizing the contingent cultural commodity. *New Media & Society*, *20*(11), 4275–4292.

Packer, J., & Stoneman, E. (2021). Where we produce one, we produce all: The platform conspiracism of QAnon. *Cultural Politics*, *17*(3), 255–278.

Pereira, P. S., da Silva Silveira, A., & Pereira, A. (2020). Disinformation and conspiracy theories in the age of COVID-19. *Frontiers in Sociology*. https://doi.org/10.3389/fsoc.2020.560681

Perry, B., & Scrivens, R. (2016). Uneasy alliances: A look at the right-wing extremist movement in Canada. *Studies in Conflict & Terrorism*, *39*(9), 819–841.

Quandt, T. (2018). Dark participation. *Media and Communication*, *6*(4), 36–48.

Rafail, P., & Freitas, I. (2019). Grievance articulation and community reactions in the men's rights movement online. *Social Media+ Society*, *5*(2), 2056305119841387.

Rogers, A. E. (2020). Evil™—Islamic State, conflict-capitalism, and the geopolitical uncanny. In *"Who's afraid of ISIS?"* (pp. 118–135). Routledge.

Srnicek, N. (2017). *Platform capitalism*. John Wiley & Sons.

Statista. (2021, December 9). Number of monthly active WhatsApp users 2013–2020. https://www.statista.com/statistics/260819/number-of-monthly-active-whatsapp-users/

Stewart, N. K., Al-Rawi, A., Celestini, C., & Worku, N. (2023). Hate influencers' mediation of hate on telegram:" "We declare war against the anti-white system". *Social Media+ Society*, *9*(2), 20563051231177915.

Telegram. (2022). FAQ. https://telegram.org/faq

Tingley, D., & Wagner, G. (2017). Solar geoengineering and the chemtrails conspiracy on social media. *Palgrave Communications, 3*(1), 1–7.

Trujillo, M., Gruppi, M., Buntain, C., & Horne, B. D. (2020, July). What is BitChute? Characterizing the. In *Proceedings of the 31st ACM conference on hypertext and social media* (pp. 139–140).

Urman, & Katz, S. (2020). What they do in the shadows: Examining the far-right networks on Telegram. *Information, Communication & Society,* 1–20. https://doi.org/10.1080/1369118 X.2020.1803946

Uscinski, J. E. (2018). *Conspiracy theories and the people who believe them.* Oxford University Press.

Van Dijck, J., Poell, T., & De Waal, M. (2018). *The platform society: Public values in a connective world.* Oxford University Press.

Wimmer, R. D., & Dominick, J. R. (2013). *Mass media research.* New York: Cengage.

Zeng, J., & Schäfer, M. S. (2021). Conceptualizing "dark platforms". Covid-19-related conspiracy theories on 8kun and Gab. *Digital Journalism, 9,* 1–23.

4 Conclusion

There are varied groups that can be categorized based on their ideological backgrounds, with many Canadian Right Wing Extremism (RWE) groups having regional and transnational links to other RWE groups. Based on the combination of literature and research conducted, we have developed insights to better understand RWE groups in Canada, as well as highlight possible avenues for future research. As a means to explore conspiracy theories and better conceptualize their main components, we provide a historical, geographical, ideological, and conduit mapping of RWE (and their conspiracy discourses) in Canada. We present four main categories to cover the range of conspiracy theories including: topics, actors, targets, and concerns. This operationalization of conspiracy theories is useful in understanding their intentions and nature, and we hope that this type of conceptual mapping is a productive empirical tool for other researchers to examine how far-right actors participate within the full dark platform ecosystem.

We show how BitChute serves as an alternative video-hosting platform within the dark ecosystem, where far-right actors can freely spread conspiracies and hate. We used a manual content analysis approach to analyze the top 500 BitChute videos from a dataset of 35,153 videos in total, and we found the majority of these videos focused on spreading misinformation related to the COVID-19 pandemic, while also targeting prominent liberal figures such as Justin Trudeau.

As for Telegram, we used a mixed-methods approach, combining traditional content analysis as well as a digital method to analyze a dataset of 270,806 posts collected from 21 Canadian RWE channels. Our analysis illustrates a migration of RWE actors to Telegram as well as an increase in conspiratorial topics. Pandemic-related messages on Telegram represent the highest percentage of posts as well as views. Our manual assessment of the data illustrated a propensity of RWE actors to delegitimize the legitimate with everything from COVID-19 to technology and the Great Awakening.

Using manual reverse engineering, we found that Google searches and many traditional social media sites enable RWE groups to be mainstream by posting controversial hashtags that refer to conspiracies related to QAnon, such as #WWG1WGA, other conspiracies #TheGreatAwakening and #TheGreatReset, COVID-19 conspiracies, i.e., #CovidHoax, #Covod1984, and populism hashtags such as #MakeCanadaGreatAgain and #Canada1st. In terms of Google's subtitles

Conclusion 125

offered via its autocomplete feature, algorithms automate the search engines that people use in the functions of everyday life. but are also entangled in technological errors, and algorithmic bias, and have the capacity to mislead the public. Through a process of reverse engineering, we searched 37 conspiracy theorists to decode the Google autocomplete algorithms (Al-Rawi et al., 2022). We identified how the subtitles attributed to conspiracy theorists are neutral, and positive, but never negative, which does not accurately reflect the widely known public conspiratorial discourse these individuals propagate on the web. This is problematic because the algorithms that determine these subtitles are invisible infrastructures acting to misinform the public and mainstream conspiracies within larger social, cultural, and political structures. This study highlights the urgent need for Google to review the subtitles attributed to conspiracy theorists, terrorists, and mass murderers, to better inform the public about the negative nature of these actors, rather than always labelling them in neutral or positive ways.

We also found that some of the enablers include large companies. In the case of Amazon, its book section offers RWE members like Gavin McInnis and Lauren Southern platforms to promote and sell their books, which often contain hateful messaging and disinformation, especially targeting minorities.

In Chapter 3 and the Appendix, our study on alternative social media sites shows how dark social media platforms offer users an avenue to widely disseminate conspiracy theories. We refer to these information activities as dark participation because the main intention is to express hate, attack opponents, and spread disinformation. Alternative social media sites are rich platforms for dark participation because there is less content moderated than mainstream social media channels. Interestingly, the far-right group members often discuss being censored or deplatformed on other social media sites such as Twitter, Facebook, and Instagram, in addition to discussing alternative venues like podcasts that are used as their preferred dissemination tools. In other words, social media sites offer a space where far-right actors seek exile congregations in response to infrastructure ostracization on other social media platforms. Dark platforms allow the far-right to continue spreading their disinformation and hate without fear of censorship.

We also found that Rebel News plays a large role in discrediting and misrepresenting information related to the COVID-19 pandemic, often targeting Justin Trudeau and Doug Ford for their pandemic lockdown measures. Several of Rebel News' more popular BitChute videos (32,285 views combined) covered the quarantine hotels in Toronto, Ontario, likening them to prisoner isolation camps. Rebel News, however, freely posts its negative content on traditional social media outlets like YouTube; hence, alternative social media sites serve in amplifying content liberation and dark participation across platforms, even though sites like YouTube are still complicit in conspiratorial dissemination. Moreover, the funding solicitations on BitChute and elsewhere intertwine with concepts like platform capitalism (Srnicek, 2017) because fringe outlets provide a lifeline and alternative routes to economic survival.

We believe that our work fills a substantial gap in the literature by offering an empirical look at salient conspiratorial topics in Canada. The combination of lax moderation protocols and mass communication to users provides a safe haven for far-right actors to mobilize their followers to spread hate and misinformation without fear of legal repercussions. The technological affordances of alternative social media sites encourage dark social movements by the Canadian far-right. We highlight how the dissemination of these conspiracies cultivates dark social movements for members of the far-right to coordinate their activities, share similar ideas, and troll their opponents, especially liberals, immigrants, and anyone who does not fit their white supremacist ideology. These findings demonstrate how dark users actively diminish credible authorities and the broader implications that occur when disinformation gains traction and becomes increasingly mainstream. Delegitimization occurs across multi-modal formats including texts, emojis, and hashtags. Based on Mark Fenster's (1999) argument, the exclusion of extremists is a form of delegitimization of radicalism, creating an "Other" from the "normal" of mass society. This separation can lead to conspiracy theories that can be used by political movements to disrupt existing political parties and create new coalitions. Conspiracy theories can also be very valuable tools for populism to arise. The manual content analysis approach and the qualitative examination in combination with a digital method to analyze the whole dataset allowed us to better understand conspiracies on alternative social media sites. These conspiracy theories include those related to COVID-19 and technology, the Great Awakening, the Deep State and political polarization, #Savethechildren, and critical race and/or religion. A conspiratorial trend that we uncovered was the tendency of conspiracists to weave conspiracies into other ones.

The interwoven nature of conspiracies was particularly prevalent with COVID-19-related conspiracies. While conspiracies are timeless, there is also a degree of timeliness to them (Uscinski, 2018). Since COVID-19-based issues anchored around anti-lockdown, anti-mask, anti-vaccination, and anti-vaccination-passport policies, dark social movements pre-dating the pandemic pivoted in such a way as to co-opt or subvert these causes as their own (Amarasingam et al., 2021). Our findings show that COVID-19 conspiracies dominated discourse attempting to discredit lockdown measures, mask-wearing mandates, and vaccinations using fake experts. The 2022 Convoy protest was a clear example of how some online conspiracies were translated into offline action. For example, conspiracists often argue that fifth-generation (5G) technology spreads the COVID-19 virus and is a tool used by the evil cabal to enslave humanity. The third prominent conspiracy is the Great Awakening, which shows how conspiracies are rooted in politics and their tendencies to overlap with other ones.

RWE actors included subcategories like members of extremist groups, fake experts, and whistleblowers. This coding system is one we hope that researchers can use as a basis to analyze these mechanisms for creating fear-mongering, providing delineations of who is and is not a Canadian, and spreading distrust in government institutions for various nefarious goals. The power of RWE, conspiracy theories, moral panics, and populism "responses" to evoke social movements has become glaringly obvious in the convoy protest that occupied the nation's capital and various border crossings in early 2022. The use of fear, conspiracy theories, hate rhetoric, and the sowing of discontent and distrust in elected political leaders and the political process has had a significant impact on how Canadians understand themselves, their neighbors, and the country as a whole. Unfortunately, the convoy protest events led to an arguable increase in political polarization in Canada, some of which is caused by mainstream politicians like Justin Trudeau who once called the protesters a "fringe minority".

Interestingly, many phrases and topics used in our conspiracy theories' codebook were distinctly in use during the 2022 Freedom Convoys in Canada. While conducting our research on conspiracies and RWE, we watched the movement from social media posts to offline protests that left an indelible mark on Canada and inspired similar protests globally. The protestors came together occupying both the nation's capital in Ottawa, a border crossing between the United States and Canada in Coutts Alberta, as well as the Ambassador Bridge in Windsor, Ontario. The convoys were supported by some elected officials and politicians including MPP Randy Hillier, People's Party of Canada leader Maxime Bernier as well as other members of the Party, and by member of Parliament Andrew Scheer (Gillies et al., 2023, p. 2) Randy Hillier, an independent MPP in Ontario was vocally in support of the convoy protests, and released on official MPP letterhead that the protests were peaceful. Hillier also spoke in Ottawa at the protests, comparing their fight to that of soldiers at Vimy Ridge (Parkhill, 2022). In February 2022, Canadian Prime Minister Justin Trudeau invoked the Emergencies Act to end the "Freedom Convoy" protest. It was the first time the act was invoked since it was first introduced in 1988.

Some of the protesters who were arrested were linked to a group known as Diagolon. Diagolon envisions a white ethnostate diagonally across North America from Alaska to Florida. The group developed online by sharing antisemitic, far-right, anti-government memes (Hodge, 2022). The government of Canada has designated Diagolon as an anti-government group (Standing, 2022), and its founder, Jeremy MacKenzie, was in Ottawa at the convoys. The combination of the arrest and MacKenzie's involvement was stated as one of the reasons to support the invoking of the Emergencies Act. In addition, the Canadian Security Intelligence Service (CSIS) found that Diagolon supporter Alex Vriend had been fundraising to help transport protestors to both Ottawa and Coutts protests (Dryden & Grant, 2023).

While most individuals participating in the convoys were protesting the COVID-19 mandates, there were some leading individuals who believed in a number of conspiracies. The account below offers some details on James Bauder, Jason LaFace, Christopher Barber, BJ Dichter, Patrick King, Tom Quiggin, and Tamara Lich who were all influential in this movement.

Originally, the idea of the convoys came from James Bauder, his wife Sandra Bauder, and Martin Brodmann under a movement titled "Operation Bear Hug" organized by their group Canada Unity. Bauder has said that he began planning a convoy to Ottawa back in August of 2021 (POEC, V. 16, 2022). The initial idea was to create non-violent protests against the mandates. Prior to the convoys, Bauder had posted on his social media that the COVID-19 virus was a bioweapon created by China, and that George Soros, an individual at the center of numerous antisemitic conspiracy theories, was involved (Parkhill, 2022). On the Canada Unity website, a petition was posted calling for the end of the COVID mandates and in support of a memorandum of understanding (MOU) written by Bauder and Brodmann. The MOU called for the resignation of any elected official who supported mandates or vaccines. It also called for the Senate of Canada, the Governor General, and Canada Unity to form a government. It claimed that Canada Unity would be the "Representative of the People of Canada". In essence, Canada Unity was calling for a coup to overthrow the Canadian government, with the dissolution of the elected Liberal Party and installing themselves as the unelected government. The MOU was removed from the site in early February when researchers and members of the media began inquiring about its political aspects. Bauder posted a video in response claiming that he had hoped the MOU would trigger a referendum that would prompt Elections Canada to call for an election. This is not within the constitutional powers of Election Canada (Parkihill, 2022). The MOU also stated that if the MOU was agreed to, the convoy protest would end. When the convoys arrived in Ottawa, Bauder sent the MOU by registered mail to the Senate and the Governor General (POEC, V. 16, 2022). In the same video, Bauder made reference to the conspiracy theory that Dominion voting had changed the outcome of the 2020 US presidential election, and insisted the same machines would not be used in Canada, should an election be triggered by the convoys (Parkhill, 2022). Religion played a role in the Convoys as well, with Bauder claiming that when he was baptized, God told him to organize the convoys and go to Ottawa. He also claimed that the convoy was linked to the story of the city of Jericho in the Bible (POEC, V. 16, 2022). Canada Unity's website also hosted forums moderated by Jason LaFace. The latter, who also uses LaFaci, announced in 2020 that he planned to deface a Black Lives Matter (BLM) mural in Sudbury and called for others to join him via his social media accounts. In another social media post, LaFace posted a picture of himself wearing a jacket and baseball cap with the Soldiers Of Odin insignia as well as a recruitment image asking people to contact him to join (Antiracist, n.d.).

Christopher Barber, another convoy organizer, claimed that the idea for the convoys came from a discussion on TikTok with one of his followers in early January 2022. This follower eventually introduced Barber to the Bauders, and organizers Tamara Lich, and Patrick King. Barber's TikTok following prior to the convoy was around 30,000, and in mid-February 2022, it had grown to almost 170,000. His social media posts on TikTok and Facebook had been about the pandemic measures, primarily expressing his anger at what he perceived to be government overreach. Barber also had posted racist and anti-Islam posts prior to the convoys and had confederate flags hanging in the background of his TikTok videos, and when questioned, he said they were simply pieces of cloth and those offended needed to get over it. Using the social media accounts of various organizers, including Barber, the convoy planning, promotion, and organization took two weeks. The Bauders and Canada Unity had already been planning prior, and had the routes mapped out, and their website online (POEC, V. 14, 2022).

Another convoy organizer is BJ Dichter who once spoke at a 2019 People's Party of Canada convention to warn the audience about the dangers of "political

Islamists" and accused the Liberal Party of Canada of being "infested with Islamists". He also made an accusation that Islam was destroying Canadian society (Dichter, 2019). Lichter had previously run as a CPC MP candidate in a Toronto, Ontario riding in 2015 (Parkhill, 2022). In an interview on a Twitter Space livestream with RWE influencers Keean Bexte and Lauren Southern, Dichter, when asked about the presence of Confederate Flags at the protest in Ottawa, claimed he did not care (Parkhill, 2022). During the convoys, Dichter was interviewed by Tucker Carlson and Sean Hannity of Fox News, and on NewsMax, and podcast interviews with Gad Saad, Jordan Peterson, and Steven Crowder (POEC, V. 16, 2022).

As for Patrick King, he compared the COVID-19 mandates in a video posted on his social media to a systematic program to allegedly reduce the population of "the Caucasian race". In videos posted to his social media, King also called for the targeting of politicians' homes and said the only way to solve the issues being addressed by the convoys was through bullets. He discussed other conspiracies like the depopulation of the Anglo-Saxon race linked to the Great Replacement conspiracy theory and that Muslims plan to infiltrate the Western world via mass immigration and control the institutions of society to support the depopulation of whites (King, 2019). King was primarily a user of Facebook and Instagram, and between his website and Facebook, his live streams would have up to half a million followers/viewers. Having seen posts and discussions on social media about the planned convoys, King reached out to Chris Barber to become involved (POEC, V. 15, 2022).

Former security intelligence expert for the Canadian Centre for Intelligence and Security Studies, Tom Quiggin, acted as the self-proclaimed "protective intelligence" for the Ottawa convoy. Quiggin is known for being a proponent of anti-globalist conspiracy theories including the Great Reset. He is also the author of *The New Order of Fear*, a novel about the new world order globalists wish to create based upon Marxian totalitarianism (Parkhill, 2022). A January 28th Freedom Convoy 2022 group update, daily briefings sent out to convoy protestors in Ottawa, included references to the Great Reset, the involvement of Deputy Prime Minister and Finance Minister Chrystia Freeland's position on the World Economic Forum's Board of Trustees, and other "globalists" just as Bill Gates and President Xi of China. A similar reference was made in a February 8th, 2022 daily update (POEC, V. 14, 2022).

Finally, Tamara Lich has been a member of the Wildrose Party and the Maverick Party, as well as a regional coordinator, a member of the Board of Directors, and the Vice-President of Wexit[1] Canada (POEC, V. 16, 2022). In 2019, she also participated in the Yellow Vest[2] movement in Alberta and was an organizer of Yellow Vest rallies in Medicine Hat.[3] Lich was also the person who created the initial GoFundMe funding campaign on January 14th, 2022, and she provided an alternative email address for email money transfer donations to support the convoys. A GiveSendGo campaign was also attached to Tamara Lich's bank account, and almost $420,000 CAD was raised in email transfers to Lich's bank account (POEC, V. 16, 2022). Funds raised via email transfers for the Freedom Convoy and Adopt A

Truckers were 100% Canadian. The GoFundMe campaign was composed of 86% Canadian donors, but GiveSendGo donations were different in that donations for the Freedom Convoy were 59% from the United States, and 51% of the donations for Adopt a Trucker were American. Based on the actual value, an equal amount from the United States and Canada were raised, with 47% each, and other countries around the world constituted the remaining funds (POEC, V. 16, 2022).

Lich created the Freedom Convoy's fundraising campaign on the GoFundMe platform, with a description declaring the funds raised would assist with costs for fuel, food, and lodgings for the protestors. Any unused funds, according to Lich's description, would go to a veteran's organization chosen by the donors (POEC, V. 16, 2022). Concerns were flagged by the platform itself, that with the sheer number of donors no consensus could be reached as to what veteran's organization to donate to. They reached out to Lich and meetings were held for over a week. After these meetings, the platform released some of the money to Lich. To receive these funds, Lich and other organizers had to create a financial committee, and Chris Barber was added as a signatory to her bank account. A second bank account with both Lich and Barber was also created. The decision to release the funds was made on January 28th by the crowd-funding platform, but the money was only released until February 1st. During the time period between the decision and the funds' release, GoFundMe was made aware of media reports that some convoy protests were not peaceful, and a few unlawful acts were occurring. GoFundMe announced in February 2022 that it would cease payments to the organizers of the convoy after having already released 1 million dollars to the organizers, and it would refund all donors, due to the protest violating the site's terms of service on violence and harassment. This move by the crowd-funding platform led the convoy leader, Tamara Lich, to inform supporters to donate to a campaign started on the GiveSendGo platform.[4]

In addition to crowd funding and email transfers, the convoy organizers had access to a number of cryptocurrency campaigns. One attached to an "Adopt a Trucker" campaign, Pat King established a new cryptocurrency associated with a Freedom Convoy Token and the HonkHonk Hold campaign. The latter campaign had several people associated with it including Dichter, and it raised a total of 22 bitcoin, or an approximate value of $1.2 million CAD at the time of the convoys. About $800,000 of this was distributed (POEC, V. 16, 2022).

As for social media engagement, Al-Rawi found that Twitter posts were primarily focused on perceived social justice, freedom of movement, anti-mandates, and freedom of speech. The tweets expressed support for the Canadian Conservative Party, the People's Party of Canada, and the GOP in America including Donald Trump and his political base. The posts also expressed negativity toward legacy media, liberal governments, and Prime Minister Justin Trudeau. A smaller number of posts about the Convoys were linked to conspiracy theories and disinformation like using hashtags reflecting the Great Reset, Social Credit System, the Great Awakening, Queen of Canada, and save the children, conspiracy theories (Al-Rawi, 2022, p. 6). On Twitter, American right-wing influencers were found to hold the most liked messages regarding Convoy posts including individuals such as former actor and a well-known vocal right-wing social media user, Rob Schnieder and

Daily Wire's Candace Owens (Al-Rawi, 2022, p. 8). Users on Twitter who posted the most about the convoys were also found to have been posting disinformation on the pandemic, vaccines, and or on climate change (Al-Rawi, 2022, p. 14). Al-Rawi mentioned that the top ten most active users on Twitter posting about the Freedom Convoys included David Freiheit and Maxime Berner, the leader of and a political candidate for the People's Party of Canada. Another high-use poster was Andy Ngo, a vocal American conservative, who is also the editor of the Canadian far-right publication, *Post Millennial* (Al-Rawi, 2022, p. 15). On Facebook and Instagram, the most active posters about the Canadian convoys were supportive of the protests, including many American users. While they predominantly posted about American issues, the Canadian convoy protests positioned them as an inspiration (Al-Rawi, 2022, p. 16). On Instagram, conspiracy theories were more prevalent than content found on Facebook, with some users including hashtags on the Great Awakening, Save our children, and the QAnon phrase "WWG1WGA" (Al-Rawi, 2022, p. 18). As for Telegram, convoy-related posts were mostly requesting funding for the convoys through their GoFundMe page (Al-Rawi, 2022, p.24). On this platform, more references to conspiracy theories were found, including that Prime Minister Justin Trudeau is the illegitimate child of Margaret Trudeau and the Cuban leader Fidel Castro. Others were related to Queen Romana Didulo, the Great Reset, and other conspiracies related to Bill Gates (Al-Rawi, 2022, p. 25).

We believe that organizations such as Anti-Hate Canada, the Centre on Hate, Bias, and Extremism, and the Canadian Network for Research on Terrorism, Security, and Society (TSAS) working in tandem can play an integral role in providing expertise, research, and guidance on the harmful nature of some online content. However, more work needs to be done in the areas of disinformation, conspiracy theories, and extreme forms of nationalism. The propagation of nationalist tropes and disinformation is a conduit to the spreading of RWE beliefs, social movements, and anti-social dissent in society. Following this, we need to better understand the motives and recruitment strategies RWE groups use to spread ideas. It is also helpful to further investigate the economic relationships that make the RWE sustainable in Canada and the larger historical context in which these groups emerge. RWE groups and individuals have adapted their use of social media platforms, both mainstream and alternative, to both gain traction and create offline movements, as well as in some cases evade being labelled as an RWE or break the platforms' terms of services and be deplatformed. Their use of memes, emojis, online videos, images, and simple text-based posts is fashioned to present at times racist, violent, and misogynist messaging under a veneer of political critique and populist ideas. Recalling Brubaker (2006), these can be understood in terms of strategic group-making projects, which create an "Other" to blame for issues facing individuals who may not normally engage in with RWE messaging. As highlighted throughout this book, the nature of RWE and conspiracy theories ebbs and flows with social change. Economic change, perceived religious persecution or exclusion, cataclysmic events, and even global pandemics can lead to an increase in RWE recruitment and engagement. Development and adherence to conspiracy theories may also increase in such moments. An increase in perceived fear can impact the growth of RWE and conspiracy theories; hence, increased monitoring and awareness of internet activity can detect the growth in RWE groups and new influencers in these areas.

It is also important to explore the historical and current RWE groups within Canada to understand how their ideas and practices replicate in current and possibly future entities. The local contexts and historical trajectory of groups and the subsequent RWE that offshoot from original groups should not be taken lightly. While Canada First or the Ku Klux Klan (KKK) may not be visibly active in Canada today, it is clear the historical roots of hate organizations play a role in subsequent RWE groups in, for example, defining Canada or reproducing hierarchical approaches to race. In other words, studying the history of the groups can assist in understanding their current development and evolution. In the Canadian context, these must be rooted in the local contexts and conservative Christian history of the country. This may help guard against importing approaches to RWE that disregard local historical and practical realities.

Ironically, the Canadian government is actively trying to combat foreign interference in collaboration with other G7 countries, yet the discussions and debates are solely centered around nation-state roles, while regional and transnational RWE groups are not discussed even though these non-state foreign actors exert symbolic and cultural power and influence politics in Canada and vice versa. For example, RussiaToday, which is a news organization run by the Russian government, financially supported Tenet Media, a far-right news organizations in Canada. This organization is managed by Lauren Chen and Liam Donovan, frequently offering Lauren Southern a venue to spread her ideological messages (CBC News, 2024). In addition, Rebel News, which is one of the most active spreaders of misinformation in Canada (Al-Rawi & Fakida, 2023), has been instrumental in supporting far-right groups in Canada, the US, and the UK such as the case of favorably covering Tommy Robinson's anti-Islam activities.

While the deplatforming of unwanted RWE users on mainstream platforms has now become common, there has been relatively little research into understanding the scale, scope, and impact of deplatforming (Ali et al., 2021). While mainstream social media companies deplatforming terrorist groups such as ISIS drew the ire of free speech advocates in calling for the need for an effective international framework (Yu, 2018), deplatforming RWE groups is not a simple and straightforward matter. Deplatforming RWE groups from social media sites simply leads to the migration of these organizations to other platforms. This type of infrastructure ostracization is not necessarily the answer to nip the problem in the bud because it will be like playing a whack-a-mole game.

Others have found that deplatforming may have unintentional negative consequences (Ali et al., 2021; Aswad, 2018; Rogers, 2020). For example, Ali et al. (2021) in their examination of banned Reddit and Twitter users migrating to Gab found that the process itself further radicalized them. They note that in the case that they examined while banning the users may have decreased their ability to reach a wider audience, the banned users became more active online (Ali et al., 2021). Deplatforming of RWE users and groups is perceived as a form of censorship that provides alternative platforms such as Telegram, BitChute, Parler, Gab, and others a rhetorical edge in being able to advertise their services as being based on principles of "free speech".

Our findings show that deplatformed groups and individuals can and do circumvent current regulations on social media platforms. Individuals and groups can post the same material across numerous platforms, under various names and their content branding. Though alternative social media platforms and formats appear and disappear from time to time, the content posted by RWE groups/actors is relatively consistent across channels. The mediums used to provide their content are not simply deplatformed, as they can be accessed through podcast providers, the person's personal site, and from "fans" or group members reposting the content. Expansion of definitions of deplatformation is needed as well as punitive measures. As it currently stands, social media platforms may ban individual users, but not their content, which increases their reach. Deplatforming may also play into the conscious and strategic adoption of RWE groups and individuals as having "a marginalized position within society, following and defencing alternative rules and norms" (Campana & Tanner, 2014, p. 35). As stated above, deplatforming RWE groups/actors from social media platforms is often ineffective especially that it can be weaponized to present RWE members as victims of mainstream society and censorship. Deplatforming commonly results in platform migration to alternative sites, leading to discussions about the need to find better ways to govern hate speech.

Even though the United Nations' Universal Declaration of Human Rights protects the right of freedom of expression in Article 19, many countries limit certain forms of expression, including protections against hate speech (Walker, 2018, p. 1). Canada is no different with a variety of federal, provincial, and territorial restrictions on freedom of expression otherwise guaranteed in the Canadian Charter of Rights and Freedoms (Walker, 2018, p. 1). Hence, it is tempting to argue that clearer legislation will solve the problem of hate speech in Canada. In this framing, we could suggest the Canadian government to be more active in holding social media companies accountable for the content hosted on these sites, and fines must be implemented for any violations of the proposed legislations on hate speech, which may be one way forward. If this is to be proposed, further policy research is needed to look at what this would look like in actual practice, for defining where normal speech ends and hate speech begins is fraught with practical and legal difficulties.

The provisions themselves emerged in Canada in the 1960s after public organizations wanted laws to protect against hate speech publications in the context of a perceived growth in hateful publications (Kaplan, 1993). In the late 1950s, Canada did not have today's hate speech crimes but was experiencing an upsurge in hateful speech (Nesbitt, 2021, p. 51; Walker, 2018, p. 4). Some of which was a result of the country's proximity to U.S. hate groups such as the KKK, which was in the throngs of a revival in the age of the civil rights movement (Nesbitt, 2021, p. 51). With pressure on the Canadian government from civil society, such as the Jewish Congress, the Minister of Justice created the Special Committee to study hate propaganda (the Cohen Committee) in 1965 to study the problem of hate speech and come up with recommendations, which led to the criminalization of certain types of hate speech (Nesbitt, 2021, p. 51; Walker, 2018, p. 4). In 1970, after Pierre-Elliot Trudeau had become Prime Minister (a former Committee member), these recommendations were imputed to the Canadian Criminal Code by the addition of new offenses of advocating genocide (s. 318), public incitement of hatred likely to lead to a breach of the peace (s. 319(1)), and willful promotion of hatred (s. 319(2)) (see *R. v. Keegstra, 3 S.C.R. 697*, 1990). Under Section 318, a Rwandan immigrant was found guilty of advocating genocide and was sentenced in 2015 to deportation. Under section 319(2), a handful of cases have been pursued. Perhaps most famously, it was used in a Supreme Court case with James Keegstra (1934–2014). Keegstra was a public high school teacher in Eckville, Alberta, and was accused of promoting hatred against the Jewish people.

Today, hate promotion offenses can be found in sections 318 to 320 of the Canadian Criminal Code (Walker, 2018, p. 4). While an analysis of these laws is beyond the purview of this book, in his assessment of the function and assumptions of Canada's hate propaganda laws, Braun (2004) argues that they face a series of dilemmas in attempting to legally define the limits of speech and politically defend the practice of censorship. Moreover, it may provide a "slippery slope" for political use and abuse (Braun, 2004). As Nesbitt (2021) argues, the ways in which the laws are written require tremendous evidence from the part of prosecutors in order to ensure that there is no abuse of the laws which, in many cases, make it so that the charges are never filed in the first place.

In 2021, the Canadian federal government released a technical paper to propose a new framework for the Act of Parliament, which aimed to address harmful online content, and asked for community consultation (Government of Canada, 2021). The regulatory framework addressed issues of harm such as child trafficking and potential policies to regulate hate speech online. While a contentious topic, events such as the convoy protest are evidence of the harsh reality of offline results of online mobilization. While consultations have now concluded on the proposed Act, it is important that research continues in online RWE, hate speech, and conspiracy theories, and that policymakers and lawyers engage with consultations (as well as its findings) and that researchers continue to examine harmful online content, going beyond theoretical and absolutist discussions on free speech and the Charter of Rights.

In February 2024, Bill C-63, the Online Harms Act, was tabled in the House of Commons. The Act introduces a new legislative and regulatory framework, in an attempt to reduce harmful content on social media platforms (House of Commons, 2021; Canadian Heritage, 2024). The Bill covers a few areas that can directly affect RWE on social media such as content that instigates hatred or incites extremism or terrorism and violence. The Act will impose on social media platforms a duty to implement measures to mitigate risks for users to be exposed to harmful content (House of Commons, 2024). There are concerns regarding freedom of expression, especially in relation to how online hate can or should be defined in the first place.

In terms of practical legal mechanisms, it may also be the case that bringing users to account for "bad behavior" may inadvertently amplify their voice. Also worth recalling, as briefly discussed earlier, is the multiyear Canadian trials against Ernst Zündel, which allowed him to bring his own expert witnesses for testimony and gave him a platform to further spread his messaging, turning his trials into media events (Tingler, 2016). For example, the trial allowed Zündel to bring in "expert testimony" from holocaust deniers which gave them a platform to challenge other experts as if they were two sides of a debate rather than truth facing off with conspiratorial falsehoods. More recently, the Canadian RWE figure, Ezra Levant, used his experience responding to the Alberta Human Rights Commission for inciting hatred when he republished cartoon images of the prophet Mohammed to write a book that became a national bestseller (Walker, 2018, p. 13). It is also worth recalling that many mainstream social media platforms already engage in commercial censorship related to questions of copyright (Hilderbrand 2007; Clay, 2011) and other matters that are outlined in platform guidelines.

Under the guise of freedom of expression, we are witnessing today active mainstreaming of hate against Equity, Diversity, and Inclusion (EDI), indigenization, and immigration policies as well as sexual and gender minorities (SGM) often using universities as venues. For example, Lindsay Shepherd invited Ricardo Duchesne who runs the Council of European Canadians, a Euro Canadians group (https://www.eurocanadians.ca) as well as Faith Coldy for public talks at university campuses (CBC News, 2018; Chiose, 2018). Together with a few other like-minded people, Shepherd was soon after invited by a university professor from Simon Fraser University to talk about gender identity with a focus on transgender people on November 2, 2019. While these groups appropriate freedom of speech debates, they do not consider numerous other pro-social issues like anti-racist initiatives, equity, and human rights valid or worthy of discussions or attention because these causes do not align with their far-right ideologies. While such public talks followed the law during these talks, some of these figures publicly hold anti-immigration sentiments and often express hate and animosity against racialized people.

Moving away from more theoretical discussions, focusing solely on this "legal fix" approach may reduce the "problem of RWE" to simply being a matter of changing laws rather than engaging the actual terrain and experiences of people that make them identify with or organize around RWE values in online ecosystems.

A key observation here is a clear lack of designation or clarification assigned to so many RWE groups in Canada. In addition to the existence of government-led definitions for a public terrorist entity, there should also be a Canada "hate designation" system that is independently developed, monitored, and regularly updated within Canada. This would help avoid leaving so many RWE groups without any official or institutional designation. Though more initiatives are needed within Canada, Anti-Hate Canada working with the Southern Poverty Law Center (SPLC) has developed criteria for RWE and hate group designations based on human rights laws in Canada, which is of benefit to communities researching RWE in the country.

While heightened levels of governance and hate group designations make it easier to study RWE groups, it also encourages groups to disband, as is evidenced above with Proud Boys and the Soldiers of Odin. The designation of the Proud Boys as a terrorist group by the Canadian Government was unique in that this was the first time the government provided forewarning that they were going to do so. This allowed the Proud Boys to disband, and delete bank accounts, social media, and web sites, and any evidence of their actions. Normal procedures for listing a group as terrorist or hate groups do not include the public discussion prior to, as witnessed with the Proud Boys. The secretive nature of the designation prevents the groups from disbanding to evade law enforcement, media, researchers, and opponents of the movement; however, disbandment simply leads members to migrate to other violent groups or encourages the formation of new groups, as we see with the Canadian Infidels.

Finally, and returning to the problem of deplatforming RWE outlined earlier, there are contexts where deplatforming on one platform may inadvertently increase the awareness of and possible monetization of alternative platforms. This highlights the need for researchers to examine the conduits that make the spread of RWE possible. When YouTube purged some but certainly not all RWE users in 2018, actors migrated to BitChute and Rumble, profiting greatly in media attention and in an increase in users. This adds weight to Roger's (2020, p. 2) concern that when deplatforming social media celebrities they simply migrate to alternative platforms which "are given a boost through media attention and increases in user counts". In fact, the analytical term "platform" places an emphasis on the participatory opportunities of these technologies may further cloak the reality that these organizations are mere businesses. Despite this, many social platforms require user-generated content for their business model to be sustainable and profitable (Andrejevic, 2009), which adds to longstanding discussions on the benefits of approaching these companies in terms of technological platforms or as simply being publishers (Vadde, 2021). This definitional problem has a real impact on questions of governance and legalities.

There is no doubt that this book has numerous limitations. For example, our focus is on Canadian far-right groups, so it is necessary to compare them with other under-researched groups, such as those active in Australia and/or New Zealand in order to better understand the salience of topics, concerns, targets, and actors in RWE conspiracy theories. We believe that the increasing deplafromatization of far-right members from mainstream social media outlets makes it difficult to fully map the growing trajectory of conspiracy theories because these actors simply migrate to new emerging platforms. In other words, the study of conspiracy theories will evolve to fit the affordances of new social media sites, gaming platforms, cross-platform dissemination, and their varied moderation policies.

Because "conspiracy theories are often difficult to parse" (Chess & Shaw, 2015), more attention to the salience of conspiracy topics in Canada is needed across different sites. Future studies should look at a range of discourses (text, memes, images, emojis, etc.) and closely explore these conspiratorial topics on alternative platforms, like Rumble, Gettr, and Gab, which are frequented by the Canadian far-right. There is also a need to study conspiratorial topics by French-speaking RWE groups. Topics may need to be added or removed from the conceptualization as discourses evolve. Conspiracy theory as a mainstream phenomenon is a global concern, but given the lack of literature within this area, it is particularly important for further research to focus on conspiracy theories within the Canadian context.

Researching the national, and possibly international funding structures, of the RWE individuals and groups in Canada is an area for further research. The means by which they fundraise has evolved as substantially as their online promotion. Things have changed substantially from RWE reliance on event fees and merchandising sales in the digital world (Keatinge et al., 2019, p. 18). While mainstream online payment processing companies such as PayPal, Apple Pay, and Google Pay have increasingly declined to process payments made to RWE blogs and websites (Keatinge et al., 2019, p. 19), cryptocurrencies and crowdfunding sites such as GiveSendGo provide alternative funding opportunities for RWE that are difficult to trace. Further collaboration is needed with researchers such as RWE scholars and programming professionals to understand the fundraising opportunities presented to RWE groups and individuals. Indeed, studying the funding sources for RWE groups and individuals proved difficult in this project. It is recommended that relationships between government agencies, universities, and think tanks be developed to assist in further researching the significant funding behind RWE groups and individuals. Such analytical tools would allow researchers to understand the role of foreign investors in political and social movements in Canada, and provide transparency in the role of financial backers within alternative media companies, RWE influencers, and extremist Canadian groups.

Notes

1 Wexit is a movement for western provinces to exit the nation of Canada.
2 The Yellow Vest (Gilets jaunes) movement was an offshoot of a European movement. In Canada, the group supported oil and gas investments, and was anti-immigration, and xenophobic. In January 2019, the Gilets jaunes du Québec (GJQ) Facebook page called for a protest against the Trudeau Government, which resulted in a 20-person protest. Among those members, La Presse found many known members of La Meute at the protest and discovered that the chosen location for the protest was a site owned by a La Meute member (Gruda, 2019). GJQ has not been deplatformed on social media sites. The largest Gilets Jaunes Quebec Facebook page (glquebec) had a little over 2k members in January 2019 (Gruda, 2019) and over 2,000 members in January 2022. The page is still open but not that active. It also requires an email verification before being allowed to join the group. On January 14, 2022, the smaller GJQ Facebook page (giletsjaunesduquebec) had almost 1,300 followers with its last post occurring on June 26, 2021. The GJQ began protesting every month in front of the TVA building in Montréal, owned by the Quebecor Media group, to denounce the network's allegedly biased journalism (Montréal Antifasciste, 2020). An anti-fascist organization found members from Storm Alliance, Front Patriotique du Québec (Patriotic Front of Quebec), and the owner of the Les Manchettes French-language RWE conspiracy "news" website present at GJQ TVA protests (Montréal Antifasciste, 2019).
3 The Yellow Vest group in Medicine Hat had to eventually change its name after Prime Minister Trudeau received death threats from the Yellow Vest Canada movement (POEC, V. 16, 2022).
4 GiveSendGo was also the crowd-funding platform used by those involved in the events on Capitol Hill on January 6th, and this involvement led PayPal to block the site from payments by users. Prior to the shut down by GoFundMe the convoys had garnered 120,000 donors and had raised almost 10.1 million dollars (Boisvert, 2022), while the GiveSendGo account had raised $12.4 million CAD (POEC, V. 16, 2022).

References

Al-Rawi, A., & Fakida, A. (2023). The methodological challenges of studying "fake news". *Journalism Practice, 17*(6), 1178-1197.

Al-Rawi, A. (2022, December). *An empirical assessment of the convoy protest on six online sites*. Public Order Emergency Commission (POEC), Government of Canada. https://publicorderemergencycommission.ca/files/exhibits/COM00000864.pdf?t=1669938874

Al-Rawi, A., Celestini, C., Stewart, N., & Worku, N. (2022). How Google autocomplete algorithms about conspiracy theorists mislead the public. *M/C Journal, 25*(1). https://doi.org/10.5204/mcj.2852

Ali, S., Saeed, M. H., Aldreabi, E., Blackburn, J., de Cristofaro, E., Zannetou, S., & Stringhini, G. (2021). Understanding the effect of deplatforming on social networks. In *Proceedings of the ACM Web Science Conference*, 1–9. https://doi.org/10.1145/3447535.3462637

Amarasingam, A., Carvin, S., & Phillips, K. (2021). Anti-lockdown activity: Canada country profile. *ISD*. Available online at: https://www.isdglobal.org/wp-content/uploads/2021/12/Anti-lockdown-canada-ISD.pdf (last accessed at: 010323).

Andrejevic, M. (2009). Exploiting YouTube: Contradictions of user-generated labor. *The Youtube Reader, 413*(36), 406–423.

Antiracist Sudbury. (n.d.) Soldiers of Odin gain a member. Retrieved from https://antiracistsudbury.com/2020/05/07/soldiers-of-odin-lose-a-member-gain-a-member/

Aswad, E. M. (2018). The future of freedom of expression online. *Duke Law & Technology Review, 17*(1), 26–70.

Boisvert, N. (2022, February 4). GoFundMe ends payments to convoy protest, citing reports of violence and harassment. *CBC News*. https://www.cbc.ca/news/politics/gofundme-stops-payments-1.6340526

Braun, S. (2004). *Democracy off balance: Freedom of expression and hate propaganda law in Canada*. Toronto: University of Toronto Press.

Brubaker, R. (2006). *Ethnicity without groups*. Cambridge: Harvard University Press.

Campana, A., & Tanner, S. (2014). The radicalization of right-wing Skinheads in Quebec. *TSAS: Canadian Network for Research on Terrorism, Security and Society*, No. 14-07. https://doi.org/10.13140/2.1.5093.5681

Canadian Heritage. (2024). Proposed bill to address online harms. Retrieved from https://www.canada.ca/en/canadian-heritage/services/online-harms.html

CBC News. (2018, April 23). Laurier won't censor speech, says draft statement on free expression. CBC. https://www.cbc.ca/news/canada/kitchener-waterloo/laurier-university-freedom-expression-lindsay-shepherd-1.4631756

CBC News. (2024, September 6). Meet the right-wing Canadian influencers accused of collaborating with an alleged Russian propaganda scheme. https://www.cbc.ca/news/investigates/russian-influence-election-tenet-media-chen-southern-1.7314976

Chess, S., & Shaw, A. (2015). A conspiracy of fishes, or, how we learned to stop worrying about #GamerGate and embrace hegemonic masculinity. *Journal of Broadcasting & Electronic Media, 59*(1), 208–220.

Chiose, Simona. (2018, April 26). Campaign against campus appearance by far-right activist Faith Goldy raises over $12,000. The Globe and Mail. Retrieved from https://www.theglobeandmail.com/canada/article-campaign-against-campus-appearance-by-far-right-activist-faith-goldy/

Clay, A. (2011). "Blocking, tracking, and monetizing: YouTube copyright control and the downfall parodies". In *The Video vortex reader II: Moving images beyond YouTube*.

Dichter, B. J. (2019, August 19). Shocking, courageous, honest speech at the PPC convention in Quebec by Benjamin Dichter. https://www.youtube.com/watch?v=-ct-kwjHS38

Dryden, J., & Grant, M. (2023, February 17). Border protests in Coutts, Alta., a concrete manifestation of risk to Canada: Rouleau. *CBC News*.

Fenster, M. (1999). *Conspiracy theories: Secrecy and power in American culture*. University of Minnesota Press.

Gillies, J., Raynauld, V., & Wisniewski, A. (2023). Canada is no exception: The 2022 freedom convoy, political entanglement, and identity-driven protest. *American Behavioral*.

Government of Canada. (2021, February 3). Canada gazette, Part 2, Volume 155, Number 2: Regulations amending the regulations establishing a list of entities. https://www.gazette.gc.ca/rp-pr/p2/2021/2021-02-03-x2/html/sor-dors8-eng.html

Government of Canada. (2021, July 29). Technical paper – Canada.ca. Technical Paper. https://www.canada.ca/en/canadian-heritage/campaigns/harmful-online-content/technical-paper.html

Gruda, A. (2019, January 14). Les «gilets jaunes» québécois se réunissent à Victoriaville. *La Presse*. https://www.lapresse.ca/actualites/regional/201901/13/01-5210898-les-gilets-jaunes-que-becois-se-reunissent-a-victoriaville.php

Hilderbrand, L. (2007). "YouTube: Where cultural memory and copyright converge". *Film Quarterly*, 61(1), 48–57.

Hodge, E. (2022). Online networks of hate: Cultural borders in aterritorial spaces. *Borders in Globalization Review*, 4(1), 79–82. https://doi.org/10.18357/bigr41202221162

House of Commons. (2021). Bill C-36. Retrieved from https://www.parl.ca/DocumentViewer/en/43-2/bill/C-36/first-reading

House of Commons. (2024). Bill C-63. Retrieved from https://www.parl.ca/DocumentViewer/en/44-1/bill/C-63/first-reading

Kaplan, W. (1993). Maxwell Cohen and the report of the special committee on hate propaganda. *Law, policy, and international justice: Essays in honour of Maxwell Cohen*, 243–274.

Keatinge, T., Keen, F., & Izenman, K. (2019). Fundraising for right-wing extremist movements: how they raise funds and how to counter it. *The RUSI Journal*, 164(2), 10–23.

King, Pat. (2019, August 9). Twitter video. https://twitter.com/VestsCanada/status/1159997274900041729

Montréal Antifasciste. (2019, April 8). Report back on the March 16 solidarity vigil/counter-demo in Montréal. *Montréal Antifasciste Info*. Retrieved from https://montreal-antifasciste.info/en/2019/04/08/report-back-on-the-march-16-solidarity-vigil-counter-demo-in-montreal/

Montréal Antifasciste. (2020, May 9). 2019 In review. *Montréal Antifasciste Info*. Retrieved from https://montreal-antifasciste.info/en/2020/05/09/2019-in-review/

Nesbitt, M. (2021). Violent crime, hate speech or terrorism? How Canada views and prosecutes far-right extremism (2001–2019). *Common Law World Review*, 50(1), 38–56.

Parkhill, M. (2022, February 22). Who is who? A guide to the major players in the trucker convoy protest. *CTV News*. https://www.ctvnews.ca/mobile/canada/who-is-who-a-guide-to-the-major-players-in-the-trucker-convoy-protest-1.5776441?cache=?clipId=89531

Public Order Emergency Commission. (2022, November 1). Public Hearing, Volume 14.

Public Order Emergency Commission. (2022, November 2). Public Hearing, Volume 15.

Public Order Emergency Commission. (2022, November 3). Public Hearing, Volume 16.

R. v. Keegstra, 3 S.C.R. 697 (Supreme Court Judgment December 13, 1990). https://scc-csc.lexum.com/scc-csc/scc-csc/en/item/695/index.do

Rogers, R. (2020). Deplatforming: Following extreme internet celebrities to telegram and alternative social media. *European Journal of Communication*, 35(2), 02673231209220206.

Srnicek, N. (2017). The challenges of platform capitalism: Understanding the logic of a new business model. *Juncture*, 23(4), 254–257.

Standing Committee on Public Safety and National Security. (2022, June). The rise of ideologically motivated violent extremism in Canada. https://publications.gc.ca/collections/collection_2022/parl/xc76-1/XC76-1-1-441-6-eng.pdf

Tingler, J. (2016). Holocaust denial and holocaust memory: The case of Ernst Zündel. *Genocide Studies International*, *10*(2), 210–229.

Uscinski, J. E. (2018). *Conspiracy theories and the people who believe them*. Oxford University Press.

Vadde, A. (2021). Platform or publisher. *PMLA*, *136*(3), 455–462.

Walker, J. (2018). *Hate speech and freedom of expression: Legal boundaries in Canada* (Publication No. 2018-25-E). Library of Ottawa.

Yu, J. (2018). Regulation of social media platforms to curb ISIS incitement and recruitment: The need for an international frame- work and its free speech implications. *Journal of Global Justice and Public Policy*, *4*(1), 1–29.

Appendix
RWE sites

The Appendix provides an overview of how right-wing extremist groups use and rely on a variety of digital platforms and other digital sites. In addition to covering Telegram and BitChute in Chapter 3, the analysis of social media platforms here includes mainstream sites such as Twitter Facebook, YouTube, and Instagram, as well as other alternative platforms such as Gab, Discord,[1] Getter,[2] Rumble,[3] Tumblr,[4] and 4chan. Other online sites like the Google search engine and the Dark Web are also included, and all the entries in this Appendix are listed alphabetically.

Deplatforming users have historically been the norm, but, more recently, scholars argue it limits understanding of how online cultures form and propagate on fringe platforms (Trujillo et al., 2020). In 2019, Facebook deplatformed groups and individuals "engaged in promoting hate, including Faith Goldy, Kevin Goudreau, Canadian Nationalist Strikeforce, Wolves of Odin, and the Soldiers of Odin (also known as Canadian Infidels)" (CBC News, 2021). While most far-right groups/actors were deplatformed by Facebook/Meta in 2019, the platform only deleted Quebec's far-right group Atalante Quebec in 2021 (CBC News, 2021). As of early February 2022, the Facebook group for La Meute was still active, though experts have deduced that Facebook may lack the "necessary language skills needed to identify accounts circulating extremist content in Quebec" (CBC News, 2021).

We wanted to ensure we had a mixture of mainstream and alternative, and a diversity of mediums; therefore, the work below represents an analysis of video, text-based, visual mediums, and forums. Various digital tools were used to download the data and analyze it. We catered our research methods and analysis techniques to the different objects of study. We generally classified these sites into three main categories: alternative Social Networking Sites (SNS), mainstream SNS, and other sites.

A1 Alternative SNS sites

A1.1 4chan

4chan was founded in 2003 by then 15-year-old Christopher Poole, better known through his online handle, "moot". The original purpose of the imageboard website was to be a space where anime was the primary topic of discussion. It soon expanded to be a wide range of topics including politics and webcamming. 4chan is the place where memes and viral ideas such as Lolcats and rickrolling, an online prank in which a clickbait title would lead to a clip from the Rick Ashley video for "Never Going to Give You Up", initiated. According to the social media company, it has over 30 million unique visitors monthly. According to 4chan data, these unique visitors post on average 900,000–1,000,000 posts per day. The average user is between the ages of 19–34, and 70% of users are male, with the majority of users from the United States (47%) with a much smaller percentage of Canadian users (4%). The majority of users are currently enrolled in college or have attended college (4chan, 2021a). The rules governing posts are broad and hate speech is not even defined, while "racism" is theoretically not allowed in posts outside of /b/ threads (4chan, 2021b).

With its relatively simple interface, the site allows users to post threads via image and/or text, and to reply to the threads. There is no registration process for 4chan, so the level of anonymity allows users to be anonymous, even across numerous threads and boards. Users are referred to as 'anons', short for anonymous, due to this. The posts and threads on 4chan are not automatically archived and the rate of user post turnover is very quick (Fathallah, 2021).

Known for its content, users engage with humour and memes to propagate right-wing and extremist views. 4chan is also the originator of the interconnected conspiracies of Pizzagate and QAnon. Pizzagate originated on 4chan boards and soon spread to other online platforms such as InfoWars, Reddit, YouTube, Twitter, and Facebook (de Zeeuw et al., 2020). In 2014, 4chan along with Reddit became well known due to Gamergate, an online harassment campaign against women in computer gaming. Gamergate consisted of elements mixing traditional attributes of right-wing extremism and misogyny. The main board used by extremists and conspiracists is /pol/ (politically incorrect) (Conway et al., 2019).

Q also initially began on 4chan's /pol/ board where users began to expect Q to post "drops" of information. The conspiracy soon spread from the confines of an online /pol/ board to becoming a mainstream newsworthy concern. In this way, other RWE can be interpreted as having become a source of broader cultural engagement through the use of memes and inclusion of "youth culture" symbols and language (Bouko et al., 2021).

As has been noted, content on digital platforms don't simply become 'viral' and are passed passively along networks but also may generate further participation and content production from users who may engage the material through a variety of means, from spoofing to creating memes (Burgess, 2008).

In addition, as mentioned earlier, RWE groups have adapted to the banning of language to avoid violating terms of service or hate speech policies on social media sites. Through the use of these "cloaking strategies", extremist material is allowed to remain on these sites. This cloaking provides a sanitized version of their material. This sanitization is created through the use of humour rendering harmful material as "fun" or "harmless" rather than extreme or violent (Bouko et al., 2021). This results in problematic and often "cloaked" but nevertheless hateful material being easily shareable.

Appendix: RWE sites   143

These "cloaking strategies" do not mean they are without potential dire consequences. On April 23, 2018, Alek Minassian, a self-described Incel, drove a rented van down a sidewalk in Toronto targeting women pedestrians, killing 10 people and injuring 16 others. Eight of those killed were women. Incels, also known as involuntary celibates, are a community of people who believe they have been rejected by women and often voice their angst and desires for revenge on the internet, including 4chan (Regehr, 2020). While linking the spread of online material as being the cause of offline behavior is fraught with difficulties, Regehr (2020) argues that the Incel community on 4chan uses humour, video content, and fan art to normalize "extreme anti-feminism and mass violence". In fact, Minassian met and engaged with Elliot Rodger, the perpetrator of the 2014 Isla Vista killings, on 4chan, as well as with Chris Harper-Mercer who killed nine people and injured eight in Oregon in 2015 (Regehr, 2020). Prior to the attack, Minassian posted on 4chan and Facebook (Hoffman et al., 2020).

Regarding Canadian RWE content on 4chan, we could not find any specific active community or a large amount of recent relevant content. We found, instead, a limited number of unrelated Canadian content in the "International" and "Weapons" boards. The site is popular for gaming, dark memes, porn, and artistic content from Canada and elsewhere in the world. Further, the Q origins research project (https://dchan.qorigins.org)/ has archived some old 4chan posts in relation to the conspiracy group, QAnon. However, there is little evidence of enhanced Canadian activity.

A1.2   8kun

8kun was created in November 2019 after the fall of the 8chan imageboard and was known as a more extreme version of 4chan. It was created after the founder of 4chan, Christopher Poole, banned GamerGate discussions on the boards. Fredrik Brennan, a user of 4chan, saw this as an opportunity and created 8chan. He used GamerGate as a catalyst, promising his users that there would be less moderation, and that alone cemented the site as a safe haven for right-wing extremists (RWEs). By 2014, 8chan had grown from 100 posts a day to 5,000 per hour (Conway et al., 2019). 8chan was removed from the internet following Brenton Tarrant's attack on two mosques in Christchurch, New Zealand in 2019.

Tarrant used 8chan and posted a manifesto and links to a live Facebook feed on the site prior to the attack. Two months following this attack, two shooters, John Earnest and Patrick Crusius, followed Tarrant's steps and posted their manifestos on the imageboard (Baele et al., 2021). Earnest killed a woman in a synagogue in Poway California in April of that year, and Crusius killed 22 people in a mass shooting in a Walmart in El Paso, Texas. Both Earnest and Conway made references to the racist theory of the "great replacement" in their manifestos (Conway et al., 2019). The great replacement theory is a white nationalist conspiracy theory that cultures other than whites will replace white people both culturally and demographically through immigration and a drop in birth rates among white people. After Crusius's attack, 8chan shut down (Baele et al., 2021). Currently,

8kun's imageboard allows users to post text and images. 8kun, unlike 4chan or 8chan, does not have a /pol/ board. Instead, Brennan created a /qresearch/ board which was dedicated to the QAnon conspiracy theory, and 8kun became one of the main sources for posts from the conspiracy theorist "Q" to their followers (Zeng & Schäfer, 2021). Some of the most popular boards are /qresearch/(QResearch), /pnd/ (Politics, News, Debate), and /qrb/ (QResearch Bunker), which collectively had 15,750,753 posts as of early December 3, 2021.

Regarding this study, we searched for relevant Canadian issues using an automated search option. Specifically, we searched the following four relevant conspiracy boards: "/ qresearch/", "/pnd/", "/qpatriotresearch/", and "/qresearch-2gen/". The search was conducted from November 20, 2019, when 8kun was created until December 3, 2021. We used 38 search terms representing different Canadian issues, figures, and places. This resulted in a data pool of 64,482 relevant posts. We deployed Python software to process the over 14 million words of the posts to extract the most recurrent terms and phrases (Al-Rawi & Shukla, 2020). As expected, the board /qresearch/ contained most of the relevant posts (n = 62,934).

The digital analysis shows that the major issue discussed is COVID-19 (n = 21,403) followed by vaccine (n = 11,018). Though the search focused on Canadian issues, we found that the most referenced figures are actually US politicians starting with Trump (n = 18,532) and Biden (n = 16,961). There was also a focus on the 2020 US presidential election and Trump's indictment.

As will be shown below, the site is popular with the use of 'dank' (potently viral) memes as this word was among the 30 most used terms (n = 14,298) especially in relation to USMCA memes (United States, Mexico, and Canada Trade Agreement) (see below), Pardon Flynn memes as well as memes ridiculing and attacking Kamala Harris, Hunter Biden, and Joe Biden. In fact, one of the most recurrent phrases used is "meme warfare operations" (n = 1,937).

As of early December 2021, the top Canadian board on 8kun is /canada/ (https://8kun.top/canada/index.html), which had 4,156 posts that mostly engaged RWE issues. To retrieve the data, we downloaded all the relevant posts and analyzed the textual messages found on this board because most of the multimedia files were removed by the platform using the label 'JOIN or 404'.

Since the posts are relatively limited, our subsequent insights on this board were limited in the face of a great deal of spamming. For example, one of the most recurrent phrases on the board is "Hail Hitler" (n=178) because this was mostly used by a few users and repeatedly posted in a long series of messages. One user, for example, mentioned the following: "Canada: Its time for Nazi Basketbakk", "Canadian/ OUR SPORT, WHITES ONLY, HAIL HITLER !", and "OUR MASCOT WILL BE THE NAZI CARE BEAR WITH A BASKETBALL, HAIL HITLER !".

There is obviously a pun in the use of the first basketball word to indirectly refer to The Ku Klux Klan (KKK). Another popular phrase is "MEET MORE RED-PILLED PPL" (n = 37), which references conservative users as being "redpilled". In general, 8kun seems to be a site for posting memes with a clear polarized and hateful nature. For example, one user posted the following:

A Thread for Propaganda Memes designed to get Canadians to Take Out the Trash.

- Anti-Immigration memes
- Anti-Refugee memes
- Anti-Liberal (Wynne, Trudeau, etc.) memes
- Anti-Religion of Cuck™ memes Spread any at any opportunity you can.

A1.3 Gab

When logging into Gab, users are greeted with the words "Welcome to Gab. A social network that champions free speech, individual liberty, and the free flow of information online. All are welcome" (Gab, 2020). The focus on free speech and individuality has to be understood in the context of the banning of prominent right-wing and extremist personalities from popular social media sites such as Twitter, Facebook, and YouTube. In fact, the founding of Gab itself was in response to deplatforming.

Initially founded in August 2016, (Zannettou et al., 2018) Gab saw an increase in users during the presidential election that year, but since then the platform's users have reflected a more globalized and diverse membership base (Jasser et al., 2021, p. 1735). Gab has similar functionalities to Twitter, with users making posts and others able to like, share, or comment on the posts. The site also supports hashtags and the @function to tag users. Lima et al. (2018) analyzed Gab users and their posts when the platform first emerged. They found that the users were predominately white, conservative, males and the researchers were able to identify many of the Gab users as those who were listed as extremists by other social media platforms (Lima et al., 2018, p. 1). Gab initially was an invite-only platform, and four months after going online, the site had a waitlist of over 130,000 people (Kor-Sins, 2021, p. 2).

Gab marketed its platform as a "free speech alternative" as right-wing celebrities such as Milo Yiannopolous and Richard B. Spencer were banned for their hate speech on mainstream media (Kor-Sins, 2021, p. 2). The banning of right-wing and white nationalist accounts shortly after the election of former President Trump led to some conservatives articulating that they felt censored on popular social media platforms. There were calls that the deplatforming of conservative voices was undemocratic and was against freedom of speech. As Gab emerged as one of the "free speech" platforms, using a green frog as its icon many associated this logo with the white nationalist Pepe the Frog (Kor-Sins, 2021, p. 7). When it was discovered that a mass-shooter in Pittsburgh in 2018, had posted anti-Semitic material, Gab's web-hosting platform removed Gab. Within a week, Gab was back online with another hosting company (Kor-Sins, 2021, p. 7).

Content policy on the site forbids members from posting pornography but there is no specific policy regarding hate speech. Gab's directive towards offensive speech is to reiterate the importance of the First Amendment of the United States Constitution, and to encourage users to be "cordial and civil" (Gab TOS,

2020) This adherence to the First Amendment and non-regulation of language or posts have allowed the social media site to characterized as a far-right or extremist social media platform. For example, McIlroy-Young and Anderson (2019, p. 2) in their analysis of Gab posts found that the topics were predominately politically based and included anti-Semitic terms. Additionally, Zannettou et al. found in their research that Gab is used for sharing and discussing news and world events, but it also attracts far-right users and conspiracists (Zannettou et al., 2018, p. 1). Since its inception, Gab has welcomed those who have been banned from other social media sites, even those for hateful conduct and racist language. As those who study Gab social media have found that there is a high level of hate speech and racism. The freedom in which this language goes unmonitored and unconstrained on this platform led both Google and Apple to ban the Gab mobile app from their stores in 2017 (Zannettou et al., 2018. p. 1). Gab does not rely on advertising for monetization. Instead, Gab is monetized through user donations and the purchase of "pro" accounts. A pro account gives the user access to additional features such as live-stream broadcasts, account verification, extended character count, and formatting of posts, all for a monthly fee (Gab Pro., 2022).

On Gab, we found hundreds of Canadian RWE users. There were also some users who employed collective usernames such as: @ Bringbackcanada1, @Canada1stPartyofCanada, @AwakenCanada, @The_Myth_is_Canada, and @Keep_Canada_Free.

To better understand Gab, we used 11 hashtag searches in early December 2021 including:

#CanadaQanon,
#CDNqanon,
#QanonCanada,
#qanonCDN,
#CandianPatriots,
#WWG1WGAcanada,
#CanadaWWG1WGA,
#Canada1st,
#CanadaFirst,
#MCGA,
#MakeCanadaGreatAgain.

In this respect, we used a Python script to programmatically collect the data having in mind that there is no official API access. The total number of Gab posts we collected was 2,424. As can be seen in Table 5.1, most of the top 20 most-used hashtags indicate support for RWE causes and support for Maxime Bernier's People's Party of Canada (PPC).

Interestingly, the most mentioned users are @faithgoldy (n = 1,695), @awakencanada (n = 1,074), @peoplespca (n = 1,074), and @grain_of_truth (n = 198).

Table 5.1 The most recurrent hashtags

No	Hashtags	Count
1	#texasfirst	1,791
2	#communistsupremacy	1,694
3	#mcga	1,370
4	#cdnpoli	1,297
5	#ppc	1,171
6	#maximebernier	1,118
7	#madmax	1,103
8	#berniernation	1,080
9	#recrucifixion	1,074
10	#bernier2019	1,074
11	#liesfirst	1,074
12	#canadafirst	866
13	#reddemocracy	422
14	#canada	251
15	#openborders4israel	220
16	#freespeech	212
17	#toronto	205
18	#faithformayor	198
19	#swallowredpill	198
20	#makecanadagreatagain	182

Source: Created by the authors.

A further search completed on hashtags found very few relevant posts. Follow-up analysis of hashtag use on the platform found very few users including Canadian-specific hashtags but choosing instead to use more universal hashtags such as #QAnon, #StopTheLockDowns, and #TwoTierSociety. Some of the users included provincial hashtags, but when analyzing these we found a mixture of posts including anti-vaccine mandates, anti-COVID, cottage pictures, and tourism.

A1.4 Parler

Parler was launched in 2008 as an alternative social media site to Twitter (Munn, 2021), and to a lesser extent, other traditional platforms like Facebook and Instagram. The perception among some conservative and right-wing Twitter users was that Twitter was shadow-banning their tweets (Kelsey, 2018). Shadow banning is the process of limiting viewers of posts. At the time of Parler's launch, many mainstream social media platforms were under pressure to regulate and moderate their content; many users were blocked, suspended, or banned from the sites, and in doing so, the time period became known as "the Great Purge" to deplatform extremists and controversial figures. To counter this perceived censorship, Parler became the "free speech" social media site for these affected users. The new social media site promised its users that they would never be censored.

Table 5.2 Some of the popular hashtags on Parler

#canadalockdown	#WAKEUP-CANADA	#WakeUpCanada	#trudeaufailedcanada	#SaveCanada
#savecanada	#canada1st	#CanadaFirst	#godblesscanada	#covidcanada
#canada1stparty	#canadafortrump	#corruptcanada	#freecanadafromt	#makecanadagreat
#peoplespartyofcanada	#kanada	#kanadahasfallen	#incovidiankkkanda	#kkanada

Source: Created by the authors.

Parler's headquarters is in Henderson, Nevada, USA, and was initially created as a social media site allegedly "built on a foundation of respect for privacy and personal data, free speech, free markets and ethical, transparent corporate policy" (Parler, 2021). Parler's community guidelines state that while the First Amendment does not apply to private companies its platform has a mission to "create a social platform in the spirit of the First Amendment to the United States Constitution" (Parler Guidelines, 2021). As such, Parler does not provide a hate speech policy. It does prohibit users from posting content that is a "tool for crime, civil torts, or other unlawful acts" (Parler Guidelines, 2021). The community guidelines governing the platform also state that the company will not curate content on the site, instead offering muting or blocking functions that allow users to curate their own social media feed (Parler Guidelines, 2021).

Similar to Twitter, users post "parleys" that are capped at 1,000 characters. Users can comment and vote (like) parleys posted by those they follow. Each user has their own news feed where they interact with others and can comment, echo (share the material on their own account), and search for hashtags and other users. Many right-wing individuals soon established their presence on the new platform as did groups such as the Proud Boys and the Boogaloo movement. For example, many of the individuals involved in the January 6th uprising at Capitol Hill posted onsite videos on Parler due to its connection to this event. As a result, Amazon Web Services terminated its web hosting services and Apple and Android phone providers stopped hosting the app (Munn, 2021). After the deplatforming of Parler, many users shifted to other social media platforms, including Rumble and Gab. In February of 2021, Parler returned online, but not to a phone app (Baines et al., 2021).

While writing this book, the website of Parler was no longer stable and its public API was not working, so no bulk data download was possible. We, however, manually examined the site for any relevant content as many controversial figures are actively present on the site. Our manual examination of the site found hashtags that addressed the COVID-19 pandemic and the Canadian preventative measures, such as lockdowns and hashtags regarding the political parties vying for the Federal election. Examples include the following (Table 5.2).

A1.5 Reddit

Before the widespread migration of RWE actors and groups to other social sites, the social media platform Reddit has continued to be a hotbed for the far-right in

Canada. Reddit was founded in 2005 and is a social content aggregator website, where users can post new content, comment on other's content, and upvote or downvote posted material. According to Reddit's analytics, the platform has over 52 million daily active users and over 50 billion monthly views of the posts on the site (Reddit, 2021). On Reddit, there are smaller communities known as subreddits, dedicated to specific topics. To date, there are over 100,000 unique subreddits on the platform (Reddit, 2021). Each of these subreddits is subjected to rules created by their subreddit moderators, who are responsible for ensuring the posted comments are related to the overall theme of the community. Posts can be in any media format, and there are no restrictions as to the medium for the posted content. Anonymity is prevalent on the site and users can, and often do, create "throwaway" accounts to post material. To create an account, users only need a unique name and password. There is no email validation process. Initially created as a place on the internet for free speech, Reddit has needed to adopt policies that inhibit hate speech and offensive content in an attempt to protect users from harassment These changes were not welcomed by some subreddit communities and in June 2015; the administration of Reddit had to ban five communities for hate speech (Newell et al., 2016).

In brief, the unique feature of Reddit is the fact that users follow communities (subreddits) in which they share common interests rather than following specific people who would post information related to those common interests. There is a lack of customization and identification markers on a user's person- al page so the only way you would recognize them is if they consistently contribute to a specific community and generate a lot of "karma" to the point where you would remember their username. This is the reason anonymity is more prevalent.

The prevalence of hate speech on Reddit resulted in the company quarantining subreddits propagating extremist opinions. Once a quarantine was placed on a subreddit, viewers had to "opt in" to read the posted content. The subreddit was not banned, but instead viewers had to accept the possibility of what they might encounter in that particular community. One particular subreddit created in 2015, r/The_Donald, was a home for offensive and extremist views until it was banned from the site. r/The_Donald was a community where misogyny, racism, and alt-right opinions flourished. Misogyny or the "manosphere", which is a term for a wide breadth of male-dominated communities from men's rights movements to Incels (Mamié et al., 2021) can be a conduit to extremism or far-right belief systems.

With regard to this study, we found a few subreddits like r/metacanada (38,500 members), r/altrightcanada (91 members), and r/Canadafree-speech (416 members) as well as the r/PeoplesPartyofCanada (3,700 followers) or the PPC official Reddit channel subreddits that contain disinformation posts on COVID-19, the liberal government of Justin Trudeau, immigrants, and many other issues.

Using Pushshift API, we retrieved all the available posts and their associated comments from these subreddits that were posted from the beginning until October 1, 2021, when the last search was made. We got a total of 1,487,435 Reddit posts from the following datasets: r/metacanada (n = 1,446,782), r/altrightcanada (n = 35), r/Canadafreespeech (n = 3,072), and r/PeoplesPartyofCanada (n = 37,546). The number of posts by the subreddit administrators was 119,135 in total.

It is important to note here that the moderation policies on Reddit are almost non-existent as almost any kind of speech is allowed even if it contains misinformation on public health issues and hate against minorities. Though the social media platform claims to be actively moderating posts, the reality is that the platform is a thriving ground for hate and racism. To save money and effort, Reddit gives many responsibilities to the subreddit administrators to moderate content, which means that hate speech will thrive if the administrators are themselves racists or are not interested in moderating these issues. The first rule regarding behavior and speech on Reddit is: "Remember the human". The site's policy states that no one should have to face threats of violence, bullying, or harassment, while on the site, and anyone inciting violence or promoting hate based on identity or vulnerability, will be banned (Reddit Policy, 2021).

Using the API of Hatebase which automatically classifies hateful content, we found that 264 posts on the subreddit r/Canada-freespeech contain some type of abusive content. This constitutes 8.5% of total posts. Most of the posts were Islamophobic, anti-liberal, anti-LGBTQ, and sexist. For example, some of the top ten most recurrent terms used in this subreddit are "Jihadi" (n = 30), "globalist" (n = 16), "gay" (n = 11), "faggot" (n = 7), and "bitch" (n = 6). In addition to many more sexist terms, similar abusive words were found in the analysis of the other subreddit r/metacanada which contained 127,569 abusive posts making up 8.8% of the total posts. Finally, r/altrightcanada had an extremely limited number of posts, while r/PeoplesPartyofCanada subreddit contained the lowest number of abusive terms (n = 2,292), constituting 6.1% of the total posts. To examine the r/metacanada subreddit since it is the largest one, we found that the terms that are ranked based on the abusiveness elements in them from 0 (neutral) to 100 (highly abusive) are mostly concentrated above 50, denoting the highly abusive use of language on this subreddit (Figure 5.1).

Similar to Twitter, we find political polarization and anti-pandemic messaging occurring on Reddit with a clear focus on Justin Trudeau who with Trump are the only two figures mentioned in the top 50 single words in the subreddit posts. Some of the major themes emerged in our analysis. Among them, are attacks on the Liberal government and Justin Trudeau, anti-pandemic policies, PPC supporters, defunding the CBC, Anthropocene climate change is a hoax, attacking Muslim immigrants, and expressing concerns over China and its alleged influence in Canada.

Also, we extracted the most recurrent phrases that are made up of two words, and we found some interesting insight that shows the main figures that the subredditors discuss and mention (see Table 5.3). Here, it is a love/hate relationship and even moderate conservatives like Stephen Harper and Andrew Scheer are regarded as bad actors because they are viewed as meek and reluctant to "defend the rights of white people". For example, Stephen Harper is the only person who is strongly associated with the "f***" word based on the proximity plot analysis.

When examining the most used words in all the above subreddits, we found that the word "white" is among the top 50 most referenced terms (n = 18,311). Other prominent words in the top 50 list include 'Trudeau' (n = 24,010) and 'government'

Appendix: RWE sites 151

Table 5.3 Most frequently mentioned Canadian entities and individuals on Reddit

No	Phrases	Frequency	No	Phrases	Frequency
1	Justin Trudeau	2388	26	Conservative Party	269
2	Maxime Bernier	752	27	Human Rights	240
3	Prime Minister	732	28	Social Media	240
4	Doug Ford	503	29	Toronto Star	226
5	CBC News	500	30	Asylum Seekers	192
6	Andrew Scheer	446	31	Trudeau Liberals	189
7	Climate Change	443	32	Lauren Southern	189
8	Stephen Harper	433	33	Kathleen Wynne	188
9	Party Canada	410	34	Syrian Refugees	179
10	Free Speech	368	35	First Nations	171
11	People Party	366	36	Canada Day	167
12	Fake News	355	37	Jason Kenney	167
13	Carbon Tax	338	38	Liberal MP	165
14	Looks Like	338	39	Trudeau Says	164
15	Mad Max	332	40	Sexual Assault	160
16	Donald Trump	320	41	Breaking News	158
17	Jordan Peterson	313	42	Saudi Arabia	156
18	Actual Headline	307	43	Lives Matter	156
19	White People	303	44	Federal Government	152
20	Trudeau Government	298	45	National Post	151
21	Liberal Party	294	46	Federal Election	150
22	Omar Khadr	290	47	Tommy Robinson	148
23	Year Old	274	48	Hate Crime	147
24	Faith Goldy	272	49	Tax Dollars	147
25	Ezra Levant	270	50	Diversity Strength	143

Source: Created by the authors.

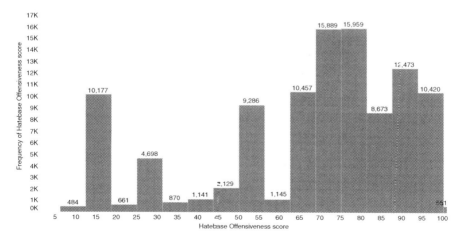

Figure 5.1 The offensiveness scores from (1–100) on r/metacanada subreddit.
Source: Created by the authors.

(n = 20,136) as well as a variety of insults like the 'f' word in different formats in association with the left and the liberal party. Again, there is a clear crossover with American politics for Trump is mostly referenced (n = 10,141) in addition to the PPC (n = 9,157) and Bernier (n = 5,794). Other prominent words that show the major topics and concerns of the far-right in Canada include "China" (n = 7,276), "immigrants" (n = 5,800), "Chinese" (n = 5,042), "climate" (n = 4,875), "Islam" (n = 4,819), and "Muslim" (n = 4,541).

A trope of the denigration of women and the racialized other was apparent throughout the data collected. As discussed earlier, the intertwining of gendering and nationalism is sometimes ignored in the analysis of RWE is prevalent in the data. This is evident from our data from Reddit. As Redditors discussed politics, politicians, and the state of Canada, the topic of women was prominent. When discussing the nation, it is often articulated in the feminine and women themselves are held as the "mothers of the nation". In this role, women are attributed with the responsibility of the nation's physical, cultural, and social reproduction. This gendering of nationalism can pose dangers for women. Pettman argues that "the nation is frequently represented as a woman under threat of penetration or domination" (Pettman, 2005). Fauldi states that the denigration of women, the focus on the manliness of men, and the calls to the return of traditional gender roles create an idealized national fantasy, that is our "constructed myth of invincibility" (Faludi, 2007). As Redditors posted about women as the feminists destroying Canada, they also articulated anger at the "feminization of men", and created a narrative of the "Other", the immigrants who were attacking or putting the women of Canada at risk. By the creation of this narrative, they were positioning themselves (the males) as the masculine heroes, the women as symbolic of the nation who were vulnerable and at risk, while simultaneously designating who the enemies were. These are common populist tactics. Populism provides a mechanism to mobilize people against established power structures and social values. Predominantly appealing to a sense of resentment against a perceived injustice or social problem in society, it calls for radical change eliminating the hierarchical structure of societies. In essence, populism provides a conduit to express unfairness and injustice, but it also serves as a recourse and remedy (Betz & Johnson, 2004).

Finally, when examining the posts and comments in r/metacanada subreddit, we find gendered references to minority groups are also frequent (👩 n = 31). Some of the hate statements against Muslim women and the LGBTQ communities are not even expressed in words but in emojis such as (👩💨🔪🏃💣💣 💣💣🖕💦) or (💧💩💧❤️💧) or (👩 💩), mostly expressing concerns about the erosion of traditional Christian values due to foreign influences such as the following emoji sequence (🕌+🇮🇳 💦 =👩).

In terms of single emojis, the fourth most referenced emoji is 💧 (n = 669). Together with Pepe the Frog 🐸 (n = 22), these two emojis are often used by far-right members on social media. The poop (💩, n = 61) and middle finger (🖕, n = 48) emojis are also among the top 50 most used ones, indicating the kind of non-verbal language communicated on Reddit.

A2 Mainstream SNS sites

A2.1 Facebook (currently Meta) and Instagram

According to Carlson and Rousselle (2020), Facebook and other American-based social media sites are not required by law to extend First Amendment protection to content shared by users. This allows American social media organizations to have the ultimate control in defining and removing content on their platforms.

This can be contrasted with other approaches. In 2017, Germany passed the Network Enforcement Act (2017), which states that any social media platform with more than two million users must remove or block content that violates hate speech within the German Criminal Code (1998). Following the 2019 Christ- church attack in New Zealand, leaders from across the globe met with the major social media sites, including Facebook, to create guidelines for hate speech, extremism, and violent rhetoric online. The United States chose not to sign the resulting "Christchurch Call", guidelines leaving its social media corporations to continue their self-regulation of content (Carlson et al., 2020).

In this respect, many EU countries do not allow attacks against religious groups, but the laws permit criticism against religions to protect freedom of speech (European Commission, 2020). The problem, however, in this law is the legal challenges of distinguishing between attacks against individuals with attacks against their faith. For example, Bleich stresses the "multidimensional nature of Islamophobia, and the fact that Islam and Muslims are often inextricably intertwined in individual and public perceptions" (Bleich, 2012, p. 182). In other words, it is not practically possible for social media platforms to distinguish between attacks on religions and on people adhering to these religions by simply allowing or blocking certain hashtags. In such cases, it is easy to see how much more advanced moderation tools are needed.

Examples of RWE groups on Facebook include the Old Stock Canadian, which was a Facebook group with more than 32,000 followers, that shared numerous anti-immigration, racist, conspiratorial, and anti-Muslim material. The group was created in 2016 and named after a popular white nationalist phrase. "Old Stock Canadians" was a descriptor used by Prime Minister Steven Harper during a leadership debate in 2015. In July 2021, the group was removed from the social media platform. Prior to July, the Old Stock Canadian group purchased an ad on the platform that promoted doubts about the COVID-19 pandemic lockdowns, and other related policies.

In October 2021, The Intercept released a list of banned RWE groups. individuals, and associated companies. On this extensive list, the following Canadians and organizations were found (Table 5.4).

A2.1.1 Hashtag policies on Meta

We followed a reverse engineering approach (Butcher, 2016) to understand the policies followed by Twitter and Instagram regarding the use of hashtags such as #fakescience, #scamdemic, #atomwaffen, or #gavinmcinne. As of late 2021 when the search was made, Instagram did not allow hashtags like # f***Christians and

Table 5.4 Canadian entities and individuals banned by social media

No	Name.	Affiliation/Location
1	Atomwaffen Division	North America, listed as a terrorist entity in Canada (Public Safety Canada, 2024). White Nationalist group
2	Earth Liberation Front North America	Canada, their first act of violence was 1995 Canada Earth Liberation Army – Burned down a wildlife museum and damaged a hunting lodge in BC (Berry, 2022). Eco-terrorism group
3	National Socialist Order	USA new name for Atomwaffen (see Atomwaffen). White Nationalist group
4	Northern Order	Canada – Atomwaffen (see Atomwaffen). White Nationalist group
5	The Base	North America - listed as a terrorist entity in Canada (Public Safety Canada, 2024). White Nationalist group
6	Vorherrschaft Division	United States - Atomwaffen (See Atom-waffen). White Nationalist group
7	Alt-knights	English US – This was a division of the Proud Boys, officially known as Fraternal Order of Alt-Knights - FOAK. listed as a terrorist entity in Canada (Public Safety Canada, 2024). White Nationalist group
8	Aryan Guard	US Canada – mostly an Alberta group. (Scheinberg, 2018). White Nationalist group
9	Aryan Nations	US-Canada. White Nationalist group
10	Canadian Nationalist Front	Canada. White Nationalist group
11	Operation Werewolf North American	White Nationalist group
12	Students for Western Civilization	Canada. White Nationalist group
13	Three percenters	Canada. White Nationalist group
14	Faith Goldy – Daily Stormer	RWE Actor
15	Gavin McInnes	RWE Actor
16	Kevin Goudreau – Canadian Nationalist Front	RWE Actor

Source: Created by the authors.

#f***Muslims, yet it allows similar hashtags against Islam and Christianity like #f***jesus, #f***christ, #f***Allah, and #f***Islam (Table 5.5). On the other hand, Twitter allows all of these hashtags to be used. When we compared similar insults against other religions, such as Judaism and Hinduism, we found the same patterns along Twitter and Instagram platforms. This policy is possibly due to potential legal implications. Twitter's hateful conduct policy specifically states that no member can "promote violence against or directly attack or threaten people on the basis of...religious affiliation" (Twitter, 2021). Similarly, Instagram does not allow "attacks on people based on their protected characteristics, including race or religion" (Instagram, 2021). For a more detailed explanation of hate speech,

Instagram directs users to Facebook's policies. Facebook is very specific in its hate speech policies but does differentiate between people, concepts, and institutions. People are protected against attacks, whereas concepts and institutions are not. A tier two offense includes "Cursing, defined as: Referring to the target as genitalia or anus, including but not limited to: c*nt, d*ck, *sshole. Profane terms or phrases with the intent to insult, including but not limited to: f*ck, b*tch, moth- erf*cker" (Transparency Center, 2022).

Regarding posts and hashtags related to the pandemic as of July 2021, Facebook and Instagram still allow the following controversial hashtags and their derivations to spread on their platforms that are mostly used by COVID-19 hoaxers. On December 13, 2020, Facebook announced they would remove all false claims about COVID-19 vaccines. This announcement supported Facebook's earlier release that the platform would be combating misinformation on the virus. In July 2020, the platform announced that it would be launching a COVID-19 Information Center to provide facts to users (Kang-Xing Jin, 2020). Yet, in October 2021, the following hashtags were still in use on the two platforms (Table A1.5).

The list of hashtags seems to evolve as conspiracies and public preventative measures such as vaccine passports are implemented. #agenda2021, #ivermectin, #covidhoax2020thegreatreset, #covid19resist, #ProjectBlueBeam, #markofthebeast, #newworldorder, and #depopulationagenda were found on the two social media platforms. In addition, on Instagram, people are using hashtags and creating accounts. So, the impact is compounded as the lack of "policing" or removal of hashtags and associated accounts increase.

While there are concerns regarding the continued appearance of the hashtags listed above, there have been recent improvements in removing "bad" content on Facebook and Instagram. For instance, the following Canadian Instagram channel, which was followed by the anti-pandemic community, is no longer available (https://www.instagram.com/keep_canada_free/).

Instagram has also worked on limiting the spread of any obvious QAnon-related hashtags stating that this material "may be associated with harmful content" and be a risk to public safety. Hashtags are hidden from the search suggestions and instead redirect users to gnet-research.org, a resource on information related to extremism and technology.

On Facebook, some conspiracy theories as well as obvious related hashtags are hidden from the search suggestions, as of late 2021. It appears that Facebook has greater control over common conspiracy hashtags compared to Instagram, although variations do exist. However, other similar accounts emerge as illustrated by this Instagram page (https://www.instagram.com/p/CH1QsRVjECO/.[5]

A2.2 Twitter (currently X)

Twitter is considered one of the most popular social media sites in the world and Canadian RWE often makes use of it. In a 2021 study, it was found that Twitter algorithms favor right-wing users, and the amplification of right-wing political leaders is the highest in Canada among the seven countries it examined including the US and UK. To test the hypothesis that left-wing or right-wing politicians are

Table 5.5 Hashtag searches using reverse engineering method

#Covid1984	#CovidHoax	#Covid_Hoax	#covidhoax2020thegreatreset	#FakePandemic
#HydroxychloroquineIsTheCure	#fakevirus	#plandemic	#plandemic2020	#scamdemic2020
#scamdemic2021	#shamdemic	#fakescience	#Covid1984	#mafiamedicine
#vaccinescauseautism	#vaccineskill	#vexit	#covidhoaxterbesardalamsejarah	#covidhoaxers
#CovidShmovid	#ProjectMockingBird	#WWG1WGAWW	#RIPScience	#NurembergCode
#FauciForPrison	#SocialismDistancing	#CrimesAgainstHumanity	#CentresForDiseaseCreation	#resisttyranny
#predictive programming				

Source: Created by the authors.

amplified differently, the authors identified the largest mainstream left or center-left and main- stream right or center-right party in each legislature, and present pair-wise comparisons between these. With the exception of Germany, we find a statistically four significant differences favoring the political right wing.

To examine Twitter, we conducted a literature review and collected a series of relevant hashtags to identify RWE Canadian users. To retrieve the necessary data, we used Twitter's academic API v.2 which pulls all available tweets. In total, we identified eight Canadian-related hashtags: #MakeCanadaGreatAgain, #MakeCanadaFreeAgain, #CanadaFirst, #CanadaQanon, #CDNqanon, #CanadianPatriots, #WWG1WGAcanada1, and #Canada1st. The term means "Where We Go One We Go All" which is a quote often incorrectly attributed to President Kennedy, but is actually from a Jeff Bridges' post from the beginning until September 12, 2021, and we retrieved a total of 28,366 tweets posted by 12,474 unique Twitter users. Some of the top 50 most active users include PPC_ON-TARIO (n = 296), PPC_Retweets (n = 146), PPCWinnipegNEDA (n = 63), OakvillePPC (n = 60), and MarkFriesen08 (n = 55) who all belong to the PPC party.

We also identified two general hashtags and the tweets referencing them: #wwg1wga and #Qanon. We found a total of 2,556,868 tweets using the first hashtag, and 4,873,865 tweets using the second one posted from the beginning until September 15, 2021. We started these Twitter searches in July 2006 because it is the earliest year we could search as it is the year Twitter launched. To extract relevant tweets, we used a Python script to identify tweets that mention Canadian issues. We found 13,488 tweets in relation to the hashtag #wwg1wga and 24,155 tweets in connection to #Qanon. In other words, we searched a total of 10 main hashtags, and we then retrieved 66,009 tweets posted between February 14, 2010, until September 12, 2021. We used the Twitter Academic API v2 to make sure we captured all the available tweets that were still available on the platform.

The search words we used included: 'canada', 'canadian', 'trudeau', 'justintrudeau', 'toronto', 'montreal', 'vancouver', 'ottawa', 'onpoli', 'polqc', 'cdnpoli', 'scheer', 'thejagmeetsingh', 'jagmeet singh', 'topoli', 'quebec', 'qcpoli', 'halifax', 'edmonton', 'calgary', 'alberta', 'ontario', 'winnipeg', 'manitoba', 'saskatchewan', and 'british columbia'. When the search was conducted (Figure 5.2), the highest number of tweets were sent on July 1, 2020 (n = 791) mostly due to the following tweet posted by one of PPC supporters (@FA_Ciardullo) calling for a rally in front of the Parliament:

(@FA_Ciardullo)
Today the People's voice will be heard on Parliament Hill.
We are the People. We are Canada.
We are strong and free.
☒ Say no to the new normal.
☒ Say no to globalism.
☒ Say no to communism.
☒ Say no to corruption.
☑ Say yes to #CanadaFirst #OurCanadaSay #FreedomRally #PPC

---

158 *The Canadian Far-Right and Conspiracy Theories*

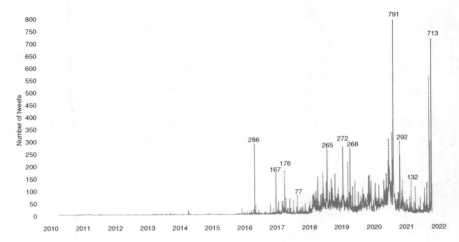

Figure 5.2 Twitter's far-right related hashtag frequencies.
Source: Created by the authors.

Though the majority of tweets show polarized political and/or related to public health issues, we found some patterns of disinformation when we searched for "fake", "false", and "hoax" with the use of another Python code. In total, we found 1,474 tweets primarily discussing conspiracy theories concerning the Canadian government and the leading Liberal Party.

When we explored some of the most used hashtags, we found some problematic ones like #covidhoax (n = 12) and #climate- hoax (n = 6). Some of the examples of such tweets include: "The Un Communist Climate Hoax Fraud in plain sight! Carbon Tax Where does the money go? Drain The Foreign Controlled SWAMP in OTTAWA! #CanadaFirst #FACTSoverFEAR https://t.co/ rBErxd7fNg".

Another one states the following:

> ☞ The Globalist Fake News Narrative PsyOp is after your Mind.
> ☞ Your Globalist Infiltrated Government is after your Body.
> ☞ What's next your SOUL?
>
> Their News is FAKE but their WAR on Canadians is REAL! #GlobalistIN-FILTRATIONvsINVASION of Canada! #CanadaFIRST https://t.co/ KO4UzFXm1t

As mentioned above, the majority of tweets referencing these 10 hashtags involve political figures, movements, or organizations. For example, the fifth and eighth most used words are "Trudeau" (n = 5,554) and "JustinTrudeau" (n = 4,317), while "Trudeaumustgo" (n = 2,382) came in the top 20. Other important top words

Appendix: RWE sites   159

include "MAGA" (Make America Great Again) (n = 4,165), "Maximebernier" (n = 3,223), "Realdonaldtrump" (n = 3,323), "Trump" (n = 2,580), "PPC" (n = 2,314), and "POTUS" (n = 1,263), indicating the ideological connection among some PPC supporters and conservative members in the two neighboring countries. As expected, we found evidence of the connection between the Yellow Vest movement and Twitter users referencing these hashtags. As discussed earlier in this book, the Yellow Vest movement is a bricolage of conspiracists, anti-immigration, and those who feel disenfranchised or left behind by the government. The movement is also a conduit for RWE groups to utilize political ideals to expand their bases through joining protests and create a political movement (Vancouver C.A.S.I.S., 2019). For example, some of the words that occurred among the top 50 ones include "yellowvestscanada" (n = 1,833), MCGA (Make Canada Great Again) (n = 1,742), and "yellowvests" (n = 1,508). The above is also corroborated when examining the most mentioned users in these tweets, for we found that once again Justin Trudeau came first (n = 3,616) followed by Donald Trump (n = 3,222), Maxime Bernier (n = 3,018), and Mark Friesen from the PPC party (n = 1,911). Finally, the top 50 most used hashtags provide a similar picture to what is presented below (Table 5.6).

Table 5.6 The most frequent hashtags used in the dataset referencing ten hashtags

No	Hashtags	Count	Freq	Hashtags	Freq
1	Qanon	14734	26	Makecanadafreeagain	581
2	Wwg1wga	8071	27	Newsoftheday	553
3	Canadafirst	7506	28	Factsmatter	569
4	Makecanadagreatagain	5518	29	USA	554
5	Canada	4523	30	Freedom	541
6	MAGA	4131	31	Toronto	536
7	cdnpoli	4103	32	onpoli	527
8	Trudeaumustgo	2380	33	Canada1st	517
9	PPC	2094	34	Oakville	516
10	Yellowvestscanada	1854	35	Followthewhiterabbit	513
11	MCGA	1740	36	Justintrudeau	511
12	KAG	1573	37	Qarmy	508
13	Yellowvests	1509	38	Qanonjapan	500
14	Trudeau	1426	39	America	408
15	TheGreat-Awakening	1281	40	Giletesjaunes	395
16	Humantrafficking	1.1226	41	Meaney4mp	385
17	Wwg1wgaworldwide	1132	42	Bluewave2020	363
18	Savecanada	1024	43	Canadians	338
19	PPC2019	993	44	Nomorelockdowns	337
20	voteppc	983	45	Wwg1wga_Worldwide	335
21	Trump	837	46	Darktolight	321
22	Q	824	47	Trump2020	320
23	Greatawakening	792	48	Canadian	317
24	Brexit	776	49	Fakenews	316
25	Wwg1gwa	745	50	Draintheswamp	315

Source: Created by the authors.

In addition to the political polarization stated above, some of the major themes we found in the dataset concerning conspiracies include the Canadian Liberal government conspiring with the United Nations (UN) and foreign governments to create unnecessary lockdowns during the pandemic and that some members of the political elite are involved in human trafficking (see Table A1.6 above, no. 16). Another dominant theme is calling for freedom of movement and expression because of the perceived injustice inflicted against the community. Professor of law, Mark Fenster states that a conspiracy theory is effective when politics are interpreted through a conspiratorial lens by those individuals and groups for whom politics are inaccessible.

This inaccessibility renders politics as something that is impenetrable or secret. Although conspiracy theories can be wrong and appear simplistic in their presentation of "answers", they may harbour a problem or issues that need to be discussed or addressed. Beneath the conspiracy could be issues such as structural inequities, an unjust political order, a dysfunctional civil society, or an exploitative economic system (Fenster, 1999). The conspiracy could provide a response to these issues for the adherents when society as a whole or the social safety net does not. Those who feel disenfranchised will seek out others who understand or feel the same and create a community or social group of like-minded individuals.

Since the PPC was featured prominently in our initial search, we collected all the tweets referencing #voteppc and #purplewave that were trending during the 2021 federal election. Interestingly, we could identify tweets referencing hoaxes using the #Purplewave hashtag. However, when we examined the other hashtag #voteppc, we found some conspiracy-related terms such as #climatehoax (n = 11), #fakepandemic (n = 4), #covidhoax (n = 3), #climatechangehoax (n = 3), and #climatechangehoax (n = 3).

As for Twitter users, we retrieved all the available Twitter data from 10 users who are either followed by, affiliated with, show sympathy towards, or belong to the far-right in Canada (see Table A1.7). There were two exceptions. Faith Goldy's Twitter account is still active, but she has made it a private account (Table 5.7).

As a result, we were not able to download her tweets from her official account whose profile picture features her smiling with Stephen Harper, the former Prime Minister. Second, Gavin McInnis does not have a public Twitter account. In the analysis, similar to the findings above, we found that Justin Trudeau is the most prominent person highlighted in the Twitter discussion (n = 14,374) coming second after Ezra Levant, while Donald "Trump" remained in the top 20 most used words (n = 7,669).

4 For #Voteppc, we collected a total of 590,945 tweets and 62,114 tweets referencing #Purplewave posted from the beginning until September 14.

The same evidence can be found in the top 20 most mentioned users, for Maxime Bernier is ranked 15th (n = 1,149) and Trudeau comes in the 18th spot (n = 1,009) with the exception of Randy Hillier (n = 1,894) who came 7th. Randy Hillier is an Independent elected Member of Provincial Parliament (MPP) in Ontario, after being ousted from the Conservative Party. During the COVID-19 pandemic, Hillier has been a leader in protests against health measures and has been arrested numerous times for his protest actions. During the 2021 Federal election, he was a vocal

Table 5.7 Far-right users and the frequencies of their tweets

No	Name	Twitter	No. of Tweets
1	Maxime Bernier	@MaximeBernier	24,638
2	Lauren Southern	@Lauren_Southern	4,538
3	Ezra Levant	@Ezralevant	170,249
4	Canadian Patriot Proud	@TQMMYLLQYD	2,719
5	Free Canuck Movement	@freecanucksca	124
6	Q Canada	@todd_branscombe	398
7	Randy Hillier	@randyhillier	18,519
8	Jean-François Gariépy	@JFGariepy	19,466
9	Keean Bexte	@TheRealKeean	8,751
10	Euro Canadians	@eurocanadians	1,824
	Total		251,226

Source: Created by the authors.

supporter of Maxime Bernier and the PPC, and his daughter was a candidate for the Party as well. Other prominent users who are highly mentioned in the top ten users' list include @therebeltv (n = 12,362), @SheilaGunnReid (n = 7,473) (the Alberta Bureau Chief for Rebel Media), @rebelnewsonline (n = 5,866), @prison-planet (n = 2,922) (Paul Joseph Watson is a regular guest host on Alex Jones' InfoWars radio show, and a YouTube Channel host), @bcbluecon (n = 2,825), @inspector4 (n = 1,668) (an account for the former Chief of Staff during the Stephen Harper administration, a past journalist and instructor in Political Science at the University of Ottawa), and @therealkeean (n = 1,452). Some of the popular hashtags found in the top ten list include #MAGA (n = 1,108), #Trump (n = 935), and #voteppc (n = 700). However, it is important to mention a marginal degree of data contamination resulting from Ezra Levant posting far more tweets than all the other accounts examined, and his tweets overwhelmed our digital data analysis due to their frequency and high level of audience interaction with them. For example, some of the most recurrent hashtags we found in the overall digital analysis included words like "#Islam" (n = 427) "#China" (n = 380), and #ISIS (n = 318) which also happens to be terms favored by Levant and his Rebel News (Al-Rawi & Fakida, 2021).

Through an analysis of the above data that we collected from specific groups, individuals, hashtags, and word searches, the findings reveal the global nature of the rise of populism, similarity in "cultural war" issues, and conspiracy theories. Just as globalized conspiracies such as QAnon are bringing together divergent groups and forging a bricolage of interlocking beliefs, the findings on Canadian-based Twitter accounts and hashtags reflect this interconnectivity. Interspersed between biblical quotes are purported evidence of collusion between international government leaders and personnel, as well as "evidence" of Satanic activities including child harm and human trafficking (see examples below).

- Bonkers, pedovore, satanic communists ruling the world are not desirable for any country. Only psychopaths want that. #Maga #CanadaFirst #ByeBye Globalism #UNFails #ElitePsychopaths https://t.co/4gKJR9H3CI

- @kwilli1046 as a Canadian, all i can do is vote in my local election next year... and pray that enough Canadians have woken up by then to vote Trugrope out. #GodHelpUsAll #TrugropeMustGo #Make- CanadaGreatAgain #MakeCanadaSafeAgain #PedophiliaIsNOT- Normal #BestialityIsNOTNormal

Within this Twitter data is a distrust in societal institutions and a strong belief in a controlling cabal. Analysis of selected hashtags reveals that spamming of tweets is the preferred method to disseminate messages. Support for Maxime Bernier's PPC and their stance on anti-COVID19 measures were very popular before and after the 2021 federal election.

These tweets also linked to conspiracy theories, such as the great reset and "the Globalist Cabal", that were also addressed by candidates from the PPC in their social media posts. This coincided with the themes of anti-tyranny, freedom, liberty, and human rights, which was the foundation of the PPC's platform for the 2021 federal election.

The language used to describe the other candidates (Prime Minister Justin Trudeau, Conservative Leader Erin O'Toole, and NDP leader Jagmeet Singh) was largely derogatory towards Trudeau, linking the leaders to the globalist cabal, with a hashtag calling for insurrection against their perceived alignment to the World Economic Forum (WEF) and the "Great Reset". Consistent themes position the candidates, who were not PPC, as shills and sympathizers for the UN, to enact the "globalist" and vaccine conspiracies associated with the organization.

As vaccine passports were announced for various provinces throughout the campaign, the hashtags reflected a deeper connection of "proof" of the Great Reset, and that Canada would adopt the Social Credit System, instituted by China. Hashtags and associated tweets also linked religious persecution, calls for limited immigration, and the silencing of Canadian citizens, all due to COVID-19 measures. These ideas were linked with hashtags #MakeCanadaFreeAgain and #TakeBackCanada.

- @DivergeMedia_ Big reset...great reset.. same globalist shit that is trying to turn Canada into a UN-led communist dictatorship with Schwab and bill gates as great leaders..#FuckTheGreatReset #FuckGlobal-ists #CanadaFirst #DefendCanada

Language consistent across the Twitter data includes the use of modified slogans and themes from the American presidential elections in 2016 and 2020. Slogans such as 'Make Canada Great Again', 'Lock Him Up', 'Canada First', and 'Drain the Frozen Swamp' were modified to represent the Canadian perspective. In addition, numerous slogans were associated with QAnon, such as 'The Storm is coming', 'WW1GWGA', and a Canadian version of the Deep State. The WWG1WGA (Where We Go One, We Go All) hashtag continued this theme of globalized distrust of institutions linked via disinformation and the QAnon conspiracy as a whole. Although begun as an "American" conspiracy QAnon has spread and has become a mainstream articulation of populism, fear, and disenfranchisement of the segments of the global population. Canadian adherents link Prime Minister Trudeau to the Deep State. Many of the taboo notions of QAnon were applied to

Liberal politicians and the wealthy, "elite" in Canada. Language attributed to the Q phenomenon was found among this hashtag including "Drainthefrozenswamp", "DraintheCana- dianSwamp", and tropes of cults, pedophilia, and human trafficking. While liberal politicians were castigated and denigrated in the tweets, Maxime Bernier and Donald Trump were both praised and tagged. (See Examples below)

- A PDF on NGOs such as Gates, Ford, OPEN Society, McArthur, and OAK foundations infiltrating the UNHCR to advance open borders/migrant crises.
- Like I've been saying. It's all conditioning and social engineering to prepare society for what is yet to come. Social Credit through technocracy with a mic of fascism and communism.
- They used COVID to usher it in, starting with vax pass.
- Even assuming our elections are 100% legitimate (they're not), when Chrystia Freeland is a member of the Board of Trustees for the WEF, and there are numerous Rhodes Scholars in positions of high power (just as two examples) we don't even have a chance anyway. They're pre-rigged.

The tweets of the Council of European Canadians (@EuroCanadians) Twitter user suggested that mass immigration of non-Europeans will lead to the collapse of the European heritage of Canada. Their belief that multiculturalism, cultural Marxism, and globalism are the conduits to the liquidation of Canada is articulated through the support of political candidates supporting these beliefs, traditional gender roles, and adherence to conspiracy theories that coincide with their dystopian vision of a multicultural nation. The EuroCanadians' tweets included references to deporting "Islamic terrorists" in response to tweets from InfoWars correspondent, and PrisonPlanetLive YouTube program, Paul Joseph Watson.

Numerous tweets provided attacks on the Black Lives Matter movement and immigration policies in North America. The great replacement theory was a consistent theme within tweets of this membership group, then with the American presidential election and the Canadian federal election soon after there was a shift. The focus of the tweets then moved to conspiracies, politics, and immigration policies. The group's tweets show support for the PPC nominee Maxime Bernier and for Incumbent President Donald Trump. Tweets from 2014 show support for Incel theories such as enforced monogamy. Consistent with their focus on traditional values, tweets regarding Christianity and the trope of Christian persecution and annihilation are very present.

They also supported Faith Goldy in her bid for the Mayor of Toronto. Consistent tropes include anti-feminism, anti-immigration, toxic masculinity personal attacks on political figures (Justine Trudeau) and anti-LGBTQ2SA, The Great Re-placement, and an infinity for celebrities among the Right, including Tucker Carlson, Jordan Peterson, and InfoWars anchors.

As the leadership includes former University of New Brunswick Professor Ricardo Duchesne, there is a great interest in white politics on campuses in Canada. The account also referenced the white nationalist Bible, The Camp of Saints by Jean Raspail.

Other Twitter accounts in the study included Students for Western Civilization which is a cluster of university student groups primarily based in Toronto and Montreal. Their website states the purpose of the group is to promote European-Canadian viewpoints in academia and the media, fight anti-white discrimination and anti-white hate speech, and preserve white cultural heritage. Keean Bexte is a former member of the Conservative Party of Canada, where he worked for Conservative MP Bob Benzen, and Alberta's United Conservative Party, he then became a reporter for Rebel News. Bexte was exposed for being involved with a company that sold Rhodesian and apartheid South African flags and war memorabilia to white supremacists online. The online store, Fireforce Ventures was part of a journalistic investigation where one Canadian military person was also linked to the enterprise (Seatter & Milton, 2018). Bexte is known for his scandals and involvement in RWE projects. This includes his campus conservative club promoting a men's rights film produced by RWE, The Red Pill. In an email promoting the film Bexte wrote "feminism is cancer" (PressProgress, 2018). During the 2018 Conservative national convention, Bexte introduced a resolution to end birthright citizenship in Canada, which was adopted by the Party platform (PressProgress, 2018).

Dr. Jean-François Gariépy is a neuroscience researcher, white nationalists, and vlogger, who promotes a white ethnostate. Randy Hiller is an independent member of Ontario's legislature, for the region of Lanark-Frontenac-Kingston. Formerly a member and representative of the Canadian Conservative Party, Hiller was expelled from the Party, and in 2021, he was closely aligned with PPC leader Maxime Bernier.

Hiller is an outspoken anti-COVID vaccine and anti-lockdown mandates, and is an outspoken member of many of the protests across Canada during the pandemic. Late in 2021, Hiller announced that he would be running for the Premier of Ontario under his new Party, the Ontario First Party (OFP). The OFP will be connected to the PPC as its provincial wing of the national party, with a mandate to fight a "cultural war" in the province (Devoy, 2021). Our data also included Twitter accounts which helped to spread conspiracy theories about COVID-19, QAnon, and anti-immigration topics. These accounts were not by prominent individuals in the RWE orbit but seem to be accounts of adherents and influencers.

A2.3 YouTube

In 2005, three PayPal employees founded the video social media platform, YouTube. Two years later, Google purchased YouTube for $1.65 billion. At that time there was a burgeoning community of user-generated content websites, including Wikipedia, MySpace, and Facebook, all showing signs of significant impact and growth in the virtual realm. More recently YouTube has become the second-most visited site in the world (Arthurs et al., 2018), and the third-most popular social media platform in Canada, following Facebook and messaging applications (Gruzd & Philip, 2020). In fact, on YouTube, 64% of Canadian adults have an account, and 61% are monthly active users (Gruzd & Philip, 2020). Additionally, Canadian men are 66% more likely to have an account than women at 62% (Gruzd & Philip, 2020).

YouTube is a social media site because of its interactive feature that allows content creators to receive comments from viewers on their videos, and live stream viewers can engage via live chat. YouTube is well known for being a platform for contrarian opinions and this is due to the platform's own mission, which is to "give everyone a voice and show them the world" (YouTube, 2021b).

The limits of who is "everyone" have been tested in the past. The Intellectual Dark Web (IDW) was created by a loose-knit group of academics and podcast hosts who the New York Times described as "iconoclastic thinkers, academic renegades and media personalities" who were discussing "controversial issues such as abortion, biological differences between men and women, identity politics, religion, immigration, etc." (Weiss & Winter, 2018). The IDW was composed of a range of thinkers such as Sam Harris, Eric Weinstein, Dave Rubin, Jordan Peterson, Ben Shapiro, Maajid Nawaz, Joe Rogan, and Ayaan Hirsi Ali, some of whom have links to far-right groups and many of whom continue to have a presence on YouTube.

In 2020, YouTube banned right-wing accounts for David Duke, Richard Spencer, Stefan Molyneaux, and in 2021, the platform banned anti-vaccine accounts held by Robert F. Kennedy Jr. (De Vynck, 2021). YouTube's hate speech policy bans all content that promotes violence or hatred against individuals or groups (YouTube Policy, 2021a). The hate speech policy is based on 13 attributes which include age, ethnicity, gender identity and expression, race, or religion. Included in this policy are concerns for conspiracy theories which state that individuals or groups are "evil, corrupt, or malicious". In addition, no posts on YouTube may include "content containing hateful supremacist propaganda including the recruitment of new members or requests for financial support for their ideology" (YouTube Policy, 2021a).

Far from ironclad, there are loopholes to YouTube's hate speech policies that allow those who the site has deplatformed to remain vlogging. Stefan Molyneaux was banned from the site in June 2020 (De Vynck, 2021). Molyneaux is a libertarian and the host of Freedomain Radio, a call-in talk show. In his videos, he openly promoted scientific racism, advocated for the men's rights movement, was critical of initiatives for gender equality, and promoted conspiracy theories such as the Great Replacement theory. While his personal account is banned, content from his show Freedomain Radio is still available on the site. A search for "Freedomain Radio" finds both historical and the most recent broadcasts. In short, while he himself has been deplatformed, his messaging has not stopped.

In terms of Canadian RWE-related content, we searched the platform in early December 2021 using some common terms such as "CanadaQanon", "CDNqanon", "CandianPatriots", "WW- G1W3Acanada", and "canadaWWG1WGA", and we found a handful of videos with very limited number of views, mostly in relation to expressions of anti-liberal views and mistrust against government pandemic policies.

It is interesting to note that some of these video posters used some titles to suggest that their content would likely be removed (see the screenshot below). However, Rebel News remains the most active and effective tool used by RWE in Canada and elsewhere to spread hate and disinformation about different issues like the pandemic and immigration. As of early December 2021, Rebel News on YouTube had 1.52M subscribers and 624,261,098 views. This is more than the number of subscribers on CBC News: The Nation- al (1.22M) and a bit less than the number of subscribers on CBC News (2.83M subscribers). The most popular video on Rebel News channel remains Gavin McInnis' clip 10 Things Canadians Don't Know About Americans (Rebel News, 2015) comparing the US to Canada which has over 5.6 million views. The second popular video channel is run by Rebel News' former journalist, Lauren Southern, who has 53,769,192 views and more than 666,000 subscribers. Finally, the PPC also has its own YouTube channel, but it is dwarfed by the above two channels, for it only has 33,500 subscribers and 1,328,001 views. In other words, YouTube remains an effective tool to disseminate RWE content to be used across different other social media platforms like Discord, Telegram, and Parler.

Reine Romana Didulo, self-professed "Queen of Canada" and the founder of the Canada1st Party of Canada, has her own channel on YouTube. Didulo, who also promotes Q-Anon conspiracy theories, recently told her supporters to "shoot to kill" those who were administering vaccines to children (CBC, 2021). Based in Vancouver, British Columbia, as of February 17, 2022, her YouTube account has 5.12 thousand subscribers and 168,900 views as is her Party's account with 2.67 thousand subscribers and 90,794 views.

Just Right Media is a radio program hosted by former libertarian Freedom Party of Ontario leaders Robert Metz and Robert Vaughan, the two hosts often spotlight discussions with fellow Freedom Party member, and PPC Candidate Dr. Salim Mansur. Mansur is a Professor Emeritus at the University of Western Ontario. Mansur is a proponent of stopping all immigration from Islamic countries into Canada. The channel provides anti-Islam, anti-globalization, and anti-feminist programming to its 4.03 thousand subscribers, material that has had 520,241 views.

The Raging Dissident III channel is the fourth attempt to keep a YouTube channel for this Raging Dissident group, which has been banned three times. The self-described bigots and bigettes hold to the motto "Pro Patria Sic Semper Tyrannis" and promote anti-government, anti-legacy media, and pro-conspiracy theories to their 4.92 thousand subscribers. The videos have had 294,972 views.

Tom MacDonald is a rapper from Vancouver who is an influencer in right-wing groups. His YouTube channel has 2.83 million subscribers and his music videos have had 722,926,572 views. MacDonald was listed as one of the top emerging artists in 2021 with his number one hit "Fake Woke" (Zellner, 2021). His songs provide a right-wing populist view of society that denigrates liberals. Song titles include "Snowflakes", "No Good Bastards", "Canceled", "Coronavirus", "Straight White Male", and "No Lives Matter" (Zellner, 2021).

A3   Other sites

A3.1   *Amazon Book publishing*

We found evidence that Amazon Books is actively involved in not only providing access to but also providing a platform for RWE groups in Canada and elsewhere.

The book section of the online retail site prints and advertises books by well-known hate group members, conspiracy theorists, and RWE pundits like Lauren Southern, Stefan Molyneux, Gavin McInnes, and Ezra Levant.

The latter, for example, mentions in his book chapter in Censored: How the West became Soviet Russia that "Laurence [sic] Southern… is banned from Britain for blaspheming against Is- lam" which is not true in terms of the reason why she is banned. McInnis continues saying: "But if Islam thrives in London, and it becomes normalised, the lefties and the liberals will be the first to go" (Jones et al., 2019, p. 79). He goes on to justify Alex Jones' conspiracy that frogs are turning gay by saying that if the facts about the increasing levels of estrogen in water are mentioned and how it affects frogs, it can become "a very boring way of telling you a true fact" (Jones et al., 2019, p. 85). In other words, it should be acceptable to claim that water is turning frogs gay because people can get easily bored by the straight facts.

McInnes then defends his creation of the Proud Boys who are shown as being victims of liberals, asserting that "it's a lie that white supremacy is the real terrorist danger" in America (Jones et al., 2019. p. 87), often picturing himself as a free speech warrior who has been forced to be deplatformed. Ironically, the book itself is printed by Amazon.ca in Bolton, Ontario.

A similar book printed by Amazon.ca is Lauren's Southern's *Barbarians: How baby Boomers, Immigrants, and Islam Screwed my Generation* (2016). The book is published with a preface by Gavin McInnes who calls her the "millennial Ann Coulter" and by Stefan Molyneaux who urged readers to "buy it, read it, share it- if you have no spine, you will surely grow one". In this book, Lauren Southern expresses a great deal of hate and animosity against liberals, Muslims, and non-white immigrants. For example, she describes Muslims as being "one particularly dangerous group" (Southern, 2016, p. 48) who are inherently evil. Islamophobia is a "retarded concept" (Southern, 2016, p. 49) because it prevents her from attacking Muslims. She further asserts that "anti-Muslim sentiments" do not make someone a Nazi. Instead, "it makes you someone who wants nothing to do with a people who are Nazis in all but name" (Southern, 2016, p. 76), while Muslim terrorists "have plenty of friends among the alleged 'peaceful Muslim majority', almost all of whom are zealous Muslims" (Southern, 2016, p. 53). According to Southern, Muslims have fundamental problems that are intrinsically related to their nature, and that they cannot be cured, probably only by converting to Christianity. She mentions, for example:

> It may be cruel to shoot a wolf charging at your child with its jaws slavering, but it is not bigoted. Wolves are predators. They pose danger to defenseless humans…. while individual Muslims can no doubt be decent and noble people, just as tame wolves do exist, the fact is that Islam the religion is by its nature dangerous to the West. We can have compassion for people who have never known any other way of thinking, just as we have compassion for cancer patients, without excusing the diseases (Southern, 2016, p. 50).

The above lines can be interpreted as promoting genocide against a whole religious group and justifying it with a perceived sense of threat. Southern elaborates stating:

> Islam's ambition has been the destruction of Christendom… since Muhammad dreamed it up between child brides… Let he who desires peace prepare for war, and let he who desires religious tolerance between the West and Islam prepare for more crusades. So while the leftists attack the Crusades as evil imperialists, I'm going to be hoisting the flag and saying 'Deus Vult'.
> (Southern, 2016, p. 56)

The style of the latter lines is similar to Biblical teachings, and her references to the Crusades as well as the reference to the Latin term which means "God wills it" clearly show Southern's militant far-right vision in which the only way to 'save' the West is through ridding the world of Islam.

Unlike McInnes who discusses culture wars, Southern actually discusses possible physical wars. Southern argues that diversity is a "weakness" and its legacy is "not peace and love, but division and hate…It must be razed, salted, and burned" (Southern, 2016, p. 8). In this respect, multiculturalism and immigration have ruined the traditional values of Western societies. Southern asserts that if the West accepts too many immigrants, "we lose the ability to assimilate them, and everything goes to s—t" (Southern, 2016, p. 37). This is because mass immigration "is the destruction of the economy, of our culture, and the very moral norms…" (Southern, 2016, p. 39). Immigrants, after all, are "hordes of uneducated fanatics and criminals" or "human garbage" that the liberals "would willingly invite" or "seek to import" (Southern, 2016, p. 80). To solve this problem, Southern suggests that the national origins of immigrants need to be factored in "so that limits on immigration from other Western countries can be removed" (Southern, 2016, p. 77). In the top list that should not be allowed to enter Western countries are Muslims "especially from the Third World" (p. 75). Hence, "pan-Western nationalism" in Southern's view is "awesome" (p. 72) as it can solve all the social problems in the West. Ironically, when she referenced Chipotle, she expressed her delight with the food but repeated the lines of Rowan Atkinson's fictional conservative voter who said: "Now we've got the recipe, is there any need for them to stay?" (Southern, 2016, p. 39).[6] It is important to note here that the funding Southern gets is not only from cryptocurrency donations, book sales, and social media activites, but also from famous figures like Elon Musk who once tweeted at her in 2024 and has covered her monthly subscription to Twitter (Hern, 2024).

Due to the limited space in this report, it is not possible to include all the details, for there are numerous other examples of how Amazon Books is promoting hate, misinformation, and propaganda by publishing the works of some fringe Canadian writers. For example, Christopher A. Shaw, a professor based at the University of British Columbia, is known for his anti-pandemic and anti-vaccine views. His book, *Dispatches from the Vaccine Wars: Fighting for Human Freedom During the Great Reset* was published in 2021 in which he spreads misinformation on the efficacy of the vaccine, and it is widely popular on Amazon books. Another notable example is a book written by Ricardo Duchesne, a former professor at the University of New Brunswick, which is entitled *Canada in Decay: Mass Immigration, Diversity, and the Ethnocide of Euro-Canadians* (2018). In this book and numerous other publications, Duchesne promotes white supremacy, hate against immigrants, and misinformation.

In brief, the books cited above clearly show the ideology of the authors in which hate, misinformation, hyper-masculinity, and White supremacy are expressed directly and indirectly. Some of these were expressed quite explicitly, while others were thinly cloaked and otherwise indirect while also providing profits for RWE authors and for Amazon to gain profits. What remains shocking is the way such books are promoted and even printed by Amazon to gain profits, while also offering sympathizers and followers the means to comment favorably on these books, creating a mini-social media site.

A3.2 Dark Web and cryptocurrency

The Dark Web is a term used to describe a section of the internet whose content is intentionally concealed. Because of its concealed nature, it has become associated with "illegal and anti-social" material (Weimann, 2016, p. 196). Dark Web pages are not accessible through popular search engines such as Google and require access via specialized software. The Dark Web, or encrypted engagement, was developed by the U.S. Naval Research Laboratory to anonymously communicate online (Weimann, 2016, p. 196). This team of computer scientists and mathematicians developed a new technology titled onion routing, which allows "bi-directional communication where the source and destination cannot be determined by a third party" (Kaur & Randhawa, 2020, p. 2132). A network that uses this onion routing process is classified as a Darknet, and a combination of many Darknets created the Dark Web (Kaur & Randhawa, 2020, p. 2132). The Naval Research Laboratory eventually released the onion routing technique to the public under an Open Source License, which in time became The Onion Router (Tor) (Kaur & Randhawa, 2020, p. 2132). Tor uses onion routing through a network of participating computers that sends user traffic through other computers, so that the original user cannot be traced as easily. In essence, the websites and the web traffic are encrypted leaving no trace of who accessed or who the website/content creator is (Weimann, 2016, p. 196). Other browsers that provide access to the Dark Web include FreeNet, Riffle, Invisible Internet Project (I2P), and Whonix (Kaur & Randhawa, 2020, p. 2133). Encryption is an important component of the Dark Web, and simply using one of these browsers is not a guarantee of anonymity, so users also use a Virtual Private Network (VPN). When exchanging information, users also employ an encryption technique known as Pretty Good Privacy (PGP) which encrypts both private and public keys when communicating (Kaur & Randhawa, 2020, p. 2134).

The Dark Web has been associated with a wide range of activities. For example, it has been associated with everything from WikiLeaks, Bitcoin, and cryptocurrency

(Weimann, 2016, p. 197) to being a means for illegal activities such as terrorism, hacking, phishing, human trafficking, child pornography among others (Kaur & Randhawa, 2020, p. 2133). The Dark Web has made headlines with nefarious activities a few times. In 2015, the online dating site for those seeking extramarital affairs, Ashley Madison was hacked and 9.7 GB of users' personal data was dumped on the Dark Web. In 2017, there were over 1.4 billion personal records retrieved by a variety of means, which were dumped by hackers on the Dark Web (Kaur & Randhawa, 2020, p. 2140). In 2019, the Dark Web site Silk Road, an online illegal drug marketplace, was shut down by the FBI, while Canadian founder Ross Ulbricht was sentenced to life in prison (Kaur & Randhawa, 2020, p. 2140). The illegal drug markets still exist, with the largest being AlphaBay (Kaur & Randhawa, 2020, p. 2140). The Dark Web is used for arms trafficking and has become the platform for criminal gangs and terrorists (Kaur & Randhawa, 2020. P. 2142). Overall, the criminal marketplace on the Dark Web has been estimated to generate around $500,000 per day (Kaur & Randhawa, 2020, p. 2156). Estimates are difficult because currency is transferred predominately by Bitcoin, which is difficult to trace (Kaur & Randhawa, 2020, p. 2156).

Cryptocurrencies, such as Bitcoin, are the monetary backbone of the Dark Web. Hatewatch (Edison & Squire, 2021) reported that some leaders of the extreme right benefited from the early adoption of the currency. The group identified over 600 cryptocurrency addresses linked to white supremacists and far-right extremists. One of the extremists identified by Hatewatch was Canadian Stefan Molyneux, an early purchaser of Bitcoin, who has profited immensely. He initially purchased Bitcoin in January 2013 and his investment as of December 2021 is worth $3.28 million (Hayden & Squire, 2021). Investments in cryptocurrencies allow the extreme right to expand their social movement and to attain, obscure, and relocate funding sources. Molyneux is a perfect example of the power of cryptocurrencies. He was deplatformed from Twitter and YouTube in 2020 and he was pushed to alternative platforms, which impacted his ability to raise funds as his overall traffic decreased. Molyneux invested early and for the long-term holding his assets regardless of the volatility of the market. His donors also donated 1250 Bitcoin tokens to him, a much larger donation than the other RWE individuals Hatewatch investigated. Through donations, Molyneux was able to increase his overall assets in cryptocurrencies (Hayden & Squire, 2021).

National and international funding remains integral to the activities of RWE in Canada and elsewhere. For example, the Christchurch mosque's terrorist donated $138.89 AUD to Stefan Molyneux's Freedomain Radio podcast on January 15 and 17, 2017 (Report of the Royal Commission, 2021, p. 180). On September 15, 2017, he made another donation of $106.68 AUD via PayPal to Rebel News Network Ltd. (Report of the Royal Commission, 2021, p. 194). It is noteworthy to mention here that Stefan Molyneux and Southern Lauren toured New Zealand in early August 2018 discussing the alleged dangers of Islam. A few months afterwards, the Christchurch attack occurred which led to the death of 51 people.

Another notable example is related to the way some US far-right groups and figures that were engaged in the January 2021 Capitol attack got more than $500,000

Appendix: RWE sites   171

USD in Bitcoin donations. Similar to the case of Christchurch attack, the donation came from abroad as it was sent by a French computer programmer who donated "28.15 BTC - worth approximately $522,000 at the time of transfer"; the donation was sent to "22 separate addresses in a single transaction" including a transfer to the digital wallet of the extremist livestreamer, Nick Fuentes (Chainalysis, 2021).

We searched the Dark Web in early January 2022 for Canadian RWE content, using some of these search engines: DarkNet Search, Kilos, Torch, Deep Search, Ahmia, TorDex, etc. However, these search engines are very limited in what they crawl, so we could not find anything specific or related to RWE activities.

Instead, we found general sites that offer links to dark markets that offer drugs, pornography, and alleged services like hired assassins to hack emails and social media accounts. Hundreds of other sites also alleged having fake Canadian passports, visas to enter Canada, driver's licenses for different Canadian provinces, permanent residency cards, and COVID-19 vaccine passports for various provinces.

Using the Beacon Dark Web search engine offered by Echosec Systems, we found, for example, over 14,000 Dark Web sites that reference 'vaccine' and 'Canada', most purportedly offering some of the above services. Using the above Canadian RWE terms, we identified 2,634 posts that reference these terms on the Dark Web after removing all duplicates. We also found that some of the RWE popular sites like 8kun, greatawakening.win, the Daily Stormer, Parler, and 4chan had mirror sites on the Dark Web that can only be accessed using software such as Tor, or the Dark Web portal. Table 5.8 shows the top ten Dark Web sites that are often used by the Canadian RWE. In terms of the frequency of using these sites, 8kun was the most frequent probably because it mirrors the site on the open web, which often gets disrupted or has content removed, which is not the case on the Dark Web.

The digital analysis of these Dark Web posts shows several references to 'Research' and 'QResearch' (over 1,000 posts) as well as bake and bread, which are related to QAnon conspiracy. As for the prominent figures mentioned, they include

Table 5.8 The top Dark Web sites for Canadian RWE content

No	Site
1	8kun
2	8chan Community
3	Dancing elephants: Welcome to the forum
4	The Great Awakening - WWG1WGA!
5	Daily Stormer
6	Rocksolid Light - rocksolid
7	Endchan
8	KOHLCHAN
9	9chan
10	DeepPaste
11	Stronghold Paste
12	Parler
13	4chan

Source: Created by the authors.

Donald Trump, Justin Trudeau, Joe Biden, Maxwell Ghislaine, and Romana Didulo, including her Canada1st Party of Canada. In fact, Didulo was mentioned 103 times in the comments. Some of the comments are highly problematic such as the following one: "QAnon's 'Queen of Canada' Calls for Followers to 'Kill' People Vaccinating Children | QAnon influencer Romana Didulo told her 70,000 followers that 'duck-hunting season is open' and by ducks she means healthcare workers, politicians, and journalists" (Lamoureux, 2021).

Romana Didulo is a prominent QAnon figure based in Victoria, B.C. Didulo claims to be the 'sovereign of the republic of Canada' and uses her channels to amplify her desire to halt COVID-19 vaccinations and control measures. In summer 2021, Didulo's followers sent cease-and-desist letters on her behalf demanding a stop to COVID-19 restrictions. In November 2021, Didulo started directing her followers to "shoot to kill" anyone who administers vaccines to children. Shortly after, Didulo was detained for 48 hours by the RCMP under B.C.'s Mental Health Act. Didulo has also built a network of supply chain outlets for her 'subjects', which respond to their requests regarding food banks, farm supplies, and preparations for the "end times". Her followers request her intercession as a monarchy, but also as a saint-like figure to answer their prayers. Didulo has created a social movement based upon both a self-created hagiography and a political heritage, creating a position for herself that crosses into a superhuman realm. Also, the #wwg1wga hashtag was the most frequent one in the dataset.

In terms of RWE cryptocurrency funding, we checked the following website https://www.blockchain.com/btc/address/ as of December 1, 2021. The details column in Table 5.9 offers the total amount of funding in Canadian dollars these figures and entities received. However, the site does not consider the different cryptocurrency values according to the respective dates they were received. As a result, we consulted another site called https://blockchair.com/ in early January 2022 to identify the differences in these crypto values. As we can see, Stefan Molyneux received a total of $77,714,597 in cryptocurrencies, but when calculated based on their respective value, the amount is about $2,126,340 which is still a very large sum of money. Jordan Peterson follows with an amount of $142,196 and then Lauren Southern with $72,712. In terms of the number of transactions, however, Lauren Southern comes second with 548 times only preceded by Stefan Molyneaux who transacted 5,056 times (Figures 5.3 and 5.4).

Interestingly, both Faith Goldy and Lauren Southern received one Bitcoin, which is equivalent to an amount of $14,224 (precisely $14,223.60) on the same day of January 11, 2018. The only difference was the timing as Southern received this amount about 10 minutes earlier (21:13:18) than Goldy (21:23:43).

Southern received her payment from a sender, who used different digital wallet identifiers (1Akbn2ahsSCPbqBtWdiCiXYD7dntTBr5NM). A few days earlier, the same sender made 1 Bitcoin payment to the far-right provocateur, Rebecca Hargraves, on January 2, 2018, and made another payment on September 13, 2019. Both payments were equivalent to $17,080 at that time. Hargraves is also known as the "Blonde in the Belly of the Beast". Hargraves became popular with a YouTube video about her journey into being "redpilled". In her video, she expressed popular

Appendix: RWE sites 173

Table 5.9 Cryptocurrency wallets and amounts for RWE groups, media, and individuals

Name	Funding 1	Details
Faith Goldy	Bitcoin: 1Ej6qC5zu-NAz4xhBjowx-DWD9XRjzSpadVm / Etransfer: FaithGoldy@gmail.com	This address has transacted 140 times on the Bitcoin blockchain. It has received a total of 2.08204881 BTC ($129,121.38) and has sent a total of 1.97317389 BTC ($122,369). The current value of this address is 0.10887492 BTC ($6,752). Blockchair estimates: Total received: ($26,458), total spent: ($16,717).
Stefan Molyneux	Bitcoin: 1Fd8RuZq-JNG4v56rPD1v6r-gYptwnHeJRWs / https://www.freedmain.com/donate/	This address has transacted 5,056 times on the Bitcoin blockchain. It has received a total of 1,250.71995999 BTC ($77,714,597) and has sent a total of 1,250.56253887 BTC ($77,704,816). The current value of this address is 0.15742112 BTC ($9,781). Blockchair estimates: Total received:($2,126,340), total spent:($4,150,848).
Lauren Southern	1JLM6GJwaPdNv4d-M8K5KkcFHeziXXX- MGKT // https://mypatriotsupply.com/pages/contact-us	This address has transacted 548 times on the Bitcoin blockchain. It has received a total of 9.04808060 BTC ($560,291) and has sent a total of 9.04808060 BTC ($560,291). The current value of this address is 0.00000000 BTC ($0.00). Blockchair estimates: Total received: ($72,712), total spent: ($72,710).
Rebel News	Bitcoin: 3F8Gmf-brVqSTP5djjTsqB-BwDnzxJ7nsErF //// 34XQ6FcaYiU-VzMWZu54Hs2Vp-J9cUreHo5t /// 0x21cb746bc1af-b651a839abf4d69f-4f75ae478e3f // qrakj0p9l8aufgdzkzn-n43adhhl8yz42ey5ed-vtp5v//// DGBmYH-kTustZfCsajenEYM-vTV32ZkWk5bM /// MCQpZdHoHjvnWkq-jnsArCB7i5Qc3Sm5iPo /// https://www.paypal.com/paypalme/Rebel- News	These addresses have transacted 0 times on the Bitcoin blockchain. They have received a total of 0.00000000 BTC ($0.00) and have sent a total of 0.00000000 BTC ($0.00). The current value of these addresses is 0.00000000 BTC ($0.00).

Source: Created by the authors.

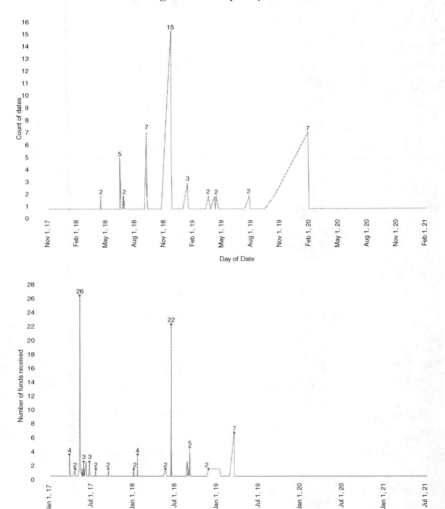

Figure 5.3 Faith Goldy (a) and Lauren Southern's (b) dates and number of cryptocurrency funds they received.

Source: Created by the authors.

racist tropes about people of color and promoted the decline of Western civilization. (Lewis, 2018. p. 28) Now an influencer on both YouTube and alternative social media, Hargraves uses her personal testimonial as a tool to influence others, by describing her process of destabilization and the "clarity" she now has. There is a high probability that all the above payments made to female RWE members (Lauren Southern, Faith Goldy, and Rebecca Hargraves) were deposited by the same sender.

Appendix: RWE sites 175

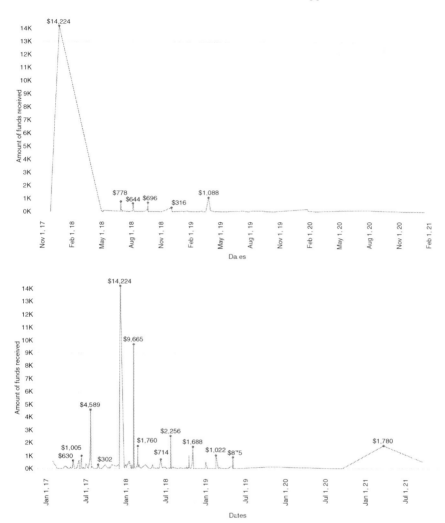

Figure 5.4 Faith Goldy (a) and Lauren Southern's (b) amount of cryptocurrency funds they received.
Source: Created by the authors.

A3.3 *Google search*

In this section, we provide empirical evidence on the problematic nature of Google's algorithmically produced autocomplete subtitles.[7] A subtitle is a fixed label that appears when a popular figure's name is typed into the Google search bar. Subtitles are useful because they allow Internet users to retrieve snippets of information when searching for certain figures (Al-Rawi et al., 2022). However, when one searches Google for the names of terrorists, extremists, and provocateurs, one can find that they mostly have no subtitles associated with them on Google's search engine. For example, we cannot find any subtitles for the world's most notable terrorists, including Abu Bakr Al-Baghdadi (ISIS former leader), Osama Bin Laden (Al-Qaeda former leader), Ayman Al-Zawahiri (Al-Qaeda current leader), Khalid Sheikh Mohammed (planned 9/11), Alexandre Bissonnette (Quebec mosque attack), Brenton Tarrant (Christchurch attack), Nathaniel Veltman (London, Ontario terrorist attack), and Faith Goldy (far-right provocateur). However, these are only exceptions. In this study, we show how the majority of other subtitles provide neutral or misleading labels for a variety of bad actors such as white supremacist Stefan Molyneaux, Randy Weaver of the Ruby Ridge Standoff, Jake Angeli (QAnon Sha-man), Jim Jones leader of the People's Temple massacre, Jerad Miller Las Vegas mass shooter, James O'Keefe of Project Veritas, Gavin McInnes founder of the Proud Boys, Fred Phelps former leader of the Westboro Baptist Church, David Koresh of Camp Davidian, Cliven Bundy leader of the 2014 Bundy Standoff, and William Pierce author of The Turner Diaries (see Table 5.10).

To empirically conduct our research, we used manual reverse engineering (Bucher, 2018) to understand how over 100 bad actors, including terrorists, mass killers, conspiracists, religious leaders, and hackers, are described by Google's algorithms. We employed VPN technology to change our location and compare whether similar subtitles are used in Canada, the United States, and the Netherlands as algorithms frequently cater to specific country's Internet laws. Our findings show that Google's subtitle feature systematically promotes and presents bad actors in neutral and sometimes in positive ways. We argue that these algorithmic subtitles are highly problematic because they mislead the public by offering controversial figures and bad actors' publicity and sometimes credibility. All of these searches on Google were conducted during the week of October 18, 2021.

Table 5.10 Canadian individuals searched on Google and subtitle results

Name	Google Subtitle	Personality Description
Lauren Southern	Canadian Activist	Alt-right political activist, white nationalist, and YouTuber. In 2015, Southern ran as a Libertarian Party candidate in the Canadian federal election
Gavin McInnis	Canadian Writer	Canadian writer, podcaster, and far-right political commentator. Get Off My Lawn podcast, on the online video platform Censored.TV, which he founded. He co-founded Vice in 1994 and founded the Proud Boys
Ezra Levant	Canadian Activist	Far-right political activist, writer, and broadcaster, who founded Rebel News and Western Standard

(*Continued*)

Appendix: RWE sites 177

Table 5.10 (Continued)

Name	Google Subtitle	Personality Description
Stefan Molyneux	Canadian Podcaster	Irish-born Canadian far-right white nationalist, podcaster, blogger, and banned YouTuber, who promotes conspiracy theories, scientific racism, eugenics, and racist views
Paul Fromm	N/A	Canadian white supremacist, neo-Nazi, and perennial political candidate
Faith Goldy	N/A	White Nationalist and Social Media Influencer, former Rebel News
Marc Lemire	N/A	Works with Paul Fromm - webmaster of Ontario-based Freedom-Site founded in 1996
Terry Tremaine	N/A	Founder of NSP of Canada, white nationalist who posted on forums like Stormfront
Ernst Zündel	German Pampleteer	Holocaust denier and revisionist
Kevin Annett	Canadian Writer	Former Minister, writer. He wrote a book exposing the atrocities to Indigenous Communities, and now is a conspiracist and vlogger
Sheila Gunn Reid	3. Author	Alberta – Rebel News
Viva Frei	N/A	Far-right member and promoter of COVID-19 conspiracies
Chris Sky	N/A	Anti-COVID Leader
Gus Stefanis	N/A	Leader of the Canadian Nationalist Party/White Lives Matters
Tyler L. Russell	N/A	Plaid Army - Vlogger
Jeremy MacKenzie	N/A	Plaid Army - Vlogger
Keean Bext	N/A	Rebel Media
Alek Minassian	N/A	An Incel charged with murder with a vehicle for purposely running over individuals in Toronto
Patrik Mathews	N/A	Canadian Military White Supremacist
Mark Lepine	N/A	Montreal University massacre shooter
Alexandre Bissonnette	N/A	Quebec Terrorist Attack
Nathaniel Veltman	N/A	London Ontario Terrorist Attack
Serge Monast	Journalist	Creator of the Blue Beam Project Conspiracy
William Guy Carr	Canadian Author	Illuminati/Third World War Conspiracy
Michael Chossudovsky	Canadian Economist	Founder of the Centre for Re- search on Globalization a conspiracy site
Barry Zwicker	Canadian Journalist	9/11 Conspiracist/filmmaker

Source: Created by the authors.

Notes

1 Discord is a messaging app that was created as a voice and text chat platform for gamers. Discord soon developed into a system for RWE to engage. According to Conway et al. (2019), there are three reasons that allowed the takeover by RWE: (1) the app allows users to create private, invite-only chat groups that cannot be discovered by non-users of Discord; (2) it is related to its anonymity; and lastly; and (3) administrators of these private group chats can create their own moderation rules. Discord came into the spotlight as the platform where the Unite the Right rally was organized and logistics such as ride-sharing and accommodations were made (Conway et al., 2019). In the aftermath of the rally, a left-wing media collective, Unicorn Riot, leaked almost 800,000 messages from the app. The leaked messages contained rampant racism, anti-Semitism, and political mobilization in support of the Republican Party (Conway et al., 2019). Discord does not define itself as a social media platform. Discord (2021) claims "there is no algorithm deciding what you should see, no endless scrolling, no news feed". The app does acknowledge the existence of RWE on its platform and has included a comment regarding safety for users on the app. However, the statement is nebulous and not impactful: "We don't sit back and simply wait for reports, but instead act to protect everyone on the platform. We know that there are cases where bad actors are acting to cause violence or harm in the real world, and we make it clear to them that there's no place for them on Discord" (Discord, 2021). The Discord guidelines define the rules governing the channels and include rules forbidding the organization, promotion, or coordination of servers around hate speech. Hate speech is defined as attacks on a person or community based on "race, ethnicity, national origin, sex, gender, sexual orientation, religious affiliation, or disabilities" (Discord Guidelines, 2021a). Further, the rules governing content, explicitly state that users "may not use Discord for the organization, promotion, or support of violent extremism" (Discord Guidelines, 2021a). In researching Canadian RWE on Discord, not much right-wing content was found. The servers that were found to have been created specifically for hate speech, racism, or extreme right-wing content purport to have Canadian members, but it was almost impossible to discern the geographical location of users, mostly because of the simple fact that each user is allowed to select their own representative country flag regardless of where they are actually located. On some servers, we find relevant RWE content including posts, specifically the memes and commentary on these servers were racist, homophobic, transphobic, and promoted RWE ideology.

2 Getter was launched by Jason Miller, a former aide and spokesperson of President Donald Trump's team. The site officially launched on July 4, 2021. The site promotes itself as a "Marketplace of Ideas" and like many alternative social media platforms, states that it is founded on free speech, as well as the rejection of censorship and cancel culture (Paudel et al., 2022. p. 1). The platform resembles Twitter where users follow each other, can share posts, and comment, and like Twitter there is a character limit for posts. Users can use hashtags and can link their posts together as a thread. Users can also keep aware of trending topics and hashtags on the site. Demographics of users show Brazilians as the most active, and Canadians being 0.13% of users (Paudel et al., 2022, p. 3). Getter's launch was not without issues. Shortly after its launch hackers used the site's API to scrape the email addresses, birth dates, names, and usernames from over 85,000 users (Hatmaker, 2021). Getter's funding also caused some negativity in that one of the funders was Guo Wengui, a Chinese businessperson, and a close associate of Stephen K. Bannon. Wengui was associated with a significant web presence and spreading of anti-COVID-19 vaccine material, election fraud claims, and with spreading QAnon conspiracies. Paudel et al. (2022) were one of the first teams to analyze the platform and its users and found that the posts were predominately political, focusing on Trump's 2020 campaign and Brazilian Presidential nominee Bolsonaro's campaign. The initial research into the platform found that the engagement with users was on a steady decline since its launch but a core of well-known right-wing individuals and early adopters

had become active users. Paudel et al. (2022, p. 6) also found that although there was a high level of toxicity on the site, it was lower than that on similar sites such as Gab and 4chan. Getter's terms of use regarding language and conduct open with the phrase "GETTR holds freedom of speech as its core value and does not wish to censor your opinions" (Gettr TOS, 2021). It does have a far more robust set of rules than other "free speech" social media platforms such as Gab, Reddit, or Telegram. Content deemed offensive by GETTR includes obscene, lewd, filthy, pornographic, violent, illegal, threatening or abusive. In this context users may not post material that is deemed "hateful, racially, ethnically or otherwise" (GETTR TOS, 2021). Although the Terms of Service does state that Gettr can "address content" but "does not commit" to doing so. Unfortunately, we did not have a programmatic method to extract data from this platform.

3 Rumble is a Toronto-based, video-sharing platform and was founded in 2013 by Canadian tech entrepreneur Chris Pavlovski (Harwell, 2021). It grew in popularity amongst conservative, right-wing social media users and conspiracy theorists after Dan Bongino and California Republican David Nunes promoted it in October of that same year. Based on their support, the number of users went from 800,000 in August to 25 million users in October of the same year (Lonas, 2021). A similar boost in the number of users occurred after the event of January 6, 2021, on Capitol Hill, in reaction to the banning of users from Twitter and Facebook who were promoting or posting about the event (Lonas, 2021). Rumble also struck early deals with congresswoman Tulsi Gabbard, and world-renowned journalist, Glenn Greenwald, to use Rumble as their video platform of choice to help gain a user base for the platform. The deal provided a two-hour exclusivity for their content on Rumble's platform in which after that period of exclusivity Greenwald and Gabbard could post the material on other platforms. In addition, the company offered monetary payments for those posting videos which "challenged the status quo" (Harwell, 2021). These publicity and public relations strategies led Rumble to grow to almost 19 million users in May of 2021 (Harwell, 2021). American right-wing venture capitalists have shown an interest in the platform by providing financial backing in the last year. Narya Capital, co-founded by "Hillbilly Eulogy" author J.D. Vance, Colin Greenspon, and Peter Theil, co-founder of PayPal and former Facebook investor, and Colt Ventures the company of Dallas investor and former Trump advisor Darren Blanton, invested in Rumble for an estimated $500 million (Hagey, 2021). In December 2021, former President Trump's media company signed a deal with Rumble as the provider of video and streaming for Trump's new social media platform, TRUTH Social. Early in 2021, Rumble filed an anti-trust suit against Google based on an accusation that the search platform favored YouTube in search results over rivals such as Rumble. The ramifications felt by Rumble include a loss of advertising revenue and viewers. The company also accused Google of unfairly depriving Rumble of users, when phones with Google's Android operating system were sold with the YouTube app pre-installed (Schechner, 2021). In general, the platform is well known for hosting and promoting a lot of misinformation and conspiracy theories (Castaldo, 2022).

4 Tumblr is a microblogging site, where users can follow each other, but reciprocal following is not a requirement. Blogs, or posts, can be re-broadcasted to their own followers in what is termed "re-blogging." Posts can be composed of text, images, audio, or videos. In 2018, Tumblr announced a ban on all nudity on the site, banning any photos, videos, or GIGs of genitalia and female nipples. This ban also included any visualizations of sex acts. The site itself had been known as a positive space for sexual sub-cultures, as an LGBTQ2SA safe space, and adult-themed adult fiction. The microblogging site was soon criticized for its banning of adult/pornographic material but for not banning extremist or hate speech (Rosenberg, 2018). Tumblr allows all hashtags to be used such as #MakeCanadaGreatAgain (n = 3), including profanities against world religions and their adherents. RWE activities are extremely limited on this microblogging social media site, which is prominently associated with adult content and illicit drug sales (Al-Rawi, 2020a).

5 Below are the groups on Facebook and Instagram representative of the hashtags and posts described above: https://www.facebook.com/groups/664645074169552/; https://www.instagram.com/kingcashyt/; https://www.facebook.com/groups/Stand4THEE/. And other ones are still active like the 5G conspiracy theory in Canada: https://www.instagram.com/stop.chemtrails.5g.canada/; https://www.instagram.com/chattruthtillreachcriticalmass/; https://www.instagram.com/5g.spotters/; https://www.instagram.com/chemtrailsworldwide/; https://www.instagram.com/standup.worldwide/; https://www.instagram.com/perception_real/; https://www.instagram.com/sovereigncitizensociety/; https://www.instagram.com/concernedinseattle/; There is a Great Reset (QAnon conspiracy) by a Canadian Instagram channel: https://www.instagram.com/truthseekersofcanada/; While the hashtag #bonniehenryisafraud is more specific to British Columbia.
6 The satirical video clip is available on YouTube here: https://www.youtube.com/watch?v=YaGdwfykYGY.
7 This section is borrowed from a previous peer reviewed study whose details are as follows: Al-Rawi, A., Celestini, C., Stewart, N., & Worku, N. (2022). How Google autocomplete algorithms about conspiracy theorists mislead the public. *M/C Journal*, 25(1).

References

4chan. (2021a, October). Advertise. Retrieved from https://www.4chan.org/advertise

4chan. (2021b, October). Rules. Retrieved from https://www.4chan.org/rules

Al-Rawi, A., & Shukla, V. (2020). Bots as active news promoters: A digital analysis of COVID-19 tweets. *Information*, *11*(10), 461.

Al-Rawi, A., & Fakida, A. (2021). The methodological challenges of studying "Fake News". *Journalism Practice*, *17*(1): 1–20.

Al-Rawi, A., Celestini, C., Stewart, N., & Worku, N. (2022). How Google autocomplete algorithms about conspiracy theorists mislead the public. *M/C Journal*, *25*(1). https://doi.org/10.5204/mcj.2852

Arthurs, J., Drakopoulou, S., & Gandini, A. (2018). Researching youtube. *Convergence*, *24*(1), 3–15.

Baele, S. J., Brace, L., & Coan, T. G. (2021). Variations on a theme? Comparing 4chan, 8kun, and other chans' far-right "/ pol" boards. *Perspectives on Terrorism*, *15*(1), 65–80.

Baines, A., Ittefaq, M., & Abwao, M. (2021). # Scamdemic, # Plandemic, or# Scaredemic: What parler social media platform tells us about COVID-19 vaccine. *Vaccines*, *9*(5), 421.

Berry, D. T. (2022). Varieties of religion and secrecy in American white power movements. In *The Routledge handbook of religion and secrecy* (pp. 355–369). Routledge.

Betz, H. G., & Johnson, C. (2004). Against the current—Stemming the tide: The nostalgic ideology of the contemporary radical populist right. *Journal of Political Ideologies*, *9*(3), 311–327.

Bleich, E. (2012). Defining and researching Islamophobia. *Review of Middle East Studies*, *46*(2), 180–189.

Bouko, C., Van Ostaeyen, P., & Voué, P. (2021, August). Facebook's policies against extremism: Ten years of struggle for more transparency. *First Monday*, *26*(9). https://doi.10.5210/ fmv26i9.11705

Butcher, T. (2016). Neither Black nor box: Ways of knowing algorithms. In S. Kubitschko & A. Kaun (Eds.), *Innovative methods in media and communication research* (pp. 81–98). Cham: Palgrave Macmillan.

Bucher, T. (2018). *If… then: Algorithmic power and politics*. Oxford: Oxford University Press.

Burgess, J. (2008). All your chocolate rain are belong to us?' Viral video, YouTube and the dynamics of participatory culture. In G. Lovink & S. Niederer (Eds.), *Video Vortex Reader: Responses to YouTube* (pp. 101–109) Amsterdam: Institute of Network Cultures.

Carlson, C. R., & Rousselle, H. (2020). Report and repeat: Investigating Facebook s hate speech removal process. *First Monday*.

Castaldo, J. (2022, January 7). How Rumble, a Toronto-based YouTube alternative, became a refuge for the MAGA crowd (with a US$2-billion valuation). *The Globe and Mail*. https://www.theglobeandmail.com/business/article-rumble-toronto-video-platform-youtube-alternative-valuation/

CBC News. (2021, November 10). 2 years after banning other Canadian hate groups, Facebook deletes Quebec far-right group. *CBC News*. Retrieved from https://www.cbc.ca/news/canada/montreal/far-right-quebec-group-facebook-1.6244609

CBC Radio. (2021, December 6). Canada's QAnon "Queen" and her escalating rhetoric. *CBC*. https://www.cbc.ca/radio/frontburner/canada-s-qanon-queen-and-her-escalating-rhetoric-1.6274606

Chainalysis. (2021, February 16). The 2021 Crypto Crime Report: Everything you need to know about ransomware, darknet markets, and more. Retrieved from https://the blockchaintest.com/uploads/resources/Chainalysis%20%20Crypto%20Crime%20 2021%20-%202021%20Feb.pdf

Conway, M., Scrivens, R., & Macnair, L. (2019). Right-wing extremists' persistent online presence: history and contemporary trends. *International Centre for Counter-Terrorism*.

Code, German Criminal. (1998). Federal Law Gazette (I, p. 945, p. 3322).

Devoy, D. (2021, December 3). MPP Randy Hillier to head new, Ontario First Party. *Thestar. Com*. https://www.thestar.com/local-perth/news/2021/12/03/mpp-randy-hillier-to-head-new-ontar-io-first-party.html?itm_source=parsely-api

de Vynck, G. (2021, September 29). YouTube is banning prominent anti-vaccine activists and blocking all anti-vaccine content. *Washington Post*. https://www.washingtonpost.com/technology/2021/09/29/youtube-ban-joseph-mercola/

de Zeeuw, D., Hagen, S., Peeters, S., & Jokubauskaite, E. (2020). Tracing normiefication. *First Monday*.

Discord. (2021a, May 19). Community guidelines. https://discord.com/guidelines

Discord. (2021b, October). Safety principles and policies. https://discord.com/safety; https://www.cbc.ca/news/canada/calgary/coutts-alberta-diagolon-paul-rouleau-1.6751945

Edison, M., & Squire, M. (2021, December 9). How cryptocurrency revolutionized the white supremacist movement. *Hatewatch*. Accessed from https://www.splcenter.org/hatewatch/2021/12/09/how-cryptocurrency-revolutionized-white-supremacist-movement

European Commission. (2020). The Code of conduct on countering illegal hate speech online. Retrieved from https://ec.europa.eu/commission/presscorner/detail/en/qanda_20_1135

Faludi, S. (2007). *The terror dream: Fear and fantasy in post-9/11 America*. London: Macmillan.

Fathallah, J. M. (2021). 'Getting by' on 4chan: Feminine self-presentation and capital-claiming in antifeminist Web space. *First Monday*, 26(7). https://doi.org/10.5210/fm.v26i7.10449

Fenster, M. (1999). *Conspiracy theories: Secrecy and power in American culture*. University of Minnesota Press.

Gab. (2020). Terms of service. https://gab.com/about/tos

Gab. (2022). Gab PRO | upgrade to support Gab. https://pro.gab.com/

GETTR. (2021, September 25). Terms of use. https://gettr.com/terms

Gruzd, A., & Philip, M. (2020). The state of social media in Canada 2020. Ryerson University Social Media Lab. Version 5. DOI: 10.5683/SP2/XIW8EW

Hagey, K. (2021, May 19). Peter Thiel, J.D. Vance invest in rumble video platform popular on political right. *WSJ*. https://www.wsj.com/articles/peter-thiel-j-d-vance-invest-in-rumble-video-platform-popular-on-political-right-11621447661

Harwell, D. (2021, August 12). Rumble, a YouTube rival popular with conservatives, will pay creators who 'challenge the status quo.' *Washington Post*. https://www.washingtonpost.com/technology/2021/08/12/rumble-video-gabbard-greenwald/

Hatmaker, T. (2021, July 6). TechCrunch is part of the Yahoo family of brands. *TechCrunch*. https://techcrunch.com/2021/07/06/gettr-trump-social-network-hack-defaced/

Hayden, M. E., & Squire, M. (2021, December 9). How cryptocurrency revolutionized the white supremacist movement. *Southern Poverty Law Center*. https://www.splcenter.org/hatewatch/2021/12/09/how-cryptocurrency-revolutionized-white-supremacist-movement

Help Center. (2021, December 13). Twitter's policy on hateful conduct | Twitter Help. *Twitter*. https://help.twitter.com/en/ rules-and-policies/hateful-conduct-policy

Hern, A. (2024, August 20). TechScape: Why I can't stop writing about Elon Musk. The Guardian. https://www.theguardian.com/technology/article/2024/aug/20/techscape-elon-musk-nvidia-ai-safety

Hoffman, B., Ware, J., & Shapiro, E. (2020). Assessing the threat of incel violence. *Studies in Conflict and Terrorism*, *43*(7), 565–587. https://doi.org/10.1080/1057610X.2020.1751459

Instagram. (2021, February 11). An update on our work to tackle abuse on Instagram. Retrieved from https://www.facebook.com/unsupported-browser

Intercept. (2021, October 12). Revealed: Facebook's secret blacklist of "dangerous individuals and organizations". *The Intercept*. https://theintercept.com/2021/10/12/facebook-secret-blacklist-dangerous/

Jasser, G., McSwiney, J., Pertwee, E., & Zannettou, S. (2021). 'Welcome to #GabFam': Far-right virtual community on Gab. *New Media & Society*. https://doi.org/10.1177/14614448211024546

Jones, A., Gavin, M., Watson, P., Loomer, L., & Robinson, T. (2019). *Censored: How the West became Soviet Russia*. Bolton: GLJohn & RWFS Distribution. Manufactured by Amazon.co.

Kang-Xing Jin, Head of Health. (2020, December 18). Keeping people safe and informed about the coronavirus. *Meta*. https://about.fb.com/news/2020/12/coronavirus/

Kaur, S., & Randhawa, S. (2020). Dark web: A web of crimes. *Wireless Personal Communications*, *112*(4), 2131–2158.

Kelsey, A. (2018, July 26). Twitter denies conservative 'shadow banning' claims, but alters search function. *ABC News*. Accessed from https://abcnews.go.com/Technology/twitter-denies-conservative-shadow-banning-claims-alters-search/story?id=56841398

Kor-Sins, R. (2021). The alt-right digital migration: A heterogeneous engineering approach to social media platform branding. *New Media & Society*, 14614448211038810.

Lamoureux, M. (2021, November 25). QAnon's 'Queen of Canada' calls for followers to 'Kill' people vaccinating children. *Vice*. https://www.vice.com/en/article/qanons-queen-of-canada-calls-for-followers-to-kill-people-vaccinating-children/

Lewis, R. (2018). Alternative influence: Broadcasting the reactionary right on YouTube. *Data & Society*, *18*. https://edgeryders.eu/uploads/default/original/2X/6/6c1bff49d3731a13f3208b56e10e694fce85d1c6.pdf

Lima, L., Reis, J. C., Melo, P., Murai, F., Araujo, L., Vikatos, P., & Benevenuto, F. (2018, August). Inside the right-leaning echo chambers: Characterizing Gab, an unmoderated social system. In *2018 IEEE/ACM International Conference on Advances in Social Networks Analysis and Mining (ASONAM)* (pp. 515–522). IEEE.

Lonas, L. (2021, May 19). Peter Thiel, J.D. Vance investing in YouTube alternative popular among conservatives. *The Hill*. https://thehill.com/policy/technology/554406-peter-thiel-jd-vance-investing-in-youtube-alternative-popular-among

Mamié, R., Horta Ribeiro, M., & West, R. (2021, June). Are anti-feminist communities gateways to the far right? Evidence from Reddit and YouTube. In *Proceedings of the 13th ACM web science conference 2021* (pp. 139–147).

McIlroy-Young, R., & Anderson, A. (2019, July). From "welcome new gabbers" to the pittsburgh synagogue shooting: The evolution of Gab. In Proceedings of the international AAAI conference on web and social media (Vol. 13, pp. 651–654).

Munn, L. (2021). More than a mob: Parler as preparatory media for the U.S. Capitol storming. *First Monday*, *26*(3). https://doi.org/10.5210/fm.v26i3.11574

Newell, E., Jurgens, D., Lorimer, James, Saleem, H. M., Vala, H., Sassine, J., Armstrong, C., & Ruths, D. (2016, March). User migration in online social networks: A case study on Reddit during a period of community unrest. In *Tenth International AAAI Conference on Web and Social Media*.

Parler. (2021, October 9). About. Retrieved from https://parler.com/about.php

Parler. (2021, February 14). Community guidelines. Downloaded from https://parler.com/documents/guidelines.pdf

Paudel, P., Blackburn, J., De Cristofaro, E., Zannettou, S., & Stringhini, G. (2022, June). A longitudinal study of the Gettr social network. In *Proceedings of the international workshop on cyber social threats*.

Pettman, J. J. (1996). Boundary politics: Women, nationalism, and danger. In M. Maynard and J. Purvis (Eds.), *New Frontiers in women's studies* (pp. 187–202). London: Routledge.

PressProgress. (2018, August 27). Conservative delegate who led push to end birthright citizenship linked to campus 'alt- right' scandals.

Rebel News. (2015, October 16). 10 things Canadians don't know about Americans [Video]. *YouTube*. https://www.youtube.com/watch?v=XpoYWROw5BY

Reddit. (2021, January). Reddit by the numbers. https://www.redditinc.com

Reddit. (2021, October). Content policy. *Reddit*. https://www.redditinc.com/policies/content-policy

Regehr, K. (2020). In (cel) doctrination: How technologically facilitated misogyny moves violence off screens and on to streets. *New Media & Society*, 1461444820959019.

Report of the Royal Commission of Inquiry into the terrorist attack on Christchurch masjidain on 15 March 2019. (2021). Volume 2. Retrieved from https://christchurchattack.royalcommission.nz/assets/Report-Volumes-and-Parts/Ko-to-tatou-kainga-te- nei-Volume-2.pdf

Rosenberg, E. (2018, December 4). Tumblr's nudity ban removes one of the last major refuges for pornography on social media. *Washington Post*. https://www.washingtonpost.com/business/2018/12/04/tumblrs-nudity-crackdown-means-pornography-will-be-harder-find-its-platform-than-nazi-propaganda/

Schechner, S. (2021, January 12). Google sued by YouTube rival over search rankings. *Wall Street Journal*. https://www.wsj.com/articles/google-sued-by-youtube-rival-over-search-rankings-11610407969

Scheinberg, S. (2018). Canada: Right-wing extremism in the peaceable kingdom. In *The extreme right* (pp. 36–54). Routledge.

Seatter, E., & Milton, J. (2018, November 13). Rebel Media reporter worked for white supremacist web store. *Ricochet*. https://ricochet.media/en/2422/rebel-media-reporter-worked-for-white-supremacist-web-store

Southern, L. (2016). *Barbarians: How baby boomers, immigrants, and Islam screwed my generation*. Bolton: Rebel News Network Ltd. Manufactured by Amazon.com.

Transparency Center. (2022). Hate speech. *Meta*. https://www.facebook.com/unsupportedbrowser?from=https%3A%2F%2Fwww.facebook.com%2Fcommunitystandards%2Fhate_speech

Trujillo, M., Gruppi, M., Buntain, C., & Horne, B. D. (2020, July). What is BitChute? Characterizing the. In *Proceedings of the 31st ACM conference on hypertext and social media* (pp. 139–140).

Vancouver, C. A. S. I. S. (2019). Yellow vests, right-wing extremism and the threat to Canadian democracy. *The Journal of Intelligence, Conflict, and Warfare*, *1*(3), 12–12.

Weimann, G. (2016). Going dark: Terrorism on the Dark Web. *Studies in Conflict & Terrorism*, *39*(3), 195–206.

Weiss, B., & Winter, D. (2018, May 8). Opinion | Meet the renegades of the intellectual dark web. *The New York Times*. https:// www.nytimes.com/2018/05/08/opinion/intellectual-dark-web.html

YouTube. (2021a). Hate speech policy. *YouTube Help*. https://support.google.com/youtube/answer/2801939?hl=en#zippy=%2Cother-types-of-content-that-violates-this-policy

YouTube. (2021b). Our mission. *YouTube*. https://www.youtube.com/howyoutubeworks/our-mission/

Zannettou, S., Bradlyn, B., De Cristofaro, E., Kwak, H., Sirivianos, M., Stringini, G., & Blackburn, J. (2018, April). What is Gab: A bastion of free speech or an alt-right echo chamber. In *Companion proceedings of the the web conference 2018* (pp. 1007–1014).

Zellner, X. (2021, February 13). Tom MacDonald tops emerging artists & digital song sales charts. *Billboard*. https://www.bill-board.com/pro/tom-macdonald-tops-emerging-artists-chart/

Zeng, J., & Schäfer, M. S. (2021). Conceptualizing "dark platforms". Covid-19-related conspiracy theories on 8kun and Gab. *Digital Journalism*, *9*(9), 1321–1343.

Index

Note: **Bold** page numbers refer to tables; *italic* page numbers refer to figures and page numbers followed by "n" denote endnotes.

AB *see* Aryan Brotherhood (AB)
Abidin, C. 53
accelerationists 61–62
Act of Parliament 134
Adinolfi, G. 64
Adorno, T. 20
AEL *see* Asiatic Exclusion League (AEL)
AG *see* Aryan Guard (AG)
Agenda 21 35
Agenda 2030 35
Ahmed, Y. 55
Ahmia 171
Alberta 11, 12, 17, 19, 59, 60, 67, 129, 134, 135, 164
Alberta Human Rights Commission 135
Ali, A. H. 165
Ali, S. 132
alien threats 25
AlphaBay 170
Al Qaeda 50, 55, 76n4
Amazon 2; Amazon Books 166–169; Amazon.ca 167
American Civil War (1861–1865) 11
Anderson, A. 146
Anderson, B. 9–10
Anglin, A. 72
Angry White Men (Kimmel) 71
anti-Catholicism 5
Anti-Defamation League 66, 107
anti-feminism 143
Anti-Hate Canada 56, 135
anti-Semitism 14–16, 18, 25, 34, 37, 48, 61, 103, 145, 146, 178n1
API of Hatebase 33, 150
Apocalypsis Apocalypseos (Brightman) 13

Apple 87, 89, 146; Apple Pay 137
Arcand, A. 14–15; *La Republique Universelle* 15
ARM *see* Aryan Resistance Movement (ARM)
Aryan Brotherhood (AB) 17
Aryan Guard (AG) 59–60
Aryan Nations 54, 57
Aryan Resistance Movement (ARM) 17–18
Aryans 16, 17
Aryan Strikeforce 57, 60, 61
Ashcraft, K. L. 26
Ashley, R. 142
Asian Immigration 9
Asiatic Exclusion League (AEL) 9
Atalante 62–64
Atalante Québec 64
Atkinson, R. 168
Atomwaffen Division (AWD) 57, 61, 62
Aupers, S. 23, 24
Australia 116, 136
Austria 63
AWD *see* Atomwaffen Division (AWD)

Babbar Khalsa (BK) 50
Babbar Khalsa International (BKI) 50
Baker, S. A. 9, 52
Bale, J.: *Image of Both Churches, The* 13
Balleck, B. J. 68
B&H *see* Blood & Honour (B&H)
Bannon, S. K. 178n2
Barbarians: How baby Boomers, Immigrants, and Islam Screwed my Generation (Southern) 167
Barber, C. 127, 129, 130

186 *Index*

Barkun, M. 20, 24; *Culture of Conspiracy: Apocalyptical Visions of Contemporary America, A* 22
Barrie 12
Bartley, A. 57
Base, The 68
Basham, L. 23
Bauder, J. 127
Bauder, S. 127–128
Beacon Dark Web 33, 171
Beaudry, P. 65
Beauvais-MacDonald, G. 64
benevolent sexism 71
Benzen, B. 164
Bernier, M. 68, 108, 131, 160–164
Bexte, K. 129, 164
Bhindranwale Tigers of Khalistan (BTK) 50
Biden, J. 144, 172
Bill C-63 134
Birth of a Nation, The 11
Bissonnette, A. 55, 89, 176
BitChute 2, 31, 33, 34, 38, 48, 52, 53, 87–89, 93, 105–118, **106**, **116**, 124, 125, 136; frequency of posts *117*, **117–118**
Bitcoin 170–172
BK *see* Babbar Khalsa (BK)
BKI *see* Babbar Khalsa International (BKI)
Black Lives Matter 19, 36
Blair, B. 56
Blanton, D. 179n3
Bleich, E. 153
Blood & Honour (B&H) 18, 56, 57, 59, 60
Bongino, D. 179n3
Boogaloo movement 148
Book of Revelation 13
Borden, Sir R. 10
Bratish, J. 20
Braun, S. 134
Brennan, F. 143
Brightman, T.: *Apocalypsis Apocalypseos* 13
Britain *see* United Kingdom (UK)
British Columbia 8, 11, 57, 60
British Empire 5, 6, 11
British Isles 12
British Israelism 12–13
British National Party 60
British rule 5, 9, 10
Brodmann, M. 127
Brubaker, R. 46, 49, 132
BTK *see* Bhindranwale Tigers of Khalistan (BTK)

Buckley, N. 92
Burdi, G. 17

California 17
Camp, S. 60
Camp of Saints, The (Raspail) 27
Camus, R.: *Le Grande Replacement* 26–27
Canada Border Services Agency 46
Canada First 5–7, 20, 132
Canada1st Party of Canada 166, 172
Canada in Decay: Mass Immigration, Diversity, and the Ethnocide of Euro-Canadians (Duchesne) 169
Canada Trade Agreement 144
Canada Unity 127–128
Canadian Armed Forces 57, 75
Canadian Confederation of 1867 5
Canadian Conservative Party 130
Canadian Criminal Code: section 318 134; sections 318–320; section 319(2) 134
Canadian Infidels 57, 66, 136
Canadian Nationalist Party 119n2
Canadian Nationalist Strikeforce 141
Canadian Network for Research on Terrorism, Security, and Society (TSAS) 56, 131
Canadian Pacific Railway 8
Canadian Security Intelligence Services (CSIS) 16, 54, 127
capitalism 18, 61; global 9, 34; platform 87
Carian, E. K. 70; *Good Guys, Bad Guys: The Perils of Men's Gender Activism* 70
Carlson, C. R. 153
Carter, D. 46, 47
CasaPound 64
CBC News 12, 166
Center for Hate, Bias, and Extremism 56
Center for International Security and Cooperation 62
Chaput, G. S. 61
Charlottesville 27, 64
Charter of Rights 134
Chastain, J. 70
Chen, K. 90
Chen, L. 132
China 36, 37, 48, 127, 152
Chinese Benevolent Associations 5
Chinese Canadian laborers 7–8
Chinese Communist Party 113
Chinese Immigration Act 8
Christchurch 143, 153, 170, 171
Christian Identity movement 16–17
Christian nationalism 19–20

Christian National Social Party 14
Christian Zionism 13–14
Church of the Creator, The 16, 17, 49, 59
Civil Rights Movement 70
cloaking strategies 142, 143
Coady, D. 23
Coalition Avenir Québec (Coalition for Québec's Future) 65
cognitive maps 23
Cohen Committee 133
Combat 18 57, 59, 60
communism 18, 64, 109, 113, 163
Conservative Party 11, 14, 130, 160, 164
conspiracism 24, 37; improvisational 22; platformed 90–93
conspiracy belief 20, 21, 24, 52
conspiracy theories 1, 3, 89, 103; conceptualization of 24–28, *34*; operationalizing 33–38; QAnon 35, 37, 91, 144, 162–163, 166, 171; racism 112; scholarship, development of 20–23; of society 21
conspiratorial convergence 25
content liberation 30, 31, 87, 108, 112, 115, 116, 125
content moderation 31, 49, 87–89, 92–94, 115
Conway, M. 178n1
Council of European Canadians 135, 163
COVID-19 pandemic 1, 27, 28, 35–37, 48, 88–90, 94, 98–101, 111–113, 118, 119, 126–129, 144, 148, 149, 153, 171, 172; anti-vaccination 52
Covington, H. 60
Cowan, W. D. 11
Crane, N. 18
Crew 38 17
Criminal Code, Section 83.05 54
Crusius, P. 143
Cruz, T. 116
cryptocurrency 100–101, 137, 169–175; funds *174*, *175*; wallets **173**
Culture of Conspiracy: Apocalyptical Visions of Contemporary America, A (Barkun) 22

Daily Stormer, The 62, 90, 171
Darknet 169; DarkNet Search 171
dark participation 28–33, 108–109
dark social movements 28–33
Dark Web 2, 169–175, **171**
Dean, J. 20, 21
Death of Cool, The (McInnes) 74

debunking 90
Deep Search 171
Deep State 88, 102–103
Dentith, M. R. X. 20, 23, 90
deplatformization 31, 58, 87, 92–94
Derkson, J. 63
de Wildt, L. 23, 24
Diagolon 127
Dichter, B. J. 127
Did Six Million Really Die? (Harwood) 16
Didulo, R. R. 36, 166, 172
digital manosphere 72
Discord 61, 89, 116, 166, 178n1
Dispatches from the Vaccine Wars: Fighting for Human Freedom During the Great Reset (Shaw) 168–169
Donaldson, I. S. 18
Donovan, L. 132
Doosje, B. 51
Droege, W. 18
Duchesne, R. 135, 163; *Canada in Decay: Mass Immigration, Diversity, and the Ethnocide of Euro-Canadians* 169
Duke, D. 12, 165
Dunkin, C. 6
DVE (domestic violent extremist) threats 55

Earnest, J. 143
Eatwell, R. 47
Echosec Systems 33, 171
8kun 89, 143–145, 171
Elam, P. 71
El Paso 143
England 12
ethnonationalism 26
Evans, P. 52
event conspiracies 22
everyday racism 9
exclusionism 6; racial 47
exile congregation 88, 107, 108, 112, 115, 125

Facebook/Meta 2, 49, 64–66, 88, 141, 142, 164; hashtag policies on 153–155, **154**
Fakih, M. 107
Farrel, W.: *Myth of Male Power* 71
far-right influencers 51–54
fascism 14, 17, 163
Fédération des Québécois 64
Feldman, M. 48
Fenians 5, 6
Fenster, M. 20–22, 28, 119, 126
Finland 32, 66

Index

First Amendment of the United States Constitution 145–146, 148, 153
First World War (1914–1918) 10
5G 100–101, 126
Ford, D. 125
4Chan 2, 30, 74, 141–144, 171
France 5, 26, 27, 62, 99
Frank, L. 10
Freedomain Radio 165
Freedom Convoy movement (2022) 54, 126, 129, 130
freedom of speech 16, 66, 130, 135, 145, 153, 179
Freeland, C. 129, 163
FreeNet 169
Freiheit, D. 131
Frischlich, L. 31
Fromm, P. 59
Front Canadian Francais 49
Fuentes, N. 171

Gab 2, 87, 132, 145–147, **147**
Gabbard, T. 179n3
Gagan, D. P. 6
Gallant, N. 69
Gamergate 142, 143
Gariépy, J.-P. 164
Garry, A. 28–29
Gates, B. 129, 131
gender identity 56, 89, 135, 165
Generation Identity Canada/Generation Identitaire/Identitarian Movement 62–63; "Defend Europe: Alps" 63
Germany 14, 61, 63, 65, 157; German Criminal Code of 1998 153; Nazi 16; Network Enforcement Act of 2017 153
Getter 2, 178–179n2
Ghislaine, M. 172
Gilets jaunes du Québec (GJQ) 137n2
GiveSendGo campaign 129, 137n4
GJQ *see* Gilets jaunes du Québec (GJQ)
global capitalism 9, 34
Global Elite 27, 35, 37, 103
GoFundMe campaign 130, 131
Goldy, F. 49, 64, 141, 163, 172, 174
Good Guys, Bad Guys: The Perils of Men's Gender Activism (Carian) 70
Google 2, 89, 125, 146, 164, 169; Android operating system 179n3; autocomplete search engine 33; Google Pay 137; Google Translate 97; search 175–177, **176–177**
GOP in America 130

Gore, L.: "You Don't Own Me" 69–70
Goudreau, K. 141
grand replacement (great replacement) theory 64
Great Awakening 34–36, 87, 88, 94, 95, 101–102, 111, 126
Great Depression 14
Great Purge 147
Great Replacement theory 25–27, 31–32, 35, 63
Great Reset 26, 34, 35, 87, 95, 101
Greenspon, C. 179n3
Greenwald, G. 179n3
Gregor, A. J. 46–47
Groupe Sécurité Patriote 69
Guardian, The 30, 31
Guardians of Alberta 65, 67
Guterman, N. 20

Halpin, M. 74
Hamas 13
Hammerskins 17
Hargraves, R. 172, 174
Harper, S. 150, 153, 161
Harper-Mercer, C. 143
Harris, K. 144
Harris, S. 165
Harvey, D. 49
Harwood, R.: *Did Six Million Really Die?* 16
hate groups, definition of 56
hate influencers 51–54
hate speech 16, 30, 31, 51, 52, 73, 88, 92, 106, 107, 133, 134, 145, 146, 148–150, 153–155, 164; definition of 178n1; policies, in social media sites 142, 148, 155, 165
Hatewatch 170
Hayden Lake, Idaho 17
hegemonic masculinity 69
Henderson 148
Heritage Front, The 18
Heyer, H. 27
Hiller, R. 164
Hillier, R. 127, 160–161
Hitler, A. 14, 15, 18, 59
Holocaust: denialism 15–16; toxic legacies of 48
Holter, C. R. 32
homosexuality 18
HonkHonk Hold campaign 130
hostile sexism 71
Hover, I. 63

Index 189

Hudson's Bay Company 6
Hunt, T. 66
Husbands, C. T. 47

Icke, D. 112
ID Canada 62
identitarians 62–65
IDW *see* Intellectual Dark Web (IDW)
Ignatiev, N. 5, 49
Ihlebæk, K. A. 32
Image of Both Churches, The (Bale) 13
imagined community 9–10
immigration 7, 19, 20, 25, 26, 32, 35, 63, 143, 162, 166, 168; Asian 9; Chinese 8; German 15; illegal 65; Japanese 8; laws 11, 16, 18; mass 129, 163, 168; racialized policies 9; re-immigration 27
Immigration Act of 1910 10
Incels 72–74
Indian Imperial Police 10
influentials 52
InfoWars 107, 142, 161, 163
infrastructure ostracization 31, 88, 108, 112, 115, 125, 132
Innis, H. A. 7
Instagram 2, 33, 52, 64, 153–155; COVID-19 Information Center 155; hashtag policies on 154–155, **156**
Intellectual Dark Web (IDW) 165
International Sikh Youth Federation 50
internetworked social movement (ISM) 28, 29
"Introducing the Pseudopenis, or Why Female Hyenas Are Feminist as Fuck," (Tierney) 71
Invisible Internet Project (I2P) 169
Ireland 5, 12, 50
Irish Catholics 5
Iron March 61, 62, 90
Iron March Exposed 62
ISIS 50, 132
Islamophobia 28, 34, 66, 88, 153, 167
ISM *see* internetworked social movement (ISM)
Israel 12, 13, 16–17, 48
Italy 63
I2P *see* Invisible Internet Project (I2P)

Jackson, P. 48
Jameson, F. 23
Jamnisek, E. 69
Jensen, N. 74
Jessen, N. 26

Jewish Canadians 14
Johnson, K. J. 107–108
Jones, A. 55, 87, 167
Just Right Media 166

Kanishka Project 75n1
Kazin, M. 26
Keegstra, J. 134
Kennedy, R. K., Jr. 165
Khalistan Liberation Front 50
Khalistan Tiger Force (KTF) 76n2
Kilos 171
Kim, S. J. 90
Kimmel, M.: *Angry White Men* 71
King, P. 127, 128
King, W. L. M. 14
KKK *see* Ku Klux Klan (KKK)
Klassen, B. 16
Knight, P. 20, 21
Knights of Labor Society, Vancouver 71–72
Knott, D. 12
KTF *see* Khalistan Tiger Force (KTF)
Ku Klux Klan (KKK) 10, 11, 16, 57, 59, 60, 132, 133, 144

Labor Reformer 8
LaFace, J. 127
La Meute 57, 65–66, 141
La Republique Universelle (Arcand) 15
Late Great Planet Earth, The (Lindsey) 14
Laurier, W. 9
LCC *see* Liberty Coalition Canada (LCC)
Le Front Patriotique du Québec (Patriotic Front of Quebec) 64
Légitime Violence (Legitimate Violence) 63, 66, 76n3
Le Grande Replacement (Camus) 26–27
Le Patriote 15
Lepine, M. 70
Les Gardiens du Québec (LGDQ) 69
Let Goglu 14
Levant, E. 14, 114–115, 135, 160, 161, 167
Lévesque, R. 56, 63
Levitt, C. 14
LGBTQ2SA communities 19, 48, 69
LGDQ *see* Les Gardiens du Québec (LGDQ)
liberal immigration policies 18
Liberal Party 15, 114, 128, 129, 152, 158
Liberator, The 12
Liberty Coalition Canada (LCC) 19
Lich, T. 127, 129–130
Lima, L. 145

Index

Lindsey, H.: *Late Great Planet Earth, The* 13
Lipset, M. 21
Loewenthal, L. 20
Long, T. 17
lookism 74
Loomer, L. 93
Lynch, O. 55

McCarthyism 21
McCormack, J. 63
Macdonald, J. A. 6–8
Macdonald, P. G. 62
MacDonald, T. 166
McDougall, W. 6
Machiavellianism 31
McIlroy-Young, R. 146
McInnes, G. 49, 55; *Death of Cool, The* 74)
McInnis, G. 125, 160, 165, 167, 168
McKee, K. 18, 59
McLeod, K. 60
Madison, A. 170
Mahl, D. 91
male supremacy 68, 69
Malleret, T. 34–35
Maloney, J. J. 11–12
Malthouse, S. 112
Manitoba 6, 12
Manitoba Act of 1870 7
manosphere 69–75; digital 72
Manson, C. 61
Mansur, S. 166
Martin, D. E. 113, 116
masculine grievance 25, 26
masculinity 25; toxic 76n5
Mason, J. 62
mass violence 143
Matrix, The 71
Mattheis, A. A. 72
Men Going Their Own Way (MGTOW) 50, 72, 73, 107
men's right activists (MRAs) 71
Men's Right Movement (MRM) 70, 71, 73
Mental Health Act 172
Métis 6, 7, 20, 46
Metz, R. 166
Metzge, T. 18
MeWe 64
Mexico 6, 144
MGTOW *see* Men Going Their Own Way (MGTOW)
militias 67–69
militia violent extremists (MVEs) 55

Miller, J. 178n2
Minassian, A. 74, 143
misogyny 71, 142, 149
mixed-method approach 1, 93–94, 119, 124
Molyneux, S. 55, 165, 167, 170, 172
Montreal 17, 65
Morning News 71
Mosaic Institute, The 56
Moslesh, O. 58
MRAs *see* men's right activists (MRAs)
MRM *see* Men's Right Movement (MRM)
Mudde, C. 47
multiculturalism 18, 65, 163, 168
Musk, E. 93, 168
Muslim Brotherhood 65
MVEs *see* militia violent extremists (MVEs)
MySpace 73, 164
Myth of Male Power (Farrel) 71

Nadeau, F. 66
Nationalist Front/Aryan Nationalist Alliance 59, 61
nationalists 65–67
Nationalist Socialist Movement (NSM) 61
National Security, in Canada 54
National Socialist Order 62
national sovereignty 14
National Unity Party (NUP) 15
Nawaz, M. 165
Nazi Germany 16
Nazism 14
Nazi Third Reich 15
neo-fascism 46–47
neo-Nazi movements 18
neo-Nazism 59–61, 63
Nesbitt, M. 134
Nevada 148
"Never Going to Give You Up" 142
New Order of Fear, The 129
New World Order (NWO) 27, 34, 35, 102–103, 111
New Zealand 56, 136, 143, 153, 170
Noppari, E. 32
North America 10, 16, 25–26, 38, 61
Northern Guard 68, 69
Northern Ireland: battle between the British Protestants 5
Northwest Emigration Aid Society 7
Nova Scotia 4
NSM *see* Nationalist Socialist Movement (NSM)
Nunes, D. 179n3

NUP *see* National Unity Party (NUP)
NWO *see* New World Order (NWO)

Obama, B. 54, 68
Odinism 49, 57
OFP *see* Ontario First Party (OFP)
Old Stock Canadian 153
Onion Router (Tor) 33, 169
Online Harms Act 134
Ontario 7, 11, 12, 57; provincialism 6
Ontario First Party (OFP) 164
opinion leaders 52
Orangemen 5, 6, 20
Orange Order 4, 12
Order of Nine Angels 49
Oregon 6, 143
O'Toole, E. 162
Ottawa 7, 109, 127–129
overt racism 67
Owens, C. 131

Palestine 13, 15
pan-Western nationalism 168
Pardon Flynn memes 144
Parler 33, 147–148, **148**, 171
Parmar, T. S. 50
Patriarchy 71
Patriotes du Québec (Patriots of Quebec) 64
Patriotic-Protestantism 12–13
patriots 65–67
Paudel, P. 178–179n2
Pavlovski, C. 179n3
PayPal 137, 164, 170
Pegida 33, 65
People's Party of Canada 130, 131
Perry, B. 29, 58, 75
Peterson, J. 165
Pfau, M.: *Political Style of Conspiracy: Chase, Sumner, and Lincoln, The* 21
PGP *see* Pretty Good Privacy (PGP)
Phangan, M. 10–11
Pigden, C. 20, 23
Pink Floyd: "Wall, The" 17
Pizzagate 97, 110, 142
platformed conspiracism 90–93
Political Style of Conspiracy: Chase, Sumner, and Lincoln, The (Pfau) 21
Poole, C. 141, 143
Popper, K. 21, 23
populism 25, 27, 31, 112, 119, 124, 126, 152, 161, 162; conspiracy and 26; definition of 26; right-wing 11, 89

Post Millennial 131
Pretty Good Privacy (PGP) 169
Promise Keepers, The 70
Protocols of the Elders of Zion, The 15, 37
Proud Boys 56, 57, 72, 74, 135–136, 148, 167
psychopathy 31
Public Land Survey System 6
Public Safety Canada 54
Pulcher, R. 60
Pushshift API 33, 149
Python 33, 95, 144, 146

QAnon 36, 124, 142, 143, 155, 161, 172; conspiracy theory 35, 37, 91, 103, 144, 162–163, 166, 171
Quandt, T. 30–31
Quebec 5, 11, 14, 57, 64, 101, 141
Québécois 64
Quiggin, T. 127, 129

race mixing 18, 19
race riots 4
racial discrimination 10
racial exclusionism 147
racial hierarchies 17
Racial Holy War (RAHOWA) 17
racially or ethnically motivated violent extremists (RMVEs) 55
racial purity 49
racial separatism 18
racism 4, 5, 16, 25, 47, 66, 74, 106, 142, 150, 178n1; conspiracy theories 112; everyday 9; overt 67; scientific 163; sexualization of 48
Raging Dissident III 166
RAHOWA *see* Racial Holy War (RAHOWA)
Raspail, J. 163; *Camp of Saints, The* 27
RCMP *see* Royal Canadian Mounted Police (RCMP)
Rebel News 114, 115, 125, 132, 165–166, 170
re-blogging 179n4
Reconstruction KKK *see* Ku Klux Klan (KKK)
Reddit 2, 33, 74, 132, 142, 148–152, *151*, **151**
Red Pill, The 164
Red River Resistance (1869–1870) 6
Regehr, K. 143
Regina Leader-Post 12

Riel, L. 6, 7
Riffle 169
right-wing extremism 54–57
right-wing extremists (RWE) 1–38, 57, 94, 141–143; in Canada, situating 46–51; groups, in Canada 57–65, *58*; historical overview of 4–20; sites 87–119; *see also individual entries*
right-wing terrorism 54–57
RMVEs *see* racially or ethnically motivated violent extremists (RMVEs)
Roberts, G. K. 47
Robertson, D. G. 24
Rodger, E. 143
Roediger, D. R. 49
Roe v Wade 27
Rogan, J. 165
Ross, L. M. 5
Rothut, S. 52
Rousselle, H. 153
Rovere, R. 21
Royal Canadian Mounted Police (RCMP) 54, 60
Royal Commission 8, 9, 170
Rubin, D. 165
Rumble 89, 136, 179n3
Russia 30, 36, 62, 167
RWE *see* right-wing extremist (RWE)

St. Patrick's Day Toronto Riot of 1858 5
Sargent, C. 60
Saskatchewan 11, 12, 109, 157
Satzewich, V. 4
Schafer, J. S. 92
Schmegelsky, B. 60
Schnieder, R. 130
Schwab, K. 34–35
scientific racism 165
Scotland 12
Scrivens, R. 29
Second World War (1939–1945) 15
securitization 25
Sellner, M. 63
Servanthoods 49
sexism 76n5; benevolent 71; hostile 71; racialization of 48
shadowbanning 31, 92, 147
Shapiro, B. 165
Shaw, C. A.: *Dispatches from the Vaccine Wars: Fighting for Human Freedom During the Great Reset* 168–169
Shelburne 4
Shepherd, L. 135

Shils, E. 21
Sikh extremism 50
Sikh Nationalism 75–76n2
Skinheads 63
SNS *see* Social Networking Sites (SNS)
social credit system 36, 162, 163
social media scholarship 29
social movement theory 29
Social Networking Sites (SNS) 141
Soldiers of Odin (SOO) 57, 64, 65, 69, 141
solidarity 30
Sons of Odin 57, 66
SOO *see* Soldiers of Odin (SOO)
Soros, G. 127
Southern, L. 63, 64, 125, 132, 170, 172, 174, *174*, *175*; *Barbarians: How baby Boomers, Immigrants, and Islam Screwed my Generation* 167
Southern Poverty Law Center (SPLC) 19, 56, 60, 135
Spencer, R. B. 145, 165
SPLC *see* Southern Poverty Law Center (SPLC)
Steam 61
Steele, R. D. 111
Steever, J. "Hatchet" 60
Stew Peters Show, The 98
stigmatized knowledge 22
Storm Alliance 64, 65, 67, 69
Students for Western Civilization 164
superconspiracies 22–23
Sustainable Development Goals 35
Swastika Club 14
systemic conspiracies 22

Tarrant, B. 143
Tarrio, E. 53
Taschereau, Louis-Alexandre 14
Telegram 2, 19, 29, 31, 33, 34, 38, 49, 52, 53, 87–89, 93–105, 108; connecting conspiracies with other conspiracies 99–100; Deep State conspiracy 102–103; frequency of posts **104**, *105*, **105**; NWO conspiracy 102–103; political polarization 102–103; race in 103–104; religion in 103–104; #Savethechildren 103; surveillance 100–101; technology conspiracies 100–101; #TheGreatAwakening 101–102
Tempel ov Blood 49
Texas 17, 143
Thalman, K. 20

Theil, P. 179n3
Thobani, S. 9, 50
Thread for Propaganda Memes 145
Three Percenters, The 68
Tierney, K.: "Introducing the Pseudopenis, or Why Female Hyenas Are Feminist as Fuck," 71
TikTok 90, 91
Torch 171
TorDex 171
Toronto 5, 11, 18, 20
toxic masculinity 76n5
Tregget, D. (aka Dave Treg) 67
Tremaine, T. 59
Trenberth, K. 52
Trudeau, E. 16
Trudeau, J. 53, 76n2, 125, 127, 131, 137n2, 150, 160, 162, 163, 172, 178n2
Trujillo, M. 107
Trump, D. 3, 36, 37, 53, 68, 74, 94, 102, 111, 130, 144, 145, 163, 172
TRUTH Social 179n3
TSAS *see* Canadian Network for Research on Terrorism, Security, and Society (TSAS)
Tumblr 179n4
Twitter/X 2, 49, 88, 132, 142, 147, 155, 157–164, *158*, **159**, **161**, 178n2

UK *see* United Kingdom (UK)
Ukraine 36
Ulbricht, R. 170
UN *see* United Nations (UN)
Unicorn Riot 178n1
Union Jack 11
United Kingdom (UK) 60, 61, 63, 155
United Nations (UN) 87, 95, 133; Agenda 21 35; Agenda 2030 35; Sustainable Development Goals 35
United States (US) 36, 49, 56, 59, 60, 67, 142, 144, 155; 2016 presidential election 28; Christian Nationalism movement 19–20; Fenians 5, 6; First Amendment of the Constitution 145–146, 148, 153; Naval Research Laboratory 169; War of independence 4
"Unite the Right" Charlottesville rally (2017) 64
Unite the Right Rally 27
Universal Declaration of Human Rights 133
US *see* United States (US)
USMCA memes 144

Vaccine Choice Canada (VCC) 116
Vague bleu (Blue Wave) movement 69
Vahey, R. 105
Vance, J. D. 179n3
Vancouver 8, 9
vandalism 16
Vaughan, R. 166
VCC *see* Vaccine Choice Canada (VCC)
Veltman, N. 89
Veniamin, N. 111
Venne, E. 65
Vescera, Z. 60
Virginia 27
Virtual Private Network (VPN) 169, 176
Vriend, A. 127

"Wall, The" (Pink Floyd) 17
Walmart 143
WAR *see* White Aryan Resistance (WAR)
War Measures Act 10
Waters, C. 12, 60
Watson, P. J. 163
WEF *see* World Economic Forum (WEF)
Weinstein, E. 165
Wengui, G. 178n2
Western Europe 47
Western Guard Party 16
Westlund, O. 30
Wexit 129, 137n1
WhatsApp 64, 94
White Aryan Resistance (WAR) 18
white genocide 19, 59, 64
White Lives Matter (WLM) 19, 53
whiteness 10, 49, 50, 71, 72
white supremacists 1, 12, 16, 19, 57, 59–65, 68, 69, 72, 74, 75, 94, 118, 126, 148, 164, 170, 176
white supremacy 7, 10, 11, 59–61, 167, 169; defnition of 50, 59
Whonix 169
Wikipedia 164
Winnipeg 6, 12
WLM *see* White Lives Matter (WLM)
Wolves of Odin Canada Infidels (WOOCI) *see* Soldiers of Odin (SOO)
woman-obsessed separatism 73
Women's Rights movement 70
WOOCI *see* Wolves of Odin Canada Infidels (WOOCI)
Wood, G. 21
World Economic Forum (WEF) 34, 35, 129
World Health Organization 37

xenophobia 10, 25, 47, 48, 55, 59, 63, 66, 137n2

Yellow Vest (Gilets jaunes) movement 54, 137n2, 137n3
Yiannopolous, M. 145
"You Don't Own Me" (Gore) 69–70

YouTube 2, 32, 49, 61, 87–89, 93, 107, 142, 164–166, 174
You Will Not Replace Us 27

Zog (Zionist Occupation Government) 60
Zündel, E. 15, 20, 135; "Concerned Parents of German Descent, The" 16

Printed in the United States
by Baker & Taylor Publisher Services